THAT BIRD HAS MY WINGS

THAT BIRD
HAS MY
WINGS

The Autobiography
of an Innocent Man
on Death Row

Jarvis Jay Masters

HarperOne
An Imprint of HarperCollinsPublishers

HarperOne

Portions of this book have previously appeared in different forms in *The Turning Wheel: Journal of the Buddhist Peace Fellowship, Shambhala Sun,* and *Finding Freedom.*

HarperCollins books may be purchased for educational, business, or sales promotional use. For information, please e-mail the Special Markets Department at SPsales@harpercollins.com.

HarperCollins Web site: http://www.harpercollins.com

HarperCollins®, 📖®, and HarperOne™ are trademarks of HarperCollins Publishers

FIRST HARPERCOLLINS PAPERBACK EDITION PUBLISHED IN 2010

Library of Congress Cataloging-in-Publication Data
Masters, Jarvis Jay.
That bird has my wings : the autobiography of an innocent man on death row / Jarvis Jay Masters. — 1st ed.
p. cm.
ISBN 978-0-06-173048-1
1. Masters, Jarvis Jay. 2. Authors, American—21st century—Biography. 3. Prisoners—United States—Biography. 4. Buddhists—United States—Biography. I. Title.
PS3563.A826Z46   2009
818'.609—dc22
[B]   2009022124

To my life's best friend,
Summerlynn.

To all those who have lost someone by an act of violence,
to the memory of those whose lives have been cut short,
to the memory of those who have been executed on death row,
and especially to those who still have the opportunity to make choices
that will take them down a different path.

Contents

AUTHOR'S NOTE

THIS IS A WORK of nonfiction. The events and experiences detailed herein are all true and have been faithfully rendered as I have remembered them, to the best of my ability. Some timelines, circumstances, and the names and identifying characteristics of some people and institutions have been changed to protect the integrity and/or anonymity of the various institutions and individuals involved, and especially to protect the orphans and foster children I have known, who have a right to tell their own stories if they so choose.

Though conversations come from my keen recollection of them, they are not written to represent word-for-word documentation; rather, I've retold them in a way that evokes the real feeling and meaning of what was said, in keeping with the true essence of the mood and spirit of the event.

FOREWORD

Pema Chödrön

ALL BUDDHISTS TAKE A vow not to cause harm, and some go further. They vow to do anything in their power to alleviate suffering—the suffering of everyone—without giving in to biases of like and dislike, worthy and unworthy.

My dear friend Jarvis Masters has taken both these vows while on death row in San Quentin Prison. He took these vows from his Tibetan Buddhist teacher, Chagdud Tulku Rinpoche. In my thirty-five years as a Buddhist, I have rarely met anyone who took these vows as wholeheartedly as Jarvis. Yet this dedicated man, this loving and compassionate man, didn't acquire his immense empathy and courage without undergoing great suffering himself and causing great pain to others as well.

When I first read this story of his early life, it was sometimes so painful that I had to stop and take a break. I kept wanting things to go differently for this promising young boy, but the blunt truth is that things didn't go differently. The story Jarvis so compellingly tells actually happened, and it's still happening to countless other poor and traumatized children.

Jarvis told me repeatedly that he felt he had to look closely at his formative years for his own sake and for the sake of all the other children like him who would recognize themselves in his words. He hoped that by telling his story he might help them to avoid making the mistakes that had brought him to San Quentin. He knows there are millions of children just like him who are intelligent, kindhearted, and full of potential, and who can meet that potential if only they have support from their struggling families, decent schools, safer neighborhoods, and mentors to guide them. He longs to be such a mentor.

Even without this book, Jarvis is already a role model for many children. He gets so many letters from adolescent boys who are going through what he went through in one way or another that even in prison it's difficult for him to find time to answer them all. Some of these young people are in juvenile lockups, and some of them are the children of prison guards who see their fathers bringing the violence of prison home with them. Yet true to his vows, Jarvis tries to say something to each of them that will make a difference in their lives.

Once when I was visiting him at San Quentin, Jarvis told me that something was troubling him. He knew that his personal story, with all its confusion, violence, and pain, is all too common. As he put it, "Whether you ask a prison guard, an inmate, or a person on the street, they'll all agree that such a life is that of a man who is likely to end up just where I have, on death row, waiting to be killed by lethal injection. So how," he asked me, "will anyone believe I'm innocent?"

It seems, in fact, that his innocence is a miracle—a very fortunate miracle. At the age of nineteen, when Jarvis was rightly sent to San Quentin for a series of robberies, he was angry, defensive, and mean. His childhood, as you will read in these pages, had trained him to violence and abuse. So it was by luck that he never killed anyone and that, auspiciously for him, he never would.

But it was only partly by luck. This book also tells the story of a child who managed to keep alive a small flame of compassion for himself and others, thanks to the essential wholeness of his nature and the acts of kindness he experienced along the way. That Jarvis's Dickensian childhood included some people who loved him made an enormous difference. There was in this violent young man an aversion—deeply buried but still present—to killing. As you will read here, as a boy Jarvis threw away a box cutter because there was no way he could ever see himself using it to harm anyone. And as a young man, Jarvis never actually aimed and shot his gun at another human being, even while inexcusably committing armed robberies that terrified many people.

Four years after Jarvis entered prison, a gang conspiracy resulted in the senseless murder of a prison guard. Jarvis easily could have been part of that conspiracy. Yet for some reason he wasn't included in the planning and execution of the crime. Nevertheless, because of testimony that has since been shown to be false, he was convicted of participating in the planning and of sharpening the weapon that was used to stab the guard, and he was sentenced to death.

Jarvis says today that even if he is killed by lethal injection he'll die with a clear conscience, knowing that he was not responsible for the death of a good man. As he puts it, "I know my own truth, that I am totally innocent of the death of any prison guard."

The irony of this, as Jarvis well knows, is that his life turned around only after his conviction. If he had been released from San Quentin at the end of his original term, it is possible that he might have remained as sullen and rebellious as he was when he came in. The odds are very good that he would have been dead on the streets well before he reached the age of thirty.

Instead, during his murder trial two important things happened. First, Jarvis started wanting to know who he was and where he'd gone wrong. And at the same time, a private investigator working on his case taught him how to meditate and gave him tools to look at himself honestly and face his pain.

Since that time, Jarvis has dedicated his life to nonviolence and benefiting others. These have been years of deep contemplation and discovery, years that have transformed him at the core.

This powerful book is in some way a fruition of those years. It is as intimate a look at an "at-risk" childhood as you'll ever get. For Jarvis, writing about his early years was a descent into places that he'd repressed and been afraid to explore. It took him years of self-reflection to reach the point where he had the courage to go back into the painful, as well as happy, memories of his earliest life and to see with total honesty each of the times when he had lost touch with his basic intelligence and kindness and then taken a wrong turn.

It is a riveting story, told with tremendous heart, yet totally devoid of sentimentality. I know it will be an eye-opener for all who read it. It is my sincere aspiration that this story will, against all odds, have a happy ending. I pray that this autobiography of an innocent man does not end with the death chamber but with freedom.

PREFACE

O VER THE YEARS, I have been asked when it was that I "saw the light," had a dream, or heard a voice. What experience created a reverberation that transformed me from the person I was then to the person I am today? The truth of the matter is that I have never changed. Rather, I have simply discovered who I've always been: the young child who knew that his life mattered, that he could make a difference in the world, and that he was born to fly.

In spite of the pain and hurt, and however much I engaged in crazed violence and lashed out at the world for thinking it owed me something, in the center, in my heart, there was always something of a natural goodness. This may have been the place from which my tears poured when I was a young child. In that same place, the violence later grew so much larger than life that I stopped believing in myself. But I finally came into a situation where I dared myself to reclaim that natural goodness. That I reclaimed it on San Quentin's death row doesn't change who I am. I have experienced an inner journey that brought me to the life-affirming realization that my violent actions were never a reflection of who I really am.

If I had known how painful it would be to sit and write this book about my life, I doubt that I would have ever picked up my pen filler, the only writing instrument allowed to an inmate in solitary confinement on death row. It was only from not knowing what layers of memories—particularly from childhood—would slowly unfold that I innocently began to write. I remember what a friend said when I told him what I was writing. We were walking together out on the death row exercise yard.

"Man," he said, putting one arm out to bring us to a stop in the middle of the yard, "I wouldn't do that. Look at this." He raised his sweatshirt, revealing horrible, healed-over gashes—scars, he said, from dog bites.

"I still dream about this shit," he said. "You want to sit down and write all night about this kind of stuff?"

"What happened?" I asked.

"Whenever I did anything wrong, I mean anything, my pops would sic his dog Fang on me. He would hold Fang by the chain, and he wouldn't let him go. He made him bite these holes in me— here, there, everywhere."

It would have sounded strange to say "thank you" to my friend, but what he said spoke to me. It helped me realize my true purpose in picking up the thin straw of ballpoint pen filler, resting it between my fingers, and beginning to write. At first I wrote in circles, the long way around memories. Then I began to silently challenge myself: *Without anyone else having to know,* I asked, *how honest can I be with myself as I write all the scattered memories of my life? Can I do so without blame, with only a truth that has no place to go beyond these sheets of paper?* In essence, questioning my own sincerity is what inspired this book.

Many events recalled in these pages could have kept me angry my entire life; many times just the memories made me want to quit writing. I would forget about not blaming others, fearing the truth that might be triggered by the next word or sentence I wrote. At times I literally cursed the makeshift pen caught painfully between my fingers. There was no name I did not call it. It was not just that it hurt to hold it, but that it moved so slowly, forcing me to attend to every detail. I couldn't write any faster than it let me; it refused to skim lightly over the surface as I tried to breeze past the unpronounced emotions that would crawl up my throat and fill my eyes with tears. The filler's slow pace repeatedly dragged me into a swamp of unwanted memories. Only through the patience learned in meditation was I able to settle myself into a place that allowed me to keep writing.

Jarvis Jay Masters
SAN QUENTIN
2008

A hand so soft
to touch the mother
that she is.
A reason to stand,
to hold on to my prayers,
that she'll
awaken to find me
holding on to her,
my mother's hand.

—ANONYMOUS

First Memories

Aunts and Uncles

OUR PARENTS WERE ALMOST never home. The house seemed large because my sisters and I were alone and trapped in its emptiness. We made it bigger to enlarge our days there. But in fact the house was quite small. In the long days of being left alone, we got to know the interior of the house like our own bodies. It was our whole existence.

The four of us ranged in age from three to eight. My sister Charlene was the oldest, then me, Birdy, and Carlette. In this seemingly huge old house we had gone from crawling to standing to walking, like the evolution chart that shows a monkey-man developing into the first human being. Those pictures come to mind when I think about how my sisters and I grew up.

I can still see my sisters' faces from those many years ago. Yet at that time we never gave a thought to how we looked or what we wore on our tiny bodies. The only times we noticed ourselves were when I used to walk around in my stepfather Otis's shoes and when my sisters put on my mother's different wigs. Then we would prance around the house, laughing and giggling at how we looked.

Afterward, putting Mama's and Otis's things back in the exact same place where we had found them was a serious matter. If we got caught messing with their things—as happened once—we'd be beaten out of our wits. But playing with their things was not the absolute cardinal sin. The most forbidden thing of all was playing with the tiny balloons stashed in socks and hidden all over the house. These balloons were filled with heroin. I used to set out to find them, like going on an Easter egg hunt. I'd open the socks and play with the colorful balloons as if they were my secret toys. They were like marbles. I liked to put them in piles—all the blue ones together, the reds together, the yellows together. Whichever color there were the fewest of seemed the most special. I liked the danger of it too. I took great care to put the balloons back just as I had found them. (Even today I can look at something, take a mental picture of its position, remove it, and replace it in the exact same spot.) It made me feel grown up to handle these jewels of my parents', as if I were part of the same business as all the people I saw coming to the house; it made me feel like "somebody."

It was the late sixties, when my mother Cynthia and my stepfather Otis were among the biggest heroin users and dealers in Long Beach, California. From the outside the house didn't look like a dope house. My parents had lots of money from being in the drug underworld, so they could afford a "front house" that drew no suspicion or complaints from the neighbors. The house was a place where my parents' clientele and whomever they chose to bring with them could always, no matter the time of day, walk right in and shoot their dope indoors, off the streets. Many of their customers would nod themselves to sleep right there on the living room or bathroom floor and stay for hours and hours.

These friends and customers of my parents had a code word to use when they came to the house and only my sisters and I were there—which was most of the time. They introduced themselves as our "uncles" and "aunts." We had many, many uncles and aunts. My favorites were the ones who nodded out on the couch or in the bathroom sitting on the edge of the toilet, with saliva dripping from their mouths. Then I could steal the coins from their pants pockets or the pouches hidden inside their bosoms. I never took paper money, just coins, because the grocery store clerks gave me strange looks when I tried to buy candy bars for my sisters with paper money. Also, I didn't know the difference between a five-dollar bill and a hundred-dollar bill. So I stuck to stealing coins from pockets. I liked the dimes best.

We were too young and innocent to be afraid of the strangers who entered the house throughout the day and night. The frequency of their visits even gave us the feeling that they somehow cared for us. Sometimes they asked when we last ate, or simply noticed that we hadn't, and they would come back with boxes of doughnuts and pop. Sometimes prostitutes brought their tricks there, but my mother didn't like that. She told us to let her know if it happened so she could beat those women up.

Even with the filthy, ragged clothes on our backs, we had no comparisons to make that would tell us that our fragile lives were being neglected. How were we to know our lacking everything was any different from children's lives in other households? The clothes we wore, the way we smelled—it all fit, like junkyard guys working alongside each other, nobody thinking he smells worse than the next guy. In those long wallowing hours of hunger pangs, we lived in the same ragged clothes, the same stench, and the dry salt of our tears, but we were together. And in our misery we shared many moments of laughing and chasing one another in childish games that almost made us forget the hours, days, and weeks of abandonment.

The Attic

We found all the hiding places in the house, like closets, kitchen cabinets, and even suitcases. But the attic was our favorite. We would climb on top of the dresser in one of the closets, then onto the high closet shelf. From there we reached the ceiling and the square sheet of wood that we pushed up in order to climb into the attic. When the sunlit days in the house became too long for us, we climbed up into the night of the attic to take our naps. In the attic we felt hidden from all our fears, and we could always sleep soundly, like babies in their cribs.

The attic ceiling wasn't so low that we felt cramped. The wooden beams peaked in the middle, where we could stand straight up and play around. We made up games to forget we were hungry and alone, but we didn't talk that much. I had a serious stutter up until the age of ten or eleven, way after I had been taken from my parents. So we didn't console one another with words as much as by our togetherness.

The attic had a window that faced out over the front porch of the house. We looked out through that window at the world, as if the attic were our private tree house. There, level with the highest trees, we could see all the busyness of people. We could see a chain of stores several blocks away. Those golden arches and an empty Ronald McDonald wrapper that I kept symbolized food for me. From this attic window we watched and waited and hoped to see our mother coming home.

The emptiness of the house provided no home life for my sisters and me, but we felt no real pain other than our empty stomachs and the drafty stench of loneliness that curled us up and rolled us into tight balls of one heartbeat. Later, a television appeared in the house, and we laughed to it. Then one day the television disappeared, as if it had never been there.

An old white woman lived in a house behind us. Every morning she would put food out for us. She somehow knew that we were being left to starve in our own house. We counted on her food. Sometimes, when no adult was around the house for days, this was the only food we had.

Every evening, after the sun went down, we lay in fetal positions in the attic, looking out of the window into the night sky. We waited and waited for that next morning, so we could rush down from the attic to the porch to eat whatever the old lady had put there for us. Our idea, strange as it sounds, was that we wouldn't go to sleep at all. We were so hungry that we just felt like watching for the morning to come and feed us.

Of course we could never stay awake all night. Eventually we would fall asleep. Birdy, who was younger than Charlene and me, always fell asleep first, even before Carlette, the youngest. As soon as she woke up in the morning, she would wake the rest of us, because she was afraid of being awake while we slept.

Of all of us, Birdy was the wildest. Being neither the oldest nor the youngest, she had no special role to play, so she could just be her true self. She must have been about four at the time. We often had to chase her around the house, and if anyone got us into trouble, it was usually Birdy. She didn't worry. She didn't have to steal money or scrounge for food; Charlene and I took care of that, and Birdy made us laugh when we felt truly abandoned. She put on our mother's high-heeled shoes and danced around until she fell down. She made up games—she put one of Otis's hats on me and pulled it down over my eyes so I couldn't see. Then she led me around the house by the hand, laughing as I bumped into the furniture. Then it was Charlene's turn to have the hat on, and then Birdy's. When I led Birdy around, she walked fearlessly, knowing I wouldn't let her bump into anything.

It was Birdy who first found the attic. It was Birdy who climbed into the kitchen cabinets. It was Birdy who first ventured outside to taste the food the old lady had left on our back porch and to drink from the pitcher of milk—that girl loved milk!—that the old lady always left beside the food.

Whenever Mama was at home, we'd often see her come out of the bathroom sweating, gently touching her face with her hands, as if she were sleepy. Then she'd lie down on top of the bare mattress. The heroin in Mama's veins gave Birdy the chance to do what she loved to do. Softly raising Mama's head and bringing it down into her lap, she'd comb her hair, while the rest of us sat on the bed and watched quietly. We would just wait, watching, as if we all knew there was so much more happening than just us being there with our mother.

When my baby brother Dean was born, he was left alone with us too, even though he was only an infant. I tried to take care of him and give him his bottle. My mother said Carlette—we called her "Bug"—was Charlene's baby, and Dean was mine. Dean was supposed to take the place of another baby brother, Carl, whom my mother had put me in charge of a year or so before, but Carl had died of crib death.

One morning when Birdy was standing under a tree next to the fence, drinking her milk, I came out of the house rubbing my eyes. Suddenly out of nowhere a cat dropped down from the tree onto Birdy's back and dug in its claws. It happened so fast! My body didn't move even as my mind was reaching out, trying to wrestle the cat off my baby sister. I could feel this cat all over her and her hands above her head, trying to grab the cat and push it off. But I was frozen with fear and couldn't move.

Then the cat took off. Birdy was on the ground screaming, still trying to get the cat off her head, even though it had already gone. I was finally able to run to her, stop her arms from swinging around in the air, and reassure her that the cat was gone. Birdy still thinks her big brother got that cat off her. I never did tell her the truth.

After that we were afraid to eat outside. Being the only boy, I was elected to tiptoe out to get the food the old lady continued to leave for us. Or I would jump out of the window and run to the store to buy candy when I got coins from the pockets of the people who nodded out. But I was always scared to leave my sisters, scared to be gone in case my parents suddenly came home.

The only other person who really understood my fear was Charlene. My mother and Otis had told both of us never, ever to leave the house. If they ever caught us outside or found the front door unlocked, we would be whipped. They didn't want us to attract attention to the house in any way. They didn't want anyone to call the police to report a lost child. They feared cops stumbling into their operation, or burglars coming in to steal their heroin. I later learned that my mother feared that burglars would kill us kids so we wouldn't be able to identify them.

Whenever we were afraid of getting whipped, we would race one another to get to the bathroom first. Birdy was often the one to sound the alarm for all of us by dashing to the potty when she heard our parents coming through the front door. It was as if our parents' and their friends' constant use of the bathroom to shoot heroin had made it a sanctuary. Whoever got there first—and it was usually Birdy—was given the same level of respect as people sitting on the toilet cover with a tie around their arm.

One time my parents caught me coming back from the store carrying a whole bunch of candy bars inside the front of my shirt. Otis's face was full of anger, and my mother just said, "Don't kill him. You mustn't kill him." I don't remember too much after that. The extension cord Otis used tore right through the pillow that I held against my body, and the beating seemed to go on forever.

My Father's Shoes

OTIS WAS MY STEPFATHER. The only memory I have of my biological father is also one of my earliest. That memory still has the power to raise its head from a pool of painful childhood events, just like my mother raising up her head from the floor, blood pouring out of her face.

We were all in the bedroom, where Mama had been trying to pack our stuff in a chaotic frenzy. My father—whose name I never knew—banged open the front door, yelling, "Where are you, bitch? I'm gonna kill you and your kids!" Panic-stricken, Mama grabbed me, jerked my face up to hers, and shook me, saying, "If anything happens to me, you take care of your sisters." Then she crammed the three of us under the bed one by one—with me on the outside.

Now I heard my father yelling, "Where are those kids?"

Sweat dripping from her face, my mother ran out of the bedroom. Hearing the *bam! bam! bam!* of my father's fists against her flesh, I knew what happened when she got to the next room. My sisters and I shook with every blow, as if our mother's cries were our own—and when her cries stopped, we could still hear the blows. But that wasn't all we heard. Furniture was breaking and glass was flying as the pictures fell down from the walls. My father had slammed into us like a hurricane.

Then, with a kick of his foot, the bedroom door smashed open and the storm stood at our threshold. From under the bed, all I could see was these shoes—the scariest sight I'd ever seen. I raised my eyes to catch a glimpse of the man who filled the shoes, but his voice interrupted me:

"Where you motherfuckin' kids at? I'm gonna kill you too!"

Three steps in, and his shoes were level with my eyes, barely inches away. All desire to see his face evaporated as I heard the sound of my mother pouncing on his back, flailing and pounding as she screamed, "You ain't gonna kill my kids!"

In this macabre embrace, they twirled out of the bedroom once more. Now I heard the dishes breaking, and then the sinister sound of those horrible shoes kicking my mother, stomping her as she lay on the floor. I heard her yelling, "Help! Please! No!" but there was nothing I could do. As the beating went on and on, my sisters and I simply froze with fear.

Finally the pounding and stomping noises stopped. I heard my father slam out of the house. What was I to do? It was difficult to stay under the bed. I remembered Mama telling me to take care of my sisters if something happened to her. Now something had happened to her, and I wanted to help.

Trying to decide what to do, I fell into an anxious sleep. What woke me up was the sound of something being dragged across the floor. I peeked out from under the bed to see what looked like a monster crawling into the room. It was Mama, her lip swollen and dragging, her eyes hidden by a curtain of blood. She had pulled herself all the way from the next room to just a few feet away from us. I recognized her by her earrings.

She lifted her head off the floor and reached out to us with her hand, but the effort was too much. Her head fell back with a crack as it hit the floor.

Charlene and I scrambled out from our safety. I took Mama's head in my lap and tried to wipe the blood from her face, but it just continued to gush. Even with a wet towel that Charlene brought from the bathroom, we couldn't stop the blood. We looked into one another's eyes and started screaming. At the sound of our panic, Mama opened her eyes a crack. She took my hand and squeezed it really tight, and even managed a smile, as if to say that all was well. And in some way, it was: we were still together.

Hearing our screams, a neighbor came in and called an ambulance for Mama. After that I never asked about my father. But I've always remembered those shoes trying to stomp out the light of my mother, taking me to pain that has lasted forever.

CHAPTER 2

Rescue

Social Services

WE WERE LIVING IN filth and hunger when we were finally found. Someone—perhaps the old lady who set out food for us—reported us to the cops, who brought people from the social services department to see us. The sight of our torn and ragged clothes led them into the house, where every one of their senses was laid to waste.

Only now can I imagine the awful stench of our pee-stained mattresses. After urinating on them for months, we'd become immune to the smell, like a rancher to his cows. The mattresses were our playground, better than any merry-go-round. We would take them off the beds and drag them to the middle of the living room and, like a family of lion cubs, jump and wrestle there until we fell asleep.

Like the foul smell, the cockroaches were also natural to us. At our house, they came in every size, bunching together in revolving circles that would scatter when we opened the kitchen cabinet doors. This was very entertaining, and we made serious efforts to keep any of them from leaving the kitchen. When the inspector from social services opened what we called "the roach cabinet," he jumped and fell backward. Later, as Miss Ann, my social worker, was driving me to my new foster home, I giggled as she desperately tried to keep me from standing in the car seat to show her how I had seen the fat man falling.

We were removed from our house and our parents. When we arrived at social services, a black woman led me down a hallway with colorful wallpaper. I stared up at Mickey Mouse, Donald Duck, and Bugs Bunny as I walked along beside them holding that lady's hand. I remembered them from the television.

We went into a room, and I was lifted up onto a table. Two other ladies began to undress me. I started crying because the lady who had held my hand was about to leave. So she stayed and held my hand again, talking to me gently while the other two women opened up my shirt. They kept saying, "Oh my God, oh my God." The look in their eyes as they registered the condition of my young body began to scare me. I could tell they were near tears and at the same time angry. I felt a pain inside me, as if something were really wrong, but I didn't know what.

I had accepted beatings, loneliness, and near-starvation as normal because those things had helped me to survive. Now when these women undressed me, it felt like they were removing a shield that had become part of me. As they peeled off layer after layer, I began to feel my age and started crying. With my tears, I shed each fiber of responsibility I had had in caring for my sisters and brother. I was finally being cared for as a child, and so the child inside me opened wide.

After the nurses bathed me, dressed me in pajamas, and fed me, I listened like a captured cub for the voices of my siblings. Sadly, they weren't around. My sisters had to be quarantined because of the parasites found everywhere on them.

I would not see any of my siblings again for several years. We were placed in three foster homes—my baby brother and I went to separate homes, and my sisters went together to the same home.

Because of the care and affection I was given, I assumed they were getting the same, wherever they were. Later I found out that wasn't always true.

Miss Ann

While I was playing in the nursing unit of the social services department, another lady came in. Kneeling down beside me, she said she would be taking me to a nice home where I would live until my mother and father could care for me. She spoke with kindness, took my hand in hers, and assured me that when my mother was well enough, my siblings and I would all return to her again.

She explained that my sisters and my infant baby brother each had very special needs, and that those needs would not allow them to go with me to the place where I would be staying. I never really understood what all of this meant, but at least I knew that as long as she was talking to me she wouldn't leave me there in the nursery room. I kept nodding my head to show that I was grown up.

I don't know how many days I stayed in the child custody building, but Miss Ann came back to the nursery room to visit me several times. Then one day she walked me out through the halls with the cartoon wallpaper and put me in the front seat of her car to take me to a foster home.

Out the car window I saw the golden arches of McDonald's coming up. I knew them from my attic window. Sitting on my knees, I pointed and shouted to Miss Ann, "Look at those golden 'em! Dem right there!" The next thing I knew she turned off the highway and stopped at McDonald's. With my hand in hers, she took me inside and bought us both hamburgers, french fries, and Cokes. We ate inside the car, laughing. I wanted to stay with her and nobody else until my mother could come and get me.

When we got to the house, we sat in the car for a minute. Miss Ann told me that the foster home would only be temporary, that my siblings would be close by, and that my new foster parents were only doing this to help my mother in these difficult times. She told me that the best way I could help my mother was always to try to be happy, because my mother was going to be away for a while. I promised to try.

"But can't I stay with you, Miss Ann?"

"Let's visit these nice people and see how you feel about them, okay? If you stay with them, I promise to visit you and bring you news about your mother." Then she gave me a big hug and we got out of the car.

When Miss Ann rang the doorbell, I wanted to grab her by the leg and not let go. The front door opened, and an elderly black couple looked down at me. The lady knelt down to me with a smile and reached for my hand.

"My name is Mamie. And you must be Jah-vis," she said, holding my hand and looking as if she wanted to pick me up in her arms. She stared up at the elderly man beside her. "Oh, Dennis," she said to him. "Look at this child. Oh, praise God!" With tears pouring down her cheeks, she pulled me to her, gently rocking me in her arms like a mother who had just recovered her lost child.

Up until then I had never seen anyone crying out of pure joy. Whenever I had seen tears, it was out of hurt and pain. With both my arms pinned to my sides by Mamie's hug, I looked up at Miss Ann, who smiled and touched my shoulder as if to say, *You see? Didn't I tell you that you would be loved and cared for at this new home?*

When Mamie finally stood up, wiping her eyes, we all went into the living room. The adults began speaking to one another like I wasn't there. I sat silently on the couch, staring all around, up and down, as my feet wiggled in midair. I was too short for them to reach the floor.

How different from the vacant rooms where we had lived with my mother! There were tall curtains that went from the ceiling almost down to the floor, carpeting all over, big framed pictures on the walls, lamps on polished tables, and a great big black piano.

Farther back, in another room, I could see a dining table with chairs around it. I had never before been in such a house or seen so many things.

Before I knew it, I was up roaming around, touching everything. I didn't even know the object on the wall was a light switch until the lights went off in the living room. Up until then I had never even seen a light switch on the wall. Our light had come from the windows. One reason going up into the attic at night gave us comfort was that the "lights" in the house were still on when we came down the next morning. Thinking that we somehow made this happen gave us even greater comfort.

Now I flipped this light switch off and on again before running back to the couch. A few minutes later I was roaming through the house again. I poked into bathrooms and closets and explored the kitchen. I had found my way to the backyard and was wondering how to open the garage door when I heard Mamie calling out, "*Jah-vis!*" in a deep Texas accent. I would hear that call a million times more. She stood on the red porch steps, waving for me to come back inside. I ran to her. She lifted me into her arms and carried me back inside on her hip. When she put me down, I stood in the doorway of a bedroom.

"Is . . . uh . . . this all m–mine, Mamie?" I stuttered.

"Yes," she said. "But, child, oh child, that's only if you wanna stay with us. 'Cause if you don't, Miss Ann, she can find you another home until your mama comes for you."

Even at that age I could see how badly Mamie wanted me to stay. Seconds passed. I marched into the living room to give Miss Ann the news. She was still seated on the couch. "Miss Ann, will you . . . be m–mad," I stuttered, "if I stay wit' dem?" I turned and pointed at Dennis and Mamie where they stood in the doorway.

She said, "Not if you promise I can come see you. Can I get a promise?"

I felt sorry for Miss Ann. "Um–huh, I promise you can." I gave her a long child's hug. Feeling her hand softly patting my back, I figured she was okay with my decision. Before she left she gave Mamie a card with her telephone number on it.

That very afternoon I climbed a tree in the backyard. I was looking for ways to get up higher when I heard Mamie calling me again. She stood on the back porch. "*Jah-vis!*" I heard her cry.

"I'm up here, Mamie," I shouted.

"Oh, Lord—*Dennis!*" she called back into the house. "Come see this—this boy done climbed the tree! As God is my witness, I hope he don't think he flies too!"

When I climbed down, Mamie took my hand. "Come on indoors," she said. "Lord, we need to put your tail in front of a mirror, child! So you can see you don't have no wings!"

Into the Arms That Cared

DENNIS AND MAMIE PROCKS were already in their retirement years. Both were God-fearing Christians, and not one Sunday did they ever miss church. From the moment I arrived their love and nurturing began to release the child in me. Now I could run free and wild, without having to take care of my siblings. The "little man," as my mother had always called me, began to fade. All those times left alone—days passing into nights as we huddled in the attic watching for our mother to return—that life felt more distant with each passing day.

Although I was always thinking about my sisters and baby brother—and dreaming of them at night—Miss Ann and the Prockses assured me that their new homes were as happy as mine. But sometimes the old horrors appeared in my nightmares: I heard the sounds of my mother getting beaten up, and I saw her falling to the floor. In my dreams I crawled out from under the bed and looked down at her. I took her hand and felt the stickiness of her blood.

These nightmares made me wet the bed or scream into the night. I'd wake up shaking, scared sick. Immediately Dennis and

Mamie would rush into my bedroom, take me in their arms, and place a cool cloth across my sweaty face. Then they would take me into their own bed and put me between them until morning.

The Prockses took me to their Baptist church every Sunday. I hated it. I had a whole separate closet of church clothes that I hated as well—dress suits that Dennis, who loved clothes, had bought for me. In a suit and tie and polished dress shoes, I wasn't myself; I couldn't run around.

But every Sunday morning, like a ritual, we ate breakfast together and dressed for church. I was impressed by the fact that Dennis even wore garters to hold his socks up, and he liked to pop his suspenders. Mamie stood me in front of the mirror to grease my face and recomb my hair. If there was one thing Mamie said she didn't like it was "an ashy face." She liked my face to shine.

Mamie was into hats with flowers all over them. Dennis drove us to church, and Mamie's Sunday hat had its own seat in the car. At church Mamie made me sit in the very first row, in the care of her elderly women friends. Mamie was part of the church choir, and Dennis was a deacon who sat behind the pulpit, so little me sat squeezed in between these mothers of the church, all super-big women, powdered in their makeup, wearing hats and waving their church fans high in the air. I sat right under their armpits while they got started praising God, even before the services began. They couldn't wait for the Holy Spirit to enter them.

The first time the Prockses took me to church with them I didn't even know what a church was. I only knew it was special because of the clothes I had to wear. I sat in my new suit with no wiggle room, my face shining, while Mamie's friends hugged me and gave me mushy kisses, calling me their miracle child, God's gift. Every minute was pure torture.

When services finally got started, a column of singing, clapping choir singers marched up the aisle, dressed in beautiful robes. They filed into the choir stand in perfect order, singing gospel songs until the preacher, wearing a black robe, came out and stood behind the pulpit. He looked over my head as he spoke, and I turned to see who he was talking to. I was amazed to see that the church was packed with people. I had never seen so many people in one single place. They were all black folks too!

Suddenly the preacher stared directly down at me. He called my name and asked me to stand up. When I came to my feet, he told the whole church that "our beloved brother Dennis and sister Mamie" had brought me into their home. Then he asked for everyone to pray for my mother. In that moment I felt so flustered that I lost sight of Mamie—in the choir stand—and Dennis—seated by the pulpit. My chin just dropped down on my chest, and I started to cry. Mother Pearl saw my tears and pulled me back down into my seat.

She said, "God loves you, child. And don't you go worryin' about your mama, you hear? The Lord Jesus is watchin' over her now, so straighten up, child." Then big Mother Pearl hugged me to her bosom. "You's in God's house now, you hear?"

"Um-huh," I mumbled, wanting to see Mamie's and Dennis's faces again. I was scared of not seeing them when I looked up again. But my eyes found them back in their places, and I was reassured.

When the preacher gave his sermon, the whole church reverberated around me. Old folks stamped their feet and shouted, "Hallelujah," "Praise God," and "Glory be," from the back rows. Afraid, I reached for Mother Pearl's hand. But before I could take hold, I saw that her hand was shaking uncontrollably. I peeked up at her. Her eyes were shut tight, and her tongue was speaking in a strange language.

The preacher, too, was preaching his own self into a frenzy. Just as I was about to jump up and run to where Dennis was sitting, Mother Pearl slammed a hand down onto my knee. She squeezed my leg to use as a crutch and sprang straight up out of her seat like a rocket. She threw her head back and flung both arms high in the air, jumping up and down. As she turned in circles, saliva poured from both sides of her mouth. When Mother Pearl collapsed onto the church floor, I wet my pants.

The elderly woman on the other side of me also fell down in a fit, and then the one next to her. Across the aisle, others joined them. These old folks were all falling out. When I stood up to run, I just pissed more down the leg of my trousers, so I sat back down. The wetting kept me seated there the whole time. Not until the service was over and almost everyone had filed out of church did Mamie and Dennis realize what I had done. I didn't tell them the truth, only that I didn't know where the restroom was. I didn't want them to know how frightened I was by their friends.

A few days later, while Mamie was in the kitchen hand-drying the dishes, I asked her why her friends acted the way they did.

"Jah-vis," she said, "it's what happens when the Holy Ghost takes hold of your spirit."

"Is that like the bogeyman?"

"Oh, Lordy, child, no!" She smiled. "Baby, go fetch Mamie her Bible, so I can show you what the sweet Lord said."

"No, please, Mamie," I begged. "Can I go outside and play? Please?"

"Oh, so you don't want Mamie readin' you the Bible no mo', huh?"

Seconds passed. "Well, if I say yes, you will! But if I say no, you'll think I don't want you to, right?"

"Yeah, somethin' like that, honey bunch," Mamie said, still drying dishes.

"Well, Mamie, what's in between yes and no?"

"Oh, boy child!" she said. "Go on, child. Scoot your tail right on outside and play."

I gave Mamie a hug around her leg and jetted out the back door.

CHAPTER 3

A Taste of Normal

At Home and at School

IT WAS SUMMER WHEN I first went to the Prockses', and so there was plenty of time for me to get to know them and my new home. My room, right across the hall from theirs, quickly filled with clothes and children's books that Mamie read to me. Later, I got my own TV and record player. I had an abundance of toys, games, and puzzles that I loved to put together with Dennis. But my bedroom and Mamie never got along with each other. She never understood how I could find anything in the mess and chaos of my room. It caused Mamie—who maintained a very high standard of neatness throughout the house—to divorce my room. That's probably why my church clothes were kept in a separate closet.

Every night after a long day of playing, I had to take my bath. I would hear Mamie running the bathwater. Then she'd call, "*Jah-vis!* Get your tail on in here! Mamie needs to see her sweet pea before bedtime." Her voice could find me wherever I was. I hated taking baths. They were the worst part of my day. I would wallow in my sadness before stepping into the bathroom. I'd sit on the stool and slowly, slowly, unlace my sneakers.

Once I was in the tub, Mamie would scrub my face and body and say, "The Lord knows I ain't never seen so much dirt in this here tub. Good golly, child, when I was yo' age, in dem dirt fields of Texas, they didn't have dis much dirt on the whole field we played on! Just look at you, child," she'd say as she washed my hair. "The Lord must know what he doin'—yeah, I do declare—'cause after I get you cleaned up an' put some grease on this ashy face of yours, you be my sweet pea all over again." I kept my eyes tightly closed throughout the ordeal.

After my bath, I'd sit with Dennis in his lounge room and we'd watch *Gunsmoke* or *Bounty Hunter* together. He sat in his favorite cushioned armchair, and I sat on the carpet right between his legs.

I could ask Dennis about almost anything. He answered my questions with such an understanding that I believed if I kept asking, the whole world would reveal itself to me. Then I'd rest my head on Dennis's leg and doze off. Sometimes I'd feel myself being lifted up and carried into my bedroom. Dennis would tuck me in.

Other times, if Mamie caught me dozing off and Dennis failed to budge me with his knee to warn me she was coming into the room, Mamie would let me know without compromise that it was time to go to bed. Before I got in, Mamie and I would kneel on the side of the bed and pray. She always prayed the Lord's Prayer. She would ask me to pray for my mother, for my siblings, and, after I started school, for my teachers.

I prayed for everyone who came into my thoughts. But it was mainly my mother that Mamie wanted me to remember in my prayers, and praying for her like this, night after night, kept her in my heart. Mamie never let me forget to care for my mother, to love her always, and to dream of being back with her someday. And yet Mamie loved me as if she were my mother and I her only child. Dennis and Mamie never gave an inkling of regret for having me in their lives. They had never had children of their own—not until I came along.

I went to Carver Elementary School, just a few blocks away. On the first day Dennis and Mamie walked me to class and into the handshake of my first-grade teacher, Miss Williams. For the first time in my life I sat in a chair surrounded by other kids my age, all of them black.

Like all the other boys, I had a crush on Miss Williams. I sought her affection and longed to be her favorite student. But I had a bad stutter. The very few times I instantly jumped out of my seat—without knowing I had—so that Miss Williams would call on me, I found myself unable to get out the answer to her question. As I stood there I saw the other kids covering their mouths with their hands to muffle their chuckles while my stuttering grew worse and worse. After this happened several times, my hand stayed down.

I still had fun on the playground during lunch or recess. All the boys stayed together playing dodgeball, kickball, and other made-up games with marbles, Hot Wheels, and yoyos that we brought to school with us. The girls stayed together too, playing jump rope, hopscotch, and their favorite game, jacks.

Cast out by my stutter, I walked behind the other kids on the way home from school. Even though I had started lagging behind from a sense of shame, soon I was content to be isolated in my own inner space, tailing the other kids.

I never stuttered when I was alone. My best times were when I talked to my little red wagon as I pulled it behind me, or to the giant tree out in the backyard as I sat in its branches, because they listened. As far as I could see into the skies, I dreamed about what I would be someday when I grew up. I spoke clearly to my red wagon about how I would save people when I became a fireman; I spoke clearly to the tree that held me about how I was going to be an astronaut. I never once stuttered. After a while I could talk to Mamie and Dennis without stuttering. They were the ones who broke through the clouds of my past, who swung me up into their arms and loved me unconditionally. They listened to my stories about what Mr. Tree told me.

Early on in elementary school I began seeing a speech therapist. She kept me after school twice a week to help me with my stuttering. By this time I had really started liking sports. All I thought about was sports; all I wanted to do was play sports. Reporting to my speech therapist several times each week instead of playing basketball or baseball at nearby Carver Park was almost unbearable. Whatever sport was in season, from track and field to football to basketball to my favorite, baseball, I played them all. I loved wearing my green and yellow Little League uniform, which Mamie lovingly washed and ironed. I dreamed of one day playing for the L.A. Dodgers.

On the Mound

ONE AFTERNOON IN BASEBALL practice, I learned how to throw a curveball. After practice, I hung around the park with some friends, pitching and catching. When it started getting dark and I realized I was late, I ran home and slammed the front door behind me.

"Jarvis, where you been, son?!" shouted Dennis. He and Mamie looked worried, as if they had been pacing the living room floor. "It's dark, boy!"

"I was at baseball practice," I said, still trying to catch my breath. My Dodgers baseball cap dropped over one eye, and my mitt hung off my belt at the hip. I stared up into Dennis's and Mamie's eyes.

"Boy! Just look at your clothes," said Mamie, pointing at the holes in the knees of my jeans. "God Almighty, I don't know what in heaven's sweet name the Lord wants me to do wit' you. Just look at your dirty face." She gave me a hard look-over. "Child! Go clean that poor face of yours."

"But, Mamie," I said, with sweat dripping from my face, "guess what I learned at practice today!"

"What did you learn, son?" asked Dennis, who loved baseball and would sometimes play catch with me in the front yard.

"Looka' this," I said. I reached into my pocket for my baseball. "Dennis, they showed me how to throw a really fast curveball." I jumped around excitedly. "Now I can do it like we see 'em on TV. Watch this, Dennis. Let me show you the windup!"

I tucked the baseball between my knees while I unbuckled my belt to get my mitt. I hurried, not wanting to lose their attention. They smiled, seeing how badly I wanted to show off what I had learned.

When I was ready, I stood in the center of the living room, imagining myself on a big-league pitching mound. This was serious business: I was pitching for the Dodgers, and we were winning, four to three. The other team had runners at first and third, with two outs in the bottom of the ninth inning, and the batter was standing at the plate, facing me. . . .

Imitating my famous hero, Dodgers pitcher Tommy John, I stood poised on the mound, glancing over at first base, then slowly peeking over my shoulder at third base to keep the two runners from stealing.

"Dennis, what in the Lord's name is this child doin'?" Mamie wailed, now sitting on the couch in front of me. "Just look at those trousers of his."

"Hush, Mamie. Hush. Let our boy show us what he learned at the park today."

Seconds went by. Wearing my big-league face, I stood on the mound in the living room while a huge crowd of cheering fans stood up from their seats to watch me throw the winning pitch. I wound back and pretended to throw my curveball as fast as I could. But suddenly the ball released itself from my hand. It flew across the living room, over Mamie's head, and through the window. *Crash!* Mamie bent over, covered her head, and screamed.

"Uh-oh," I whispered. I stared over at Dennis's and Mamie's shocked faces. Seeing their anger beginning to glow, I took off my baseball cap. "I'm sorry, so sorry," I mumbled, looking down at the good-luck hole in my sneakers. Long seconds went by.

"Son, go straight to your room," said an angry voice. I ran to my room, closed the door, and climbed onto my bed. I lay there staring up at the ceiling, wanting to cry.

Putting my mitt back on, I pounded it with my fist, examining its leather seams. I felt so disappointed with myself. What had happened? I heard the awful boos of the crowd that had once cheered me on. I wished I had the chance to do it all over again to show them all.

Remembering my lost baseball, I got up and opened the door. Down the hall, Mamie and Dennis were sweeping up the broken glass. I watched them for a moment and then called out, "Dennis, can I go get my baseball, please?" Dennis turned and saw me peeking from my door.

"Lord, holy Jesus," said Mamie. "This child goin' to make it bad for all of heaven when he gets there." She turned and saw the "please" in my eyes. "We'll get your baseball tomorrow, son. Tonight, we ain't goin' to have no more balls in dis house! You just go get ready for your bath."

"Yes, Mamie." I turned and went back into my room, closing the door behind me. But after only a few minutes, I stuck my head out the door again. "Mamie, I'm sorry!" I cried out. "I love you. Do you still love me?"

"Yes, son. I love you," Mamie's voice answered from the living room. "Mamie still loves her sweet pea. But you ain't goin' out there to fetch that ball!"

Baseball was everything. Some mornings I'd wake up with my mitt still on my catching hand. And every day at recess we'd trade baseball cards. After school we'd play sports at the park or gather at a friend's house and play out on the street until it got dark, sometimes beyond.

A Child Who Mattered

I WAS LIVING IN a more affluent area of town than most of my friends at Carver Elementary. The neighborhood I lived in was mostly retired people, with hardly any other kids on the block. There was nobody getting up in the mornings to go to work. Dressed in robes and slippers, the elderly residents would open their front doors only to retrieve their morning newspapers or to set out their garbage.

Although my friends complained that I lived "where all the rich people stayed" and my neighborhood seemed deadly quiet to them, they loved coming over to my house to play. They lived in high apartment buildings in the projects, so my house became the center of gravity for our games. Mamie always fed us snacks and great big lunches and even made enough food for my friends to take home.

We played sports in my backyard, but sometimes we shifted to other activities. In the garage we created our own music and dance group, which always had a different name. One of our favorites was "The Young Tempting Temptations."

In the next phase, we made go-karts with scrounged-up plywood and whatever other materials we could get our hands on. We roamed through hardware stores and junkyards and begged our way into all the elderly neighborhood folks' garages. They gave us old construction tools, recording devices, wheels, lamps, empty suitcases, bowling balls, and jars of old coins. My friends and I would round up all this stuff and bring it to my backyard. There we let our imaginations go, with hammer and nails, until late in the evenings. We took things apart and made whatever we could think of—walking stilts, ladders, scooters, and even our own tree house— right up to the moment when Mamie's telephone started ringing with calls from parents who wanted their children home for dinner. The very best of our ideas always seemed to come just when the sun disappeared and the sky above us darkened.

As I grew older and more accustomed to living with the Prockses, nestled in the tight community around me, I became the child everyone looked out for. Whenever the old folks saw me jumping over fences or climbing into their fruit trees, Mamie's telephone would be ringing before I got home. Rock-throwing, climbing onto the oil pump in the back fields, or, even worse, journeying to the other side of the railroad tracks in the all-white neighborhoods—all these adventures would be reported back to Mamie.

The railroad tracks were over a mile away from the Prockses', and Mamie and Dennis made me promise never to cross them. In school, kids told ghostly stories about someone who knew someone who almost got caught by "them." "And boy oh boy, if 'they' ever catch you, they will tie you down on the tracks and let the train splatter you into pieces."

If you wanted a powerful reputation, or even to be the king of the school, you had to cross the railroad tracks with other kids as witnesses. But I never got into the inner circle of kids who stayed after school daring one another to do things. When I was challenged by other kids, my stuttering would return. Besides, I thought that Mamie and Dennis had eyes in the back of their heads to see if I wasn't where I was supposed to be. If I catwalked along the curb on my way home from school, there was Mamie reminding me what sidewalks were for, and if I dropped a candy wrapper on the ground, Mamie was there to point out the garbage bin.

One time I ran into a garden after my baseball. By the time I finally found it, I had trampled all over Mr. Smith's flowers. Mr. Smith was one of Dennis's best friends, and Dennis sent me back to apologize to him and offer to help clean up the mess I'd made. Together Mr. Smith and I cleaned up his garden and swept out his garage. He was so surprised by my help that afterward he paid me a whole dollar. I ran home to show Dennis the money I had made, explaining how Mr. Smith said I could work for him every day if I wanted to. I went back to Mr. Smith's the next day. When we were cleaning out his garage, he found an old accordion and gave it to me. I walked home with it strapped on me, squeezing for all I was worth.

After I'd worked at Mr. Smith's for a while, I started knocking on all the neighbors' doors, asking these grandparents of mine if they had any jobs for me. Soon I was mowing lawns, raking leaves, washing cars, cleaning out garbage bins, cleaning windows, and even doing some white fence painting. Always paid as soon as I finished, I was often tipped with empty Coke bottles that I took to the supermarket in a wheelbarrow to exchange for the deposit. Pretty soon Mamie took me downtown to open my own bank account. Then she taught me how to write in my very own bankbook, which she kept with hers and Dennis's.

Working like this, I got to know many of the neighbors. One of the other elderly couples, the Johnsons, even made a bedroom in their home for me, and Mr. Johnson told me to call him "Grandpa." He took me to late-night Dodgers games and Lakers games, and I would spend the night at his house afterward. I think he felt younger with me seated next to him, cheering the Dodgers and eating peanuts and hot dogs.

I had so many adults caring about me, wanting me to be part of their lives, that when Mamie and I prayed before my bedtime it took a long time to name all the people I needed to ask the Lord to watch over. "Oh, Jesus," I began, "please look over Mr. Smith, Mrs. Jones, Mr. Williams and Nanny, also Mr. James and his dog, and Mr. Will and Clara. . . ." I would go on and on until Mamie, kneeling beside me the whole time, would say, "Boy, can't you just say 'all God's children'?"

"But, Mamie, I'm almost finished," I would answer. But then, having lost my place, I'd start all over again: "Mr. Smith, Mrs. Jones, Mr. Williams and Nanny, also Mr. James and his dog. . . ." I would go on and on until Mamie and her poor old knees started "ouching" and I heard her mumbling to herself.

"Huh, Mamie?"

"Nothing, child. Go on—just got my poor knee sleepin'."

One day I was standing on a stool in the kitchen helping Mamie wash and dry dishes. I asked her if I could call her "Mama" instead of Mamie, since other kids called their parents "Mama" and "Daddy." At first, Mamie didn't say anything. It was like she hadn't heard me. Before I could ask the question again, she started to cry.

"What's wrong, Mamie?" I asked sadly. "Did I say somethin' bad?"

With the suds on her hands keeping her from wiping her eyes, she kept on washing the dishes. Then she mumbled, "Boy, the Lord knows that Mamie loves you. And if you want to, child, you can call your Mamie 'Mama' too."

Rarely, if ever, did Mamie shed a tear outside church services. I knew my question had touched something deep inside. I had long wanted to call her "Mama," but I had stumbled into an area sensitive to both of us. To keep Mamie from crying, I continued calling her by her name. We never talked about this, ever again. But in my own heart, and I know in hers, Mamie was my mother, as I was her son.

CHAPTER 4

Friends and Fights

Lisa

IN THE THIRD GRADE, I fell in love with my childhood sweetheart. So beautiful she was, sitting next to me in class. Unlike the other girls, Lisa wore yellow ribbons in her long black hair. Her brown eyes seemed to sparkle whenever she would glance over at me. Lisa was slow to raise her hand when the teacher, Miss Clark, would ask the class who knew the answer, but not one time when her hand went up was she ever wrong.

She didn't laugh at kids being teased. She didn't play around or make silly faces when the teacher wasn't looking. Instead, she tried by her facial expressions to help other kids know the answers to Miss Clark's questions.

One time when I was asked to tell the class something we had learned, I began stuttering. When the other kids started to laugh at me, I turned to put my head down and saw Lisa looking at me. She was trying to help me pronounce the answer that I was stuttering. She silently mouthed the words to show me how to slow down and pronounce my answer correctly. When I finally said it, Miss Clark congratulated me and thanked Lisa in front of the whole class for helping me. When I sat down again, Lisa and I exchanged a special look. She had seen past my stuttering.

Whenever I saw Lisa with her friends out on the playground, we looked at each other just long enough to keep our friendship growing. For a long time we never said a word to each other—not in class, not on the playground. Instead, we entrusted our secret friendship to our best friends. They were our go-betweens. I shone on the playground when I saw Lisa's best friend come running up to me. She'd say, "Lisa says she likes you." Then she'd run back to where Lisa was hiding behind the other girls, all of them giggling, protecting Lisa's shyness. I whispered my response to Lisa into the ear of Jeffrey, my best friend: "Go tell Lisa I like her dress." But he never got it right. By the time Jeffrey made it across the playground, the message had turned into: "Jarvis say he wanna have a baby with you." I wanted to duck for cover when Jeffrey told me what he had said. But when I saw Lisa and all her friends giggling in a huddle, I crawled out from under my embarrassment and took credit for everything Jeffrey had said.

Through our best friends, Lisa and I secretly made a plan to meet each other and "hook." The four of us met behind the sand pit at school to make it official. Lisa and I stood face-to-face with our pinkie fingers hooked together, and then we hugged and kissed each other in the presence of our two best friends. They were the witnesses that Lisa and I were to be boyfriend and girlfriend for life. It was the rule of this childhood marriage that our best friends had to go around the whole school to make the announcement that Lisa and I were "hooked up."

It was only after all of this that Lisa and I started talking and hanging out in the school hallways together. Whenever we were not in class, we held hands. Only on the playground did we go our separate ways, to kickball and hopscotch. When Lisa glanced over as I played, she brought out the best in me. For her I dodged balls like Flash Gordon, I kicked the ball the farthest, and I ran like lightning around the bases. I pretended I didn't know that she was watching, but all the time I was showing off for her. She made me more daring, and she took me out of my quiet loner's shell. And suddenly—just like that—I became conscious of what I wore to school.

Before, whatever Mamie put on me to wear to school made no difference at all. Lisa changed all of this overnight. I wanted to pick out my own clothes to wear at school, to comb my own hair the way it looked best to me, and to have the right kind of lunch pail to bring to school every day (Spiderman, not the Brady Bunch)—all to impress Lisa.

But because I stuttered, I was smart enough not to wear the kind of clothes or bring the type of lunches that would attract the attention of bullies. I wanted to look good, but I didn't want to stand out. So I didn't wear my favorite brand-new Dodgers baseball jersey to school, and I hid or gave away the separately packaged bags of potato chips that Mamie put in my lunch box, because they were an unwanted sign of privilege. I always tried to avoid being one of the kids who got held up against the wall after school while a group of bullies went into their pockets, taking things from them. But even so, the day came when I had to fight a bully—the bully who pulled Lisa's hair in front of me.

When someone really wanted to pick a fight with you, they wouldn't do something to you, but to your girlfriend. That's if you had one. This was a challenge you couldn't ignore.

A Fight on My Hands

THE BULLY WHO PULLED Lisa's hair was Tony. He pulled it right in front of me as we gathered in the hallway for class. Lisa screamed and started crying, and Tony looked over at me. "Punk," he said in the hushed silence, with everyone watching, "I see you after school." Then he ran down the hall to his class. Tony was a fifth grader, two grades ahead of me. Scared, I looked around. I could hear all the "uh-ohs" of the onlookers. As soon as Tony was out of sight, their whispering grew louder. They stood around as if lining up for tickets to the after-school fight. Be there or be square!

What could I say? As we filed into class, I felt sick to my stomach with fear. I could hear Lisa sniffling, trying to dry up her tears. I wished that school would never end. I didn't want to fight and lose. I saw Tony's face in my mind. He was not much bigger or taller than me, but he looked so brutal, like a snub-nosed pitbull that had already been scarred in many fights. His mugged appearance scared other kids.

The impulse to run straight home after school and not fight Tony crisscrossed my mind and tied knots in the pit of my stomach. I watched the classroom clock on the wall tick from 1:30 to 2:00 p.m., then to 2:30, and still I didn't know what I would do at the sound of the three o'clock bell. Should I run home? Stay? Go right now? Stop coming to school for good? I kept thinking these thoughts until Miss Clark asked the class to pass our books forward. The last five minutes was free time to gather up our things while we waited for the bell to release us from another day.

During those last minutes, Lisa turned and said to me—while the whole class stretched their necks out to hear her—that she would still like me if I didn't fight Tony. For Lisa to say this meant a lot. It was an offer of saving face. Everyone listening would recognize that I didn't have to fight—not for her sake, not for mine. But what I heard was something else. To me it meant that I didn't have to win. Then the school bell sounded, and we all filed out of class, down the hallways, and out into the world.

I saw Tony waiting for me across the playground, just off the school grounds, in the direction I always went home. I knew then that I had a fight on my hands. I walked across the playground. Everyone gathered around and made a circle, with Tony and me in the middle. No words. He pushed me once, then twice, knocking my books out of my hand. Then he brawled in and wrestled me to the ground.

The other kids stood behind Tony, pretending to be rooting for him, but I think it was out of fear of reprisal if they didn't. Our fight started out as a wrestling match; my dread of becoming disfigured had me wrapping up his arms so he couldn't swing any punches. Then somehow his knee smashed into my face and my nose started bleeding. Something blinked: before I knew it I was all over Tony, on top of him, punching him anywhere and everywhere. Even when I heard him hollering, "I give! I give!" I kept on punching him. I couldn't stop.

Suddenly I was lifted up into midair, like a dog being picked up by the scruff of the neck, my arms and legs swinging. It was my baseball coach who held me there until the swinging stopped. When Coach Pete finally put me down, there was no Tony. He and all the other kids had already run away. He asked me what had happened, and I told him. He sent me home and told me if I ever fought like that again I was off the team.

When Mamie saw me walking through the front door, Coach Pete had already called her and told her the news. The expression on her face sent me straight to my room. I stayed there until both Dennis and Mamie came in and sat on the edge of my bed. I explained what had happened. They listened, asked questions, and even more sternly repeated what Coach Pete had said to me: that I would *not* be able to play baseball if I fought again. Dennis went on to say that if something like that happened again, I should defend myself without fighting back, without trying to hurt the person fighting me.

When I looked at Mamie, I could see she didn't understand this. But I knew what Dennis meant. "Mamie," I said, getting up on my knees on the bed, "it's like not lettin' dem punch me. Right, Dennis? It's keepin' dem from hittin' me. You know how I said we was wrestlin' at first? Well, like dat, Mamie," I explained.

"Lord, Dennis," Mamie said. "You better watch what you sayin' to my poor baby."

"Oh, Mamie," cried Dennis. "This boy got to defend himself.

You can't let him out there with all those mannish children! Honey, he'll be all right."

Mamie gave Dennis one of her stern looks—the kind that said, *We'll talk later!* Then she changed the subject.

"Now, Jah-vis, when were you goin' to tell yo' Mamie about Lisa?" she asked, smiling at me. "Is that why you been askin' me to iron your shirts? Why you be stayin' by that mirror, combing your hair like you do every day?"

Blushing, I put my head down.

"Boy oh boy," Mamie said excitedly. "That girl must be somethin', gettin' you out there just'a fightin'. Now you go and get yourself cleaned up, and come back and tell me about her."

Relieved, I jumped off the bed and sprinted to the bathroom.

At school the next day I heard that Tony had been telling everyone that our fight had been a tie. Nothing could have suited me better. Since I didn't win, no other kid would have to challenge me for my reputation, and since I didn't lose either, I wouldn't be seen as easy prey, a kid to pick a fight with just for the opportunity to beat someone up. To come out of that fight tied against a known school bully felt like a win to me.

Tony never messed with me again. In those days, after two boys had a fight they had to be either enemies or friends. So we became friends and called ourselves "half brothers."

CHAPTER 5

Family

Visits from Mama

AFTER I WAS PLACED in foster care with the Prockses, I would dream I heard my mother's voice. She would call out my name; I'd see her face and run to jump into her arms. Then she would whisk me away to go look for my sisters and brothers. When we found them, we would all hide away from a world that had hidden us from each other.

The Prockses had created a caring home, a home to fulfill any child's dream, a place of unconditional love. They gave me what little childhood I had, and I felt like the light of their lives. Even so, I still dreamed of my mother carrying me away in her arms.

Whenever I expected one of my mother's rare visits, I would sit outside on the Prockses' porch. She would hurry from the car across the yard, pick me up, and spin me round and round. Then she would collapse into the Prockses' arms with gratitude for their care. She would sob, "He's my baby, my baby, my baby," like a mantra. The Prockses consoled her out of a deep-rooted heart connection as black Americans, a connection untainted by their knowledge of her past. And they knew it all; John Higgins, my new social worker, had told them.

I remember the first time my mother came to see me at the Prockses'. After we said our good-byes, I ran over to the window and watched as she looked over her shoulder at me in tears. When she got into the car, the distance stretched between us, and I felt like I was in prison. Yet I was more connected to her pain than to my own. I didn't know how any mother provided for her children, but I did know that the tears in her eyes came from my mother's deepest self. In her pain was a single promise: to gather us all back together again. That was the promise she had made to me. Looking back at those visits with their long talks now lost to my memory, I remember Mama always explaining why she couldn't take me with her, fighting back the tears. The secrets my mother entrusted to me made me feel older, almost as if I were grown up. Sitting in her lap with no one else around, I felt strong, as if she had given me the power to hold her rather than being held.

Then she would tell me that she was still "sick." I knew what she meant. Even as a tiny boy, I'd known that her sickness was not the kind that needed a doctor. When she said that she was very sick, I knew it meant she was not being her true self. Many times before we were separated, I had seen this sickness steal her life energy as she lay on the bed in a daze or crouched on the floor in the bedroom corner trembling, as if she were freezing.

I know now that the sickness was her heroin addiction. On my knees, peeking through the open bedroom door, I'd seen her tying off her arm with a rubber strap and shooting heroin into her veins. There were times when she couldn't get up afterward. I'd walk over and sit down next to her. If she was conscious, she would lean on me and say, "Mama is sick," using me as a crutch to get to bed, where she'd fall asleep. Now when my mother mentioned being "sick," this was the image that came to mind, and I understood why she couldn't take me home with her.

Charlene, Birdy, and Carlette

I WAS GOING INTO my fourth year at the Prockses' when Mr. Higgins thought it was time for my sisters and me to exchange visits at each other's foster homes.

I ran out the front door as Mr. Higgins's car drove up, standing on the front lawn as my sisters climbed out. It was the first time we'd seen one another since being taken away from our mother, but it was as if we'd been separated only for a couple of months instead of years. We could not stop looking into one another's smiling faces and laughing.

My sisters had gotten bigger, more independent of one another. I remembered them as one inseparable being, but now they had their own personalities. When I spoke to one, the others asked me completely different questions. They couldn't help but laugh and hold on to me. We could have stayed right there in the center of the front lawn forever and ever. But when Mamie and Dennis stepped outside, they took my sisters into their arms, praising Jesus up and down for their smiles.

Once we got inside the house, Mamie brought out the sandwiches she had made for us. We sat around the dining table doing more giggling than eating. My sisters, especially Birdy, lost their shyness right away. They felt at home, as I had felt when I first arrived at the Prockses'. And like me, they were amazed by the house. They stared at the big framed pictures on the wall and at the piano, stunned by what they were seeing.

When I took my sisters into my bedroom, they thought they had entered heaven. Because I knew they were going to visit, I had cleaned it up—probably the only time I ever did. They shared their little oohs and aahs as they saw my bike, my scooter and electric train set, the radio and record player, the television set on top of my dresser, and the toys I had stacked up in the corner of my room.

They started opening my dresser drawers, pulling out my clothes, and looking inside my closet, with more toys coming out of it. I had stuffed my closet, hoping I wouldn't have to open it. My sisters, all of them, started asking me, "Jay, is this yours? This too? Is that yours? Is all of this yours, Jay?" At that instant I realized that they must have been less fortunate than I. Until then I had supposed that they were as well off. The thought that they weren't had never crossed my mind, not even once. I felt a tinge of sadness at their reactions to all these things I had. I could see how badly they wanted them for themselves.

When we went out to the backyard to play, Charlene told me how much she hated their foster home. When I asked her why, she looked around as if to make sure nobody else could hear her. Then she said she didn't know why, only that she did.

Talking to Charlene made me want to be with our mother again. Although we never spoke of her or ventured back into the horrors of our memories, Charlene and I began to feel like adults all over again as we watched Birdy and Carlette playing not far from us. We didn't have to tell each other what we were thinking, for each of us knew we weren't alone in our passing thoughts.

After a while Mamie called us into the living room. She asked me to play the piano for my sisters. Embarrassed, I tried to get out of it.

"Boy, you sit your tail down," Mamie insisted. "And you play a song for your beautiful sisters."

"But, but, Mamie . . . ," I begged.

"No buts! You come on here," she said, taking me by the arm to the piano. That whole year, on and off, a piano teacher had come on Sunday evenings to give me lessons. I had never played the piano in front of anyone before. It just wasn't cool in the eyes of my friends to be taking private piano lessons. That was sissy stuff. I had begged Mamie not to ask me to play, not to let anyone even see my piano teacher, and she had always kept her promise—until now.

"Now you play your sisters somethin' nice. G'on, Jah-vis! You play them somethin'," she said.

Just then Mr. Higgins and Dennis walked into the living room. I looked at Dennis, my eyes begging him to get me out of this total embarrassment. Dennis waved his finger as if to say, *Go ahead and play. Can't help you this time!*

When I started to play "Amazing Grace," one of the two songs I had memorized, Mamie came and stood behind me. She placed both of her hands on my shoulders and hummed along until I finished two verses. Then I stopped. I was done. Everyone's applause was more embarrassing than the actual playing. When I stood up, I avoided looking at her.

"Now, Jah-vis! This here is your family," she said. "Boy! You can't deny your talent to your kinfolk!" She carried on in her Texas accent. "They goin' to love you no matter what! If God had made you ugly, these here girls would still love you, child. Uh-huh, that's right. Ain't that right, y'all?" She turned to Charlene, Birdy, and Carlette. They were laughing and laughing.

After a whole day of visiting, it was time for Mr. Higgins to take my sisters back to their foster home. We gave one another many hugs. Charlene asked for my sneakers, and it felt good to take them off and give them to her. At that time in our young lives, she and I wore the same size.

A few months later Mr. Higgins came to take me to visit my sisters in their foster home. I didn't know what to expect. I tried to memorize the way there so I could someday ride my bike to visit them on my own. But the distance turned out to be beyond the range of what I could remember.

The Reynoldses

WHEN WE ARRIVED, WE were welcomed by my sisters, their foster parents, the Reynoldses, and their own two daughters. As I took a seat in their living room I took a look around. The house was bigger than I had expected. I saw photographs of my sisters and other family members collaged together in frames on the tabletops.

As Mrs. Reynolds introduced herself and asked me how I was, I could see a tiredness around her eyes that made her look mean. She spoke fast, really fast. She seemed a lot stricter than Mamie and Dennis. I had seen other mothers like her at my friends' homes. Their eyes alone could tell you exactly what you were supposed to be doing and not doing, and how you were supposed to behave when guests were present. Mrs. Reynolds had those kind of eyes. When she told my sisters to take me outside in the backyard so that she could speak to Mr. Higgins, I was happy to go. We all started laughing once we got outside.

The backyard was like a day care center, with a swing set and a big blow-up wading pool. We talked to each other as we swung on the swings. It was a different atmosphere than at the Prockses', but it was still fun to be with my sisters.

When I asked my sisters to show me the room they shared, Charlene put a finger over her mouth to shush me as we crept back indoors. Inside their room we wrestled and played, and they showed me their dolls and other toys. But every time we got noisy my sisters would catch themselves and muffle their laughter with pillows over their faces.

The very best part of our time together was when we raced down to the candy store, ate a bunch of candy, and then took the long way back to their house. It was not the candy that was special; it was the very first time we had all walked anywhere together.

That first time I met the Reynoldses they barely spoke to me, even when we sat together around the dining table and ate dinner.

Later on, after I returned and spent whole weekends with my sisters, I got used to the Reynoldses. Mrs. Reynolds was much younger than Mamie. She insisted on order in her home. One time when she left us alone to run a quick errand, we started horseplaying in a way that would never have happened if Mrs. Reynolds had been home. It became a wild circus that resulted in Carlette needing stitches to sew up a deep gash in her face.

I got to like the older daughter, who was about my age. But mostly I loved being with my sisters whenever I could.

Closing My Eyes

ALONG WITH ALL THE love and nurturing the Prockses gave me, I always thought about my mother. I saw that the world was against her—it did not understand her as I did.

To me, my mother was a hero. The older I became, the more I understood how she had protected my siblings and me when she lay bleeding on the floor next to the bed. I felt like a cub held with my sisters in my mother's jaws while she fought and fended for us alone. Her protection was not about leaving us in a clean house, dressing us in good clothes, or giving us hot baths and meals. Often she would leave us in the house only with the hope that we would survive until she returned—and not all of us had. One of us had died from crib death. Her protection was about her fierce willingness to give up her life hiding and shielding us from all the bad people outside. Because I had actually seen her do this, there was no greater person than my mother for me to look up to. And because of her protection, I had no greater fear than my mother being harmed.

The world not knowing how much I loved my mother made me love her that much harder. Wherever she was, I wanted my mother to feel me loving her. She needed me to love her just as much as I needed the Prockses to love me. And while they kept on loving me, they kept me always praying for my mother.

Because the Prockses loved me without asking me to love them back, they gave me who I was; they gave me myself. And I loved them for who they were too. Soon, nestled in Mamie's lap, I could close my eyes and be truly carefree. Seated on the floor between Dennis's legs, I felt safe enough to let my imagination go, to wonder and ask about whatever I wanted. Dennis always gave me understanding and patience. They taught me how to feel like a child, to add and subtract on my own fingers, to say things like "please" and "thank you." But most of all, they taught me to believe in myself, whatever my mind clung to.

One night in 1969 the three of us sat around the television and watched Apollo 11 land on the moon. When we saw the astronaut take man's first steps on the moon, I turned to Dennis and Mamie and said that I too would someday be an astronaut, that someday I wanted to fly to the moon.

Instead of chuckling, Dennis and Mamie looked at me with the same surprised seriousness that I felt. They took my dreams into their hearts in a way that made me believe in those dreams. Later, Mamie gave me a poster of the moon to put on my bedroom wall, and she found stories about astronauts and the moon to read to me at bedtime. As far as they were concerned, they were there to help me explore all the possibilities of what I could be. No matter how silly my dreams were, Dennis and Mamie made me believe that what someone else had become, I could become as well. Their faith in the power of true loving hearts gave me the best years of my childhood, somehow erasing many of the horrors I had experienced before I walked into their lives.

Mr. Higgins

EVERY FEW MONTHS MY social worker, Mr. Higgins, would come to the house to check up on how things were going. One day I was sitting at the piano, playing "Doe, a Deer" with all of my fingers, while Mr. Higgins talked with Mamie in the kitchen. They always sat and talked in the kitchen. Bored with practicing, I noticed their voices dropping to mere whispers. This caught my interest, and I began to eavesdrop as I continued softly playing the piano.

> *Mr. Higgins:* "At some point he's going to have to leave. I need to prepare him."
> *Mamie:* "Well, my health is very good at the moment. . . ."
> *Mr. Higgins:* "Your age . . . but we don't know for how long. . . ."
> *Mamie:* "Well, we still have lots of time."
> *Mr. Higgins:* "We need to think of 'what if,' . . . possibly move him now. . . . "
> *Mamie:* "Lord knows . . . can't tell him. How are we supposed to tell him?"
> *Mr. Higgins:* "Well, we still have time."

As my fingers tried to keep playing, the rage in my heart suddenly burst into unannounced tears rolling down my cheeks. The jolt of everything I had heard slammed both of my hands down hard on the keys, hard enough to break what felt broken in my heart. With that thunderous noise, I jumped up and ran out the front door before Mr. Higgins and Mamie could get into the living room to find out what had happened.

I ran down the block, crossing streets as fast as I could. I kept running, far enough to know what it was going to feel like to be alone again. I crossed the railroad tracks and ran into the night of my mind until I finally stopped running, lost. "Why was Mamie sayin' this?" I said aloud to myself.

I sat down on the curb between two parked cars and cried. Why didn't Mamie say she wanted me? Why didn't she tell Mr. Higgins he couldn't take me, not even "over her dead body," as she had always said to me? "Why didn't she?" I cried, pulling my T-shirt up over my knees and stuffing my head down inside it. "How could she not love me no more? What did I do? Please tell me, Mamie, what did I do? I'll clean my room . . . I'll do anythin', Mamie. Please, whatever you want, I'll do!" I cried and cried. I rocked myself down into the crushing depths.

Minutes passed. I thought of my mother. If my mother could see me sitting there alone . . . *She'll come and pick me up*, I thought to myself. I remembered the times she told me, "Don't trust anyone!" I could still see her face when she said this. This memory now served as a reminder that my mother knew best: I could not take people for what I needed them to be. But Mamie wasn't just anyone. "She's all I got! She and Dennis is all I got," I cried. Way within, I felt at such a loss. I couldn't move. I stayed between the two parked cars, curled up inside my T-shirt. I had to figure out what to do next. My heart felt so cold.

I don't know how long I stayed there, rocking myself. At some point I thought of a plan, stood up and wiped my face, and began the journey home. When I saw so many white people's faces peeking out from behind their curtains, I realized I was on the wrong side of the tracks. White folks' eyes chased me down the middle of the street and out of their neighborhood, back to familiar ground.

When I got home, Dennis and Mamie were sitting on the couch. They asked me where I'd been. I lied: "Oh, over at a friend's house." I had never lied to them like this before, but I didn't care anymore. "Dennis and Mamie," I said, "I don't wanna stay here anymore. Please, can you tell Mr. Higgins?"

"Son, let's talk about it tomorrow," Dennis said.

Then I went into my bedroom and closed the door. I lay on my bed and stared out the window. I watched the leaves of the trees swing their reflection on the glass until Mamie opened the door. She saw me lying curled up, wrapped in my silence, my back to the door. She came over and sat next to me on the bed. She placed her hand on my shoulder, then lay down beside me, at my back, and wrapped her arm around me.

"Jah-vis, boy," she whispered. "You listen: Your Mamie is sick. I'm very sick, and I don't know what the Lord's plan is, child. They say we can't keep you too much longer, that we too old, Jah-vis. And some of them don't know too much of anythin'. . . ." She pulled me tighter into her arms. "But that Mr. Higgins is a good man, Jah-vis. He been good to you and me. And if they say you can't stay too much longer, Lord, I just know he'll bring you to come see us whenever you want. 'Cause that Mr. Higgins is a good man. . . ."

I could feel the sorrow in Mamie's heart. It almost made me want to comfort her as much as she was comforting me.

"Jah-vis," she asked, "will you come visit us? Come see your Mamie and Dennis?"

With so much of my own pain dissolved by what Mamie was trying to explain to me, I could only lie there with her hugging me, trying my heart's best to understand. Was Mamie "sick" like my mother? Was I making her this way?

I felt so torn when I finally uttered my promise to Mamie that I would always come visit her. I did it because it meant I would not be leaving forever. But my promise to Mamie never understood the "why."

It happened so fast. Within days after Mr. Higgins's visit, arrangements were made for me to be placed in another foster home close to the Prockses. We all tried to pretend it was an adventure. The pain of leaving was pushed back, buried under the idea that I would be able to visit as often as I wanted. Beneath it all, I stood scared. I didn't want to leave. I started to strike out against Mamie and Dennis. I did things to irritate them, digging and scratching my nails into their facade while I was hurting inside. As always, they knew what I was doing and only loved me more.

When Mr. Higgins came to pick me up and take me to my new foster home, the floodgates opened. With my suitcases placed in the car and the rest of my things boxed up and stored in the garage to follow later, Mamie and I faced each other on the porch. As Dennis stood behind her, Mamie kneeled down in front of me. It was just as she had done five years before. Shaking, tears streaming down her face, Mamie pulled me into her arms with a hug that would have to last a lifetime.

"Jah-vis, you be good now, okay?" She squeezed me tightly. We both sobbed. "And at night, you start sayin' a prayer for me and Dennis, okay? Will you promise me to do this?"

"Uh-huh," I mumbled, holding on tight.

For long seconds we just swayed in our hugging from side to side. We hugged as if to remember this hug forever.

"It'll be all right, son, you just watch and see," said Mamie. "You'll be here visiting us in no time, in no time at all," she sobbed.

I felt Mamie's kiss on my cheek as we finally let go of each other. Then I ran around Mamie and jumped up to hug Dennis. When he put me down, it was the first time I'd ever seen his eyes well up.

We all looked at one another one last time. I got one more hug and kiss from Mamie before I ran off the porch and out to Mr. Higgins waiting in the car. We drove off with everyone waving. I looked back and I kept looking back, now only in my mind, to see how Dennis comforted Mamie back into the house.

CHAPTER 6

A Rude Awakening

The Duponts

WITH A DEEP SENSE of foreboding, I trudged up to the front door of my new foster home. Something in me wanted to run, but I held tightly to Mr. Higgins's hand as the Duponts opened the door and welcomed us inside. As they led me into their living room I walked past the stairs that led to the upper floor. Several kids were sitting there watching me. When Mrs. Dupont raised her voice and declared in a Creole accent that she'd be talking to Mr. Higgins and myself, she didn't need to say more. In perfect order, all the kids—each different in size and color—filed down the stairs and out of sight down a hallway. As they passed I wondered if they were all my foster brothers.

When Earl and Florence Dupont, both black Creole, brought my attention back to them, I was seated on the couch in their spacious, beautiful living room. They expressed joy that I had come to live with them and welcomed me into their family. It seemed as though they already knew me. They spoke fondly about my good school grades, how I liked working with my hands, and how I was involved in sports.

Then, with tears in her eyes, Florence brought up Dennis and Mamie. The thought of leaving the Prockses still flooded my eyes every time it arose. Florence promised that I could visit them at any time and that the Duponts' door would always be open for the Prockses to visit me. This meant the world to me. I envisioned visiting Dennis and Mamie on the weekends and all the holidays, maybe even living the entire summer with them.

Knowing how much I loved sports, the Duponts showed me photographs of some of their other foster kids dressed in team uniforms, playing basketball, baseball, and football. They spoke about the fun they had attending games and how they hoped to watch me play. They offered to get me signed up for whatever sports I wanted. Dennis and Mamie had only gone to a few of my games, and when they did, I never really liked them to be there. They always cheered for both teams, feeling it wasn't nice to be calling the other team bad names. But the Duponts were real fans. I couldn't wait to get out on the field in my own baseball uniform with both of them cheering me from the bleachers. This was all I could think about while they talked business with Mr. Higgins.

When it was time for Mr. Higgins to leave, Earl walked him to the door. Florence called the other kids to the living room, and I met my five new foster brothers as well as the Duponts' son and daughter, Norman and Nasha. Everyone welcomed me with open arms. I was now the youngest of the boys, just a year older than Nasha. The oldest boys, Norman and Arnie, were in high school. Norman seemed shorter than he really was because he had a very squeaky voice. Skinny and curly-haired, with a good heart, he was afraid to see what was really going on in the house.

Florence asked Arnie to show me to my bedroom. He stopped me when I started upstairs.

"Hey, where you going?" he asked.

"Isn't my bedroom up there?"

"No!" He laughed. "Our room is down here. Right through there." He pointed down the hallway. "Our room is right next to the garage. That's where they keep boys like us."

The room was much smaller than my old bedroom at the Prockses'. There were three sets of bunk beds lining the walls. A row of dressers stood along the only wall with an outside window.

"Is this all of our room?" I asked.

"It sure is," he said, smiling. "When I first came here, I thought I was going to have a room somewhere upstairs too. We all did. But hey, don't worry. You'll get used to it."

"So where do you sleep at?"

"Here's my bed." He pointed to the lower bunk nearest the door. "But I don't sleep in it. Don't tell 'em, but I always take a blanket and go out and sleep."

"Where?"

"Oh, you'll see," said Arnie. "You'll see!" He was more than six years older and almost a foot taller than me. He was white, with long hair past his shoulders and freckles on his face and arms. He looked like a young hippie.

I felt squeezed in. I'd gone from having my own room to sharing a bedroom with five other foster kids. And my bunk seemed so close to the ceiling.

I started to unpack my things when the rest of the boys rushed into the room. They told me to go through my things, quick.

"What do you mean?" I asked.

"Yeah, you're only allowed four dresser drawers of clothes here. She's going to take the rest away," another kid explained. "That witch is gonna take your stuff!"

"She's a fuckin' witch!" somebody else said. "We all hate her!"

Without asking, they hurried to help me unpack my suitcases. We plowed through my clothes, took out all my Hot Wheels and other toys, and stashed them under the bed.

Arnie and the other kids—Paul, Jesse, Samuel, and Harold— told me all about the Duponts. Arnie, who had lived there the longest, explained that we weren't allowed to go upstairs. There were three bedrooms up there, and they were for the family. He said that the Duponts only took foster children in order to get money to spend on their own. I barely knew what that meant—for money? He warned me that if they ever caught me sneaking around upstairs, Earl would beat me with a big wooden paddle.

I blurted out, "Did you ever get hit with Earl's paddle?"

"They don't whip Arnie no more," said Jesse. He was the shortest of all of us. Since arriving at the Duponts', I'd had trouble keeping my eyes off him because of the thin razor scars that showed up across his jaw area. "They know he can take it. The last time—tell him, Paul."

"Oh, yeah, man," Paul spoke up. It was Paul who had seen Arnie as the real stunt man in the house. Nearly crippled in both legs, Paul was everyone's corner man in the ring of the Duponts' hard-nosed beatings. There was always a need for Paul. By not being broken himself, he made a busted lip, a swollen face, or even fear pass quickly. "We were down here in our room, you know? And we could hear Earl whipping Arnie with that fat-ass paddle. *Whap! Whap!* And then, it wasn't nothin'! We heard Arnie laughing when it was all over. You shoulda been here!"

"Is that true, Arnie?" I asked.

"Yeah, but hey, don't worry. You'll get used to being hit!"

Instantly I started looking up to Arnie. He was his own drummer; he did what he wanted. I felt drawn to him.

I was warned about other things: At the dining table I had to eat everything on my plate and keep my other hand down at my side; if Florence ever saw my non-eating arm on the table, she would take my food away. I should keep my clothes clean; if I ever came home with holes in my clothing, I would be in big trouble. I was not permitted to open the refrigerator, go into the backyard shed, or touch anything on the walls in the house. And I better not break anything in the house, not even a cup.

When I asked how many of them prayed at night, went to church, or played sports, they all laughed.

"They showed you that photograph, huh?"

"Yeah, the one with all of you in your good clothes and in uniforms."

"That wasn't us," they all answered.

"They always show new kids that picture," Harold explained. Harold was biracial, and it was obvious to me that he was very athletic. I could see that he was quick, competitive, and good. "They just do it to make you want to stay and to make your social worker feel good about bringing you here. That's all."

"Yeah, that's all they fuckin' do," Jesse added.

"So that picture wasn't real?" I asked sadly.

"It's sort of real," Harold said. "It's Norman, their stupid son's school and team photo. They always bring it down and set it out in the living room whenever a new kid is comin'."

I was dumbfounded. Then Harold, wanting to revitalize my broken spirit, told me about Washington Park nearby. At the park there was a host of sports activities. Harold, just two years older than me, was the only one who loved sports as much I did.

I felt an instant connection with my foster brothers: the fear I was feeling wasn't mine alone, it was in all of us. If they could deal with it, so could I. Joining together had something to do with our own histories as well. I wondered: Why was Arnie in foster care? What was Harold's story? How did Jesse and Paul end up here? Even though we'd just met, I didn't feel we were strangers. It was different from meeting new kids in school. We were more like train-jumpers who suddenly found themselves in the same railroad car; we shared an identity by the mere fact of being in "foster care," a new term that would come to mean more than I had ever thought.

Later that day Arnie took me outside to show me around. Just as everyone had warned, Florence went through my suitcases while we were gone. Returning from a tour of the new neighborhood,

I found on my bed only enough clothes to fit in my four dresser drawers. The rest, including the suitcases, were gone, except for the things we had hidden under the bed.

Around the Dining Table

THAT FIRST EVENING AT dinner, out of fear, I made myself swallow almost half the hated carrots on my dinner plate. I was nearly gagging when Arnie noticed my difficulty. As if in protest, he refused to eat his own portion. Earl and Florence glanced over at me with a tacit warning not to pay attention to Arnie.

When Earl asked Arnie why he wasn't eating his vegetables, Arnie shook off the question as if the answer was obvious. Silence froze the dinner table. Tension pushed all the foster kids straight up against the backs of their chairs. I followed their example as if my life depended on it.

Then, like a shark lunging forward, Earl suddenly leapt up and reached across the dining table. With both hands, he grabbed Arnie by the hair and around the neck and pulled him onto the table, knocking over everything. With food splashing the floor and plates shattering, Earl punched Arnie with his bare fists. I flinched with every blow, as if I were the one being hit.

Arnie curled into a fetal position on the table as the thudding sounds continued. My eyes rolled back in my head, and I found myself sitting on the floor, curled up and shaking. Nobody was trying to stop Earl. The beating went on and on until Earl, who was in his midfifties, became exhausted. When the dining room was quiet enough to hear him gasping for breath, Florence hollered, "That's enough!" She ordered us to our room, but I couldn't move. I sat there frozen with fear, inhaling the strange aroma of Earl's sweat. For some reason I thought I was hiding under a bed. Only when I felt someone grabbing me by my tiny Afro and dragging me into the hallway did I hear Florence screaming at me.

"Didn't I tell you to get to your room?!" she yelled.

Towering over me with her wig halfway off and a deep darkness circling her eyes, Florence raised her foot in a kicking motion that chased me away. I crawled as fast as I could down the hall into the bedroom. When I stood up, everyone was laughing. Arnie was sitting on his bed. How had he made it into the room before me? I climbed onto my bunk bed and lay there, not knowing if I was the butt of the joke or if they were all laughing at what had happened to Arnie. I didn't understand how it could be funny to anyone.

Arnie said, "I almost gave that old man a heart attack! Did you guys hear the way he was breathing?" He started mimicking how Earl had been punching him and had run out of breath. They all screamed with laughter into their pillows, twisting and kicking their feet in the air. They laughed so hard that I laughed too, but I still didn't get it. It was my first day in my new foster home, and I was not yet part of this fraternity. Since I didn't feel invited to ask questions about what had happened, I just played along. Shut off from my tears, I wanted to become just like Arnie and the others.

Finding My Sport

I ENTERED ELEMENTARY SCHOOL and became a favorite on the playground. My passion for sports served as my introduction to a lot of other neighborhood kids. When we weren't playing baseball or football on the school playground, we played out on the street—in front of anyone's home but the Duponts'. I learned very quickly to stay away from that house as much as possible. I was on time when I needed to be, I got all my chores done, and I was gone again until it was time to return in the evening.

Washington Park was my home away from home—not the football field or the baseball diamond or even the basketball court, but the swimming pool. I had never swum before I stepped into that pool. I don't think I had even known how to swim. But after splashing around in the shallow end with my friends and other non-swimmers, I ended up swimming the whole length of the pool.

My friends dared me to do it again, and then they pushed me into participating in a race the lifeguards had organized. When I reached the wall at the deep end of the pool and came up for breath, I was surprised to see the other kids still swimming behind me. Then I raced and beat the older youngsters as well. Nobody could believe that I was only ten years old and it was my very first day in a swimming pool. But my fear of being in water over my head had turned my feet and arms into fins and made me fly across the deep part to the safety of the pool's edge.

One of the lifeguards asked me to come to the pool early the next day before it was open. When I arrived, he introduced me to two swimming coaches. They wanted to time me. I knew I was doing something special when they asked each other what their stopwatches read. After they timed me for speed, the coaches asked if I would swim back and forth the length of the pool to see how many times I could do it. As I swam I thought about the Duponts and other things that were going on in my life. I could swim more easily if I focused on something besides swimming. I don't know how many lengths of the pool I swam before I stopped, because when I finally climbed out, the coaches had long since taken their eyes off me.

The coach invited me to join the team. After that, I swam every day and practiced for hours and hours on the weekends. Soon I was like a fish in the water. Coach Williams started teaching me technical strokes. I hated the butterfly and could never get it right.

With a team trip scheduled, I needed to get a permission slip signed by Florence or Earl. Telling Coach Williams that I knew the Duponts wouldn't sign it somehow spilled into admitting how abusive they had been, and he became concerned. When the Duponts found out that someone had anonymously reported them to the authorities, they blamed the other kids. Seeing how I was the one who had told Coach Williams and everyone else got blamed, I now understood what Arnie, Jesse, and Harold had told me: nobody would believe our truths. After that, the Duponts forbade us to go to Washington Park. We still went, though, without permission.

The cruelty I witnessed in the Duponts' house had me constantly scared for when my turn would come. I didn't know when Florence would drag me into the bathroom and wash my mouth out with soap because I'd said a bad word, or just because she thought I had. I didn't know when she would slap me across the face because I'd overheard her saying something on the phone. I didn't know when Earl would use his paddle or fist on me. I only knew it was coming. The Duponts' acts of violence were random; almost every day one of the foster children (never one of their own) was hit, beaten, or humiliated. My constant fear of being next was a kind of abuse in itself.

Caught in the Act

I was eating breakfast one morning. Hating the yolk from fried eggs, I had always found a way to dump it into the trash without Florence knowing. This time her daughter Nasha saw me and told her mother what I'd done. When I took out the morning trash, I was met by Florence's flat hand across my face. She slapped me so hard my ears rang, and I tasted blood bubbling in my mouth. Then she grabbed my head and stuffed my face down into the garbage bin. My eyes fell open into the mush while she ground my face in the garbage. While she was yelling at me to find the eggs and eat them, I passed out.

When I came to, I was lying in a shower with cold water running all over my face and clothes. I couldn't see because of the food in my eyes, but I could hear Florence and Earl arguing. Between screaming at each other, they asked me if I was all right. Could I see them? Far in the background, I heard Arnie calling Florence a "wicked child abuser." He screamed at Earl that he was a bastard. Their noisy exchanges sounded like a street riot.

The only real pain was in my ears. I couldn't make the ringing go away. It lasted for weeks on and off. In a weird way, I was glad that all this had finally happened. It was a relief compared to what I had been seeing in my mind. The dread that I would be next was over; I'd had my turn. It hurt bad, but it was over.

Needless to say, the Duponts never took me to see a doctor. Despite their apologies—and even keeping me out of school for a couple of weeks—they made it clear that if I ever told Mr. Higgins what had happened, I'd be sorry. It would land me in a cell in juvenile hall—which brought pictures to my mind of being thrown into Alcatraz—and I would never see the Prockses again.

These threats were not why I kept quiet, though. Ever since I'd arrived at the Duponts', Arnie and the others had been warning me not to speak to my social worker about what was going on. They said it would only get back to the Duponts. I was actually more concerned about word getting back to Arnie and the others; they'd think I was a sissy. We had our own rules to bind us: never letting the Duponts have the satisfaction of seeing us cry, never telling on each other. And if it took telling lies to help one another, we would.

It became a sport to see who had the biggest smile or the coolest walk after being hit or slapped around by the Duponts. In short, we rated our own toughness according to the violence that we endured. The more we were abused, the more we learned to tolerate the pain, and eventually we lost the cast of fear.

Up on the Roof

THE SAME NIGHT THAT Florence finally slapped me, Arnie shook me awake in the wee hours. Whispering, he told me to put on my clothes because he had something to show me. Even though my face was swollen and stinging and my eyes were popping, I got up and dressed. Arnie gave me his jacket, and we crept outside. We climbed onto the brick wall next to the house and catwalked down to a place where we could scramble onto the roof. Then we sat on a mat that Arnie had already put up there.

I asked him the obvious question: why were we sitting on the roof? Pointing his finger to the night sky, he told me to look straight up. For seconds I was speechless. All I could see were billions of bright, gleaming stars. I wanted so much to show them to Mamie, who had taught me a story for every star, with no end of more stories. I couldn't take my eyes off them. It felt like they were looking down knowing we were there. They watched us while we watched them. I could see patches of stars and also some that stood apart from their neighbors. They reminded me of myself; separated from my family, but not completely lost from myself. My heart was free of its self-protective armor. For the moment I was undisturbed by all the troubles in my life.

For the longest time I couldn't speak. Then Arnie struck a match and lit a cigarette. After taking a deep drag, he handed it to me. I had never smoked before, had never even watched how someone else smoked in order to learn. I inhaled, choked, coughed, and quickly passed the cigarette back. The ashtray taste in my mouth did not help my throbbing face. To distract myself from feeling dizzy, I asked Arnie, "Do you always come up here on the roof?"

"Yep! Every fuckin' night!" he replied, taking another drag from his cigarette. I smelled the smoke going out into the air. "This is where this fucked-up world and I meet up at."

"Who else knows about here?" I asked, gazing up. I wanted to fly out to those billions of stars, to dwell among them.

"Just you, only you."

"Man, Arnie," I thought aloud. "You think Mamie and Dennis could see these stars from where they're at?"

"Who are they?"

"They're my real foster parents," I explained. "They ain't nothin' like these people—nothin' like 'em."

"Where's your real mom and dad?" he asked. "Are they still alive?" He exhaled a long puff of smoke.

"Yeah, my mother is," I said. "But I don't know where she's at."
I started thinking about my mother—my father too. Where was he?
"What about you, Arnie? Where's your mom?"

"My mom and dad are dead. They're both dead!"

"For real?" I was at a loss for words. I'd never known anyone
whose mother and father were both dead. Arnie was all alone. How
would "all alone" feel to me?

"Yeah, they both died when I was eight years old. At least that's
what the social workers say."

"How?"

"They keep tellin' me shit," said Arnie. "But they all lie—lie,
lie, and lie, you know?"

"Well, maybe they're still alive, right?" He couldn't be all alone.
I hadn't heard of such a thing. To not have a mother or father alive
seemed more abandoned than I could ever have imagined. My
mother was still alive; somewhere she was watching the same stars
as me.

"I really don't give a shit if my mom and dad are fuckin' dead or
not." Arnie ground the cigarette butt under his sneaker, squashing
it out. "They abandoned me when I was six or seven. That's when I
went to my first foster home. Later the social workers said they were
both shot and killed. But all I really know is that my mom and dad
treated me like shit, worse than the Duponts. So you know what?
I'm glad they're dead." Arnie tilted his head far back to look at the
skies above us.

When Arnie lit another cigarette, in the quick flare of light I
thought I saw him crying. For some time we didn't say anything,
just watched the night pass through our thoughts. It was still dark
when we climbed down from the roof and sneaked into our bedroom. Now I knew why Arnie didn't sleep down there. Compared
to the fresh air on the roof, the room stank bad. The guys were
snoring and rolling around. Their limbs hanging down from the
narrow beds made a jungle I had to get through to reach my bunk.
Lying in bed, hearing the gurgling noises of the others, I wanted to

scale the heights out in the open air and befriend all the wonders of my mind as I had done on the roof.

I returned to the rooftop many times after that when I couldn't sleep or felt shook up from witnessing the Duponts' violence. Arnie was usually already there, and we'd sit like we were at the drive-in, watching the stars instead of a movie. It was on top of the roof that I started smoking cigarettes. The roof was also where I listened to Arnie describe all the places he had been. He had lived in a number of foster homes, boys' homes, and camps, and even juvenile hall for a brief while. The idea that Arnie had actually gone to "juvi" made me feel like he had been in Alcatraz.

But mostly Arnie told stories of running away and being free, all on his own in the open world. He made the way he felt then sound like the freedom we shared on the rooftop. While we watched the stars he told me many simple things, like where the airplanes landed, where the transit buses went, and where the trains met up. He described buildings as huge as city blocks—some of them under the city streets—and he said that people of all different colors would help you: all you had to do was stick your hand out and they would put money into it. He told stories about how he had snuck onto buses and trains and traveled; he'd seen so many places, it seemed to me like he'd gone all over the world. He told of being out at night in cities that never went to sleep. He loved San Francisco, downtown Los Angeles, and other places where hundreds of people slept out under the open skies. He said they'd sit around bonfires playing music and singing through the night. No one cared or asked any questions. For Arnie, this was freedom.

I listened and listened. Arnie's stories made me realize how crammed in and bunched up I was at the Duponts'. I started dreaming of running away.

CHAPTER 7

My Heart Is Broken

"Stirrin' Up Trouble"

THE DUPONTS KEPT PUTTING off allowing me to see the Prockses. They always had a reason why it wasn't a good time for me to visit. Even though I was terrified of getting caught by Florence, one day I snuck on the telephone and called Mamie, one of the two people I loved so much. Mamie was happy to hear my voice. I found out later that Florence had been telling her that I hadn't been doing too well, that I was having severe temper tantrums that stemmed from my attachment to her and Dennis. Mr. Higgins had told Mamie that the best way for them to help me was to refrain from visiting or talking to me. Now that she heard my voice over the telephone, she praised God in the belief that I must finally be doing better.

I poured my heart out to Mamie, telling her how much I loved and missed her and Dennis and how badly I wanted to come back to them. I hid behind the couch as I talked. I told her everything, hoping to hear her love through the phone.

But Mamie only listened quietly. She was less concerned about what I was telling her than about whether I was still suffering from temper tantrums. For her, the things I was saying about Florence's violence to me and the other kids could never be true. In her heart such things were not even possible. The more I kept trying to explain—in a panic for her to believe me—the harder my heart pounded.

Then she calmly asked me to call Florence to the phone! This was the very last thing I had expected her to do. "No, no! Mamie, please," I begged her. "Please, promise me, please don't tell her, Mamie."

"*Jah*-vis," Mamie said calmly. "Son, you goin' to have to get used to being there. They say you havin' problems adjustin'. If you want to visit us, Jah-vis—and Jesus knows I wanna see my sweet pea—you have to show Miss Florence you ain't stirrin' up trouble. Miss Florence is a good woman, doin' God's work carin' for all you children. You need to help Miss Florence. Before you come to visit us, child, we all—Mr. Higgins and all of us—wanna see you behavin' first."

"But I am behavin', Mamie," I cried into the phone. "I'm not stirrin' up trouble!"

In that moment I realized that Florence had turned Mamie and Dennis and Mr. Higgins against me. I was shattered into pieces, lying on the floor behind the couch, hopeless. I had walked right into Florence's trap. She was a veteran foster parent. She knew I would try to call somebody—the Prockses or Mr. Higgins—and she had already prepared the way. Arnie and the others were right: there was no sense in trying to tell anyone what was going on inside the Duponts' house. But Mamie? I had lost Mamie to the manipulations of the Duponts, and I had nothing left. My heart was broken.

Mamie's fears about my "problems" kept her from promising not to tell Florence that I'd called. For weeks I lived in a bubble of fear, wondering if Florence knew. Every time the telephone rang I jumped, afraid it was Mamie calling Florence. Then it began to fade from my mind, until finally I forgot all about it.

Without Protection

IN THE KITCHEN A month later, Florence looked down at my hands and told me to wash before I left the house. I was at the sink lathering when she suddenly came up behind me. Gripping one of my hands, she forced it down into the drain. For a split second I imagined she thought I'd dropped the soap and was wanting me to retrieve it.

Then I saw her flip the garbage disposal switch. The tips of my fingers felt bits of food bouncing off the rotating blades. I tried to pull my hand out as Florence kept pushing it down farther toward the blades. We were like two arm wrestlers. I didn't know why Florence was doing this. She was not only mean, she had become totally possessed: I could feel her evilness wanting to hear my screams. The seconds felt like minutes. Thanks to the soap, she kept losing her grip, which may have been what saved my fingers.

"If you ever," Florence said, spitting into my ear, "try calling somebody else about what goes on in this house, you won't have this hand! Don't you ever, ever . . ." She seethed through her teeth: "Do you hear me? Do you?"

"Yes, please, I won't, I won't, I promise I won't!" I pleaded, while Florence continued with all her might to force my hand down into the blades. Finally she let go. Drawing my hand out of the drain, I thought about how close I had come to never playing sports again. Florence kicked at me and cursed me out of the kitchen. Holding one hand in the other, I ran through the house and out the door.

At least I didn't have to wonder anymore whether Florence knew I had spoken to Mamie. That was over. Now I could worry about what was in front of me.

I asked Arnie if he thought Florence would have really cut off my fingers. "For sure!" he said. "Easily! You lucky as shit she didn't!"

"But wouldn't she have gotten in big trouble?" I asked.

"No."

"Why not?" I didn't understand.

"Because everyone would have thought you did it to yourself, you know, to get back to that other foster home again."

I slowly saw in my mind that Arnie was right and that Mr. Higgins, Dennis, and Mamie would have believed the Duponts before me. Even at that young age, I realized that I had no protection from the Duponts. I had lost the shield of being only a kid. After this I tried to stop thinking about visiting the Prockses. Instead, I filled my mind with the idea of running away. I went to school every morning thinking about it. One day when the time was right, I would see my chance and go. This hope of all hopes kept me from feeling permanently condemned.

Each of the other foster kids had a plan of escape too. Most relied on returning at least to their relatives, if not to their parents. Arnie counted on the day when he would turn eighteen and be out on his own. We all needed these plans; we nurtured them in order to survive.

When I had lost all hope of ever seeing the Prockses again, I became immune to the abuse. It stopped hurting. I learned how to cover myself, to deflect punches with my arms, and to curl up as tight as a ball of yarn on the floor. Oddly, just when the beatings stopped hurting, they became less frequent. Earl and Florence started treating me better, if only because they realized it was going to take a lot more hitting and punching to make a point.

When Mr. Higgins visited, the Duponts gave a performance. They started off by reporting to him that I had received "a few spankings" since his last visit—their way of deflecting any concern before they proceeded to praise me nonstop. Smiling happily, they looked like the most thoughtful, nurturing foster parents. I sat across from them in the living room while, close to tears, they told Mr. Higgins how desperately they wished I was their own child. They went on about how well I had been doing in school, how well I got along with others, how their own children loved me like a brother, and how happy and proud I always made them. Then they took each other's hands as if to keep themselves from falling apart with so much joy.

The Duponts said they were looking forward to me bringing them home a trophy from playing baseball, and they showed Mr. Higgins the shelf where they were planning to put it. Before I knew it, even I was smiling with modest pride. For a while, all the bumps and bruises on my body were forgotten and forgiven.

Florence and Earl never mentioned their reason for not letting me visit the Prockses. How could I be all of these good things and still have "temper tantrums"? These were all lies. I didn't understand how Mr. Higgins couldn't see that.

What bothered me most was the way the Duponts used me and the most sacred parts of my life history to entertain their friends. Sometimes Florence would pull me out of bed and bring me into the living room, dressed only in my underwear and a T-shirt, to stand before the glittering faces of strangers drinking alcohol from her finest crystal. As I entered the room their mostly white faces would stare in hushed sadness, a sadness that would stay in their eyes the whole time I was there. I took my seat in a chair that felt like a stage.

Florence would introduce me as the "Jarvis whom I was telling you about." She knew all about my past. She would describe the horrible conditions in which social services had found my siblings and me. She would say that my mother was a heroin addict and a prostitute, relating other details that I hadn't even known. Listening to this tale, the guests would pause in drinking from their little whiskey glasses. Florence would ask, "What kind of mother could leave a child like Jarvis that way?" She would say that my mother didn't deserve to ever get me back. She would even say that because she, Florence, had devoted her life to foster care, there was still hope for kids like me.

Then Florence would ask me to tell everyone what my sisters and I had done while my mother left us alone. What had we eaten?

And what did I think about my mother now? Whenever I started to answer—"Oh, cereal"—Florence would break in: "If they were lucky! Without no milk! And these children were wearing not one stitch of clothing when the social worker found them!" The staring white faces would look like they were going to burst into tears.

At these gatherings, I felt singled out as an abnormal specimen. They made me feel sorry for myself when I hadn't before. And I was upset that my mother was being cursed and condemned when before, at the Prockses', she had always been prayed for.

I had never stopped loving and praying for my mother, but a seed of doubt was growing. Why hadn't she come yet? Would she ever come for me? My mind had to constantly find my mother's voice and imagine her answers to these questions. I hated the Duponts more than ever. Being forced to confront my past in front of them and their guests brought my anger to a boil.

I stopped flinching when Florence raised her hand in anger at me. I almost wanted her to hit me—the harder the better. It would give me more courage to run away. Arnie had told me just about everything I needed to know about running away: how to sneak onto buses and how to avoid cops by staying close to adults so the cops would think you were with them. He said to never hitchhike by myself, but always make friends with other hitchhikers, the hippie types, whom I was sure to run into.

Most important, Arnie told me that if I was ever caught by the cops or just got lost and afraid out there, I must not tell the authorities my name and address. If I did, they would bring me back to the Duponts. But if the authorities didn't know who I was or where I'd run away from, they would be forced to take me to "McLaren Hall." Once I was there, he said, it didn't matter if they found out my name. I could tell them I would run away again if they tried to send me back to the Duponts.

The way Arnie described McLaren Hall, it seemed like I had nothing to lose and everything to gain by running away, even if I got caught. He said McLaren Hall was a place where they kept wards of the state and runaways, and although it had a fence around it, he knew I would like it there. The way he described it, it sounded like a coed camp with dormitories for boys and girls, a school, an auditorium, and a dining hall. There were sports activities and field trips, and no one would force you to eat something that you didn't like. He said when he was there and got into trouble, instead of getting his brains punched out, he just had to lie on his bed in the dormitory for hours. They had never physically touched him. Arnie said I'd think McLaren Hall was paradise compared to the Duponts' home. What Arnie didn't like about the place was the fence. He didn't like being cooped up. He didn't bother running away from the Duponts because, in a way, he owned them. He owned his own space. And soon he'd be eighteen.

Almost every detail Arnie told me remained fixed in my mind, and I started to observe the many things I would need to know when I ran away. I watched how people boarded buses to see if I could sneak onto one as Arnie said I could. Whenever I saw a hitch-hiker, I'd watch to see if a car would stop and give him a ride. I was rehearsing my plan, getting closer and closer to taking the chance to free myself.

Visiting the Prockses

ONE EVENING THE DUPONTS called me upstairs. My mind scattered with fear as I stood at their open bedroom door. They told me to put my school clothes on—they were taking me to visit the Prockses. I skidded across so many tracks in my mind: I felt guilty for contemplating running away, fearful that the Duponts somehow knew, and still determined to do it. I wondered if this was a sign, a chance to learn how to get to the Prockses on my own. At the same time, I felt troubled that I wasn't happier at the prospect of visiting them.

When I first moved to the Duponts', I had cried myself to sleep wanting to see Mamie and Dennis. But now, close to a year later, something was lost inside me. I was no longer the child that Dennis and Mamie remembered, and I was afraid they might reject me. At the same time, I was frightened that they would be able to read my mind and learn everything that had happened. This, I feared, could kill them. Worst of all, I wouldn't be able to bear the pain if they were to believe whatever performance the Duponts were about to give them. So I focused on one thing: nothing was going to stop me from running away. Determined to memorize how to get to the Prockses on my own, I paid close attention as the Duponts drove me there.

Dressed neatly in my school clothes, I walked up to the house with Florence and Earl. Ringing the doorbell, I looked around at the neighborhood that I had already started to miss again. When Dennis and Mamie opened the door, I rushed inside and hugged them with all of my ten years of life, forgetting about Earl and Florence behind me.

I was heavy now in Mamie's arms. She didn't have the strength to lift me as she once had. She cried and whispered into my ear that she loved and missed me. We all sat down in the living room, and the Duponts immediately began their performance. They started crying as they described to Dennis and Mamie all the good things about me. I think they almost believed their own lies.

Their talk forced me out of my seat, and for some reason I sneaked into Dennis and Mamie's bedroom and stole a twenty-dollar bill out of Mamie's pocketbook. I put the money in my shoe and walked back into the living room. The Duponts were still talking about what an angel I was. I guess stealing the money was my way of crossing out those lies.

I could see that Mamie had not been well. She looked worn and tired, as if she were forcing herself to sit up when all she wanted was to lie down. Then she started coughing. Keeping a handkerchief over her mouth, she appeared to be in a lot of pain. But when she glanced over at me and smiled, I could still see the face that I loved.

My visit with the Prockses was not what I had hoped for. We stayed in the living room the whole time, an hour or so, while the Duponts talked about me and their other foster children. I had no chance to talk alone with Dennis or Mamie. Although this didn't surprise me, I was disappointed. Would I have been brave enough to tell them anything? My greatest fear was that they wouldn't believe me. Then where would I run? I felt some relief in not being able to speak with them alone.

When we left after many good-bye hugs, I knew I would be returning. Now I knew my way to Dennis and Mamie's house—about twenty-five miles away. I had a twenty-dollar bill in my shoe, and I could choose my own time. The scars of hatred pressed against my heart. I was ready to actually do it! To run away! I had no one to stop me but myself. But as soon as I realized it was up to me, things at home seemed to get better. I was waiting for the Duponts to lay a hand on me one more time, to give me a final reason to go, but nothing happened. I may have unconsciously avoided their wrath, knowing what I would do.

Mamie's Passing

ABOUT A MONTH AFTER we went to see the Prockses, I was called home from school to meet with Mr. Higgins, who had unexpectedly dropped by the house. Just the two of us sat in the living room, and I knew this visit was something special. I could see from his face that he had what he thought was bad news and he didn't know how to begin. I imagined he was going to tell me I would have to leave the Duponts'. I tried to hide my joy.

Mr. Higgins placed his hand on my knee and told me that Mamie had died. I tried my best not to cry. I felt my body sliding itself down to the floor. I pulled a cushion off the sofa and held it like a shield as I curled up into a ball. I heard the loud chattering of my teeth inside my ears. My whole body shook uncontrollably, and I cried with a pain I had never felt before. I bit my tongue and blood came out of my mouth.

The image of Mamie's face flooded over me, drowning me in pain. My cries went beyond tears, and my fingers clutched the carpet. I was lying hopelessly on the ocean floor as panicked voices above tried to penetrate the depths of my despair. I felt my body being lifted up, flopping and bouncing, as if someone were carrying me while they ran.

I woke up on the big bed in the Duponts' bedroom. Florence and Mr. Higgins came into the room and told me that I had had a seizure but that I would be all right. I didn't know what that meant. My tongue hurt, and it felt like a nice-size pebble was glued to it. I didn't know if I'd be able to talk. My mind felt dead to the world. Though I heard them saying they would have a doctor look at me, their voices were like static, bunched up with other voices in the house. I was listening for Mamie's voice, calling "*Jah*-vis! *Jah*-vis!"

When they took me downstairs to my room, I lay on my bed, the image of Mamie before me. She was lying in a casket in the center aisle at church. The entire church congregation was singing and crying, as I'd seen them do so many times when one of Mamie and Dennis's elderly friends had passed away. I cried myself to sleep, listening in my mind to the gospel songs of the church choir and remembering all their words.

The next morning, instead of going to school, I found myself on the highway, hitchhiking to visit Dennis. I hadn't planned to do this; I was just doing it. The nice black man who picked me up had only intended to take me as far as he was going in my direction. But after hearing my story of being in a foster home and Mamie's sudden death, he decided to take me all the way to the Prockses' front door. Concerned for me, he made me agree that if for some reason I couldn't visit with Dennis, I would allow him to drive me back to the Duponts.

While the man waited outside in his car, I walked up to the door and Dennis let me in. I thought it would only be seconds before he went back out on the porch and waved my new friend off, letting him know that I would be staying. But it didn't happen like that.

As soon as I told Dennis I had run away from the Duponts, his attitude changed from pure happiness to complete sadness. He held me against his leg, struggling to find the words to tell me I couldn't stay. He convinced me that Mamie would have never permitted me to stay, that I should have known he could not hide me from the Duponts and Mr. Higgins. It was as if Mamie were right with us and I had disappointed them both. They were not the kind of people to hide me from anyone. That the cruelty I had experienced at the Duponts could have ever existed was unimaginable to them.

For only a short time we talked about Mamie's passing. While Dennis felt alone, he was unshaken by her passing on. He spoke of our Mamie being with God in heaven. I had forgotten this world of faith. It was only through Dennis that I felt it again inside my heart. It was so different from how I had been forced to think at the Duponts. Dennis said he wasn't going to tell the Duponts that I had been there, and he promised to speak to Mr. Higgins so that I could attend Mamie's funeral. I gave him a big, long hug and left.

My new friend was still waiting outside. In less than thirty minutes I was back at the Duponts'. He dropped me off a block away from the house, telling me sadly as he pulled away, "Take care of yourself."

When I found out Mamie had died, Arnie had predicted that I wouldn't be allowed to attend her funeral. Now, with an evil I had never known before, the Duponts refused to let me go. The harm I felt from their action broke my heart. I hadn't thought about running away that morning. My hitchhiking felt like a dream. But now I decided to run away into Mamie's arms, the arms that had loved me so much.

CHAPTER 8

Escape from Abuse

Running to Safety

WHEN IT WAS TIME to run from the Duponts, I gathered up only my courage, telling no one but Arnie of my plan to leave the following morning. He wished me luck and reminded me again never to tell anyone my real name.

I was ten years old. I walked the mile to the bus stop next to Washington Park. I stayed several feet away from the bench, as I wanted no one who knew me or the Duponts to see me waiting for the bus. When a bus pulled up against the curb and opened its door, I hid between the other people who were waiting to board. I didn't care where the bus was going.

After I dropped my fare in, I sat down at the back and looked out the window. The rough sound of shifting gears made me wonder what I was doing and where I was going. If I got off at the next stop, no one but Arnie would ever know that I had tried to run away. Now I realized that I had told Arnie my plans in order to keep myself from turning back. The last thing I wanted was to "chicken out" in his eyes. This kept me seated. With each stop it became harder to change my mind, until I had traveled so far outside the zone of ever finding my way back to the Duponts that I truly decided to be gone. Within an hour I felt lost but free. I was on my own in a seemingly vast, expanding world.

I kept changing buses, hoping for the one that would take me to downtown Los Angeles. Finally I asked someone the bus number that would take me there. To my surprise, I was told that I had just boarded it.

As night fell I could see approaching through my window the towering buildings of downtown Los Angeles. I had to tilt my head almost upside down to see how far these buildings went up into the sky. Lights glowed from their many windows, bringing the whole night sky to life.

On the curving and looping freeways, people were going everywhere in their cars in fender-to-fender traffic. I looked down into the cars beside the bus, wondering where everyone was going, almost wishing I was in the backseat going home with them. How would I find somewhere to sleep? I wondered whether my mother or anyone else I knew was in one of those cars. As I peered out the window, thinking this way kept me still. I was a gentle companion to myself. As I watched the reflections glowing into the night, life seemed so much kinder to me than it ever had with the Duponts. I wanted to ride on this bus for the rest of my life.

The underground bus terminal was just the way Arnie had described it—vast, with dozens and dozens of buses and hundreds of people getting on and off. It felt like an underground city. Most people were carrying their luggage, and there were many families with kids my age. I followed them as if I knew where I was going, up the escalator to the main lobby of the Central Greyhound Bus Station. Here I saw small gift stores and ticket counters with lines of people standing idly by while others sat around eating or waiting at their designated gates. An intercom announced boarding schedules. The station had the feeling of a place that stayed open all night.

Even with the uniformed cops walking around, I didn't need to worry about being spotted as a runaway. No one would notice me here.

For the next four nights I slept in the bus station. During the day I sneaked onto the local Rapid Transit District bus downtown and rode the elevators in the tallest buildings I could find. I went as high as they would take me and looked out of the windows over Los Angeles for a long time. There was always something else to see. Just before going back down, I would pick out a landmark on the ground that I would try to find once I was back on the street. Then once I was there I'd try to pinpoint the exact window I had looked down from to see how high I had been just moments before.

The year was 1972. The Hare Krishnas were a common sight on the L.A. street corners, but their chanting and dancing in a trance scared me. I tried to avoid them, but wherever I went they were there. I thought they were following me until I realized there were different groups of them on almost every corner. When I returned to the bus station, I was always hungry, but I hardly ever had to spend the money in my pocket because Rags took care of me.

Rags

ON MY FIRST NIGHT in L.A., I met Rags, an old black man who shined shoes inside the bus terminal. At first I didn't trust him because of all the cops who hung around his shoeshine stand. Somehow Rags knew that I was a runaway. He told me that he had seen many runaways like me coming in and out of the station. I was afraid he would tell one of his cop friends while he was shining their shoes.

A moment came when a cop casually asked me my name. As I stuttered in fear, Rags told the cop I was his sister's grandchild. Then he reached into his pocket, took out a five-dollar bill, and gave it to me, telling me to go get something to eat, as if to say, *Go before this cop finds out.* I knew he meant for me to keep the money and never come back. But for some reason I did come back, bringing two hamburgers, french fries, and Cokes for the two of us. The same cop was still getting his shoes shined. I gave Rags his change, sat on a stool, and ate my hamburger while he continued to pop his rag across the cop's shoes. He started humming, a way of saying, *Boy, you's a crazy one, ain'tcha?*

When the cop finally left, Rags looked over at me. "Boy," he said in a grumpy voice, "has you any damn mind left?"

"Didn't you say get something to eat?" I asked, and sipped on my Coke.

"Yeah, uh-huh, that's just what I said, son. But ain't you enough sense to know what I mean? They goin' to find you out, boy!" His tone of voice changed. "But until they do—well, here," and Rags threw me his shoeshine rag. "Clean this place up! Put my polish lids back on. Then wet a towel and clean off my seat." He climbed onto one of the stools and unwrapped his hamburger. Rags was just as smacking hungry as I had been.

I was thrilled. I jumped off the stool and went to work as if I'd just been hired by Rags; I placed all his polish lids back on, polishing the lids first, and cleaned up the whole area around his shoeshine stand.

Whenever Rags was not shining shoes, he was trying to convince me to turn myself in. To explain my running away, I told him my whole story, beginning to end. "Boy! Those Duponts," he said. "Sure sounds like my own pappy and mammy! But you don't have to tell the law yo' name. You just do what your friend Arnie said, and you'll go to that McHall place! 'Cause bad things sure happens out here, bein' on your own like you is now," said Rags. "And, son, you can't stay out here too long!"

Rags was that voice in the far back of my own mind, the voice of common sense. During our first long talk he convinced me that I ought to turn myself in. I didn't want to do it myself, so he said he would. Still, before I let him turn me in, I hung around for another three days, secretly hoping he would decide to keep me as his helper.

I thought I had been so free on my own, but when I made the decision to let Rags turn me in, I felt freer than ever. Roaming around downtown Los Angeles, sightseeing in stores the size of city blocks, eating hamburgers and hanging out with Rags, I felt that like everyone else coming in and out of the bus terminal I too now had someplace to go. Knowing that Rags would turn me in, I stopped fearing that time would run me out of things to do, places to go.

Rags spent most of our last day together teaching me how to shine shoes. I liked how he popped and snapped his rag as he bent over his customer's shoes, talking to them while he shined them. I asked him why he talked to the shoes. He smiled. "You see, boy," he said, "when them folks see you down low talkin' to the shoe, they know you puttin' somethin' way good into yo' work! They ain't goin' to pay a dime if you don't do it just like this here." Patting some polish onto the shoes of a customer reading a newspaper on his stand, he gave his rag another pop.

Runaway

THAT EVENING A UNIFORMED officer came for his shine, and I knew that this was the one. For a while I watched the cop and Rags talking and joking; I could see that they'd been friends beyond my years. Then their topic changed. I heard Rags say he had a problem. A look of concern came over the black cop's face, and he asked Rags if there was anything he could do for him. Rags said he had met this fine young man, pointing his finger directly at me. He told the cop my story in a way that almost had me laughing. He left out all the sensitive parts and said nothing I didn't want him to say.

"What's his name, Rags?" the cop asked.

"Well, George, as far as I can tell," said Rags, "he ain't got one yet. I've been calling him 'Woopie.' Yes, sir! The way this boy eats hamburgers!"

"Do you have a name, son?" the cop asked, looking down at me. He took a pen and pad from his shirt pocket.

"No, uh-uh," I mumbled.

"How did you get here? Did you run away all on your own?"

"I don't know," I whispered.

"Well, do you know how old you are?"

"Ten or eleven," I barely answered.

"Well, Rags, I don't think he wants to tell us anything," said the cop. "So I guess I'll have to call him in as a runaway. A lot of times, you know, we can just hold 'em—youngsters like this—until we can get in touch with their parents. See if they'll pick 'em up. But I'll have to call this one in. He's a runaway. And we'll see what happens."

The officer came down from his seat and paid Rags for the shine. I stared at his gun in its holster. He asked Rags if I'd run if he left me there for a few minutes.

"No, sir! This boy ain't going nowhere," said Rags. "Nowhere but up here on my seat." He motioned for me to climb up on the seat where the cop had been sitting. I jumped into the chair and put my favorite sneakers on the shoe handles where customers' shoes belonged.

"Okay, just keep him here for a few minutes," said the cop, "while I go make a couple of calls to see if we can get someone down here to help us out." Before he left, he turned and placed his hand on his gun. "Son, you sure you don't want to tell me your name?"

"No," I said again. With Rags there, it didn't scare me to see his hand resting on his pistol.

"Well, make sure he doesn't run, Rags, okay?"

"I sho' will, George," said Rags.

We watched the officer take out his police radio and speak into it as he walked away. When he was out of sight, Rags and I both started laughing.

"Ain't you too big to not have a name?" said Rags.

"Yeah." I smiled.

"Well, when they come getcha, you take care of yourself, you hear me? And don't let me see you no more! Okay? And, boy, don't think I taught you everything about poppin' this here rag! 'Cause there's a lot mo' you need to learn about shinin' shoes."

"Like what else?" I asked.

"First is, you need to get you some shoes, boy!" My sneakers looked so pitiful benched up on Rags's stand. My big toes had broken free through the holes.

It didn't take long before the officer returned. He explained to Rags what he thought was going to happen to me, and when I heard the words "McLaren Hall" I felt almost excited. Based on what Arnie had told me, I imagined it to be like a coed camp with dormitories, a school, and sports activities every day—and nobody slapping me around or forcing nasty food down my throat. I even felt happy about the high fence around it, because it would protect me from the Duponts. McLaren Hall was what I wanted.

A man and a woman dressed in suits, both blond, walked up to the shoeshine stand. They showed their IDs to the cop and shook his hand. Then the three of them walked away together and stood in the lobby, outside my hearing. I bit down on my fear, praying that I wouldn't be returned to the Duponts.

Finally they came back to us. The woman smiled and shook my hand. She introduced her partner and herself as being from the police division that dealt with runaways. With concern in her voice, she sweetly asked if I had any scars or bruises on my body that I wanted to show them. I told her no. She softly placed her hand on my knee and asked my name in a motherly voice. She promised me that if I told her, I wouldn't have to go back to wherever I ran away from. I looked into her eyes. She seemed so sincere, like someone

I could trust. The impulse to tell her my name pitted itself against all Arnie's warnings and before I knew it a name slipped out— something like "Jarvie." It only had the sound of my name, but it was a name all the same.

Then, with her hand still resting on my knee, she asked where I lived. Imagining trickery in the softness of her voice, again I remembered Arnie's warnings. With my head hanging down, avoiding all eye contact, I answered that I didn't remember where I lived or how I ended up in the bus terminal. I dummied up inside, no longer trusting her. Only Rags, whom I could feel glancing over at me, understood. After running out of questions, the two blond cops said they had no other choice but to take me to McLaren Hall.

I jumped down from the shoeshine stand. Rags caught me as I landed, and I felt myself missing him already. As I hugged him around the waist, I felt a hand on my shoulder, gently prying me away. The woman took me by the hand. As they led me from the station I kept looking over my shoulder at Rags, who waved his rag at me. We walked out into the lit night air, past the bumper-to-bumper line of cabs, to the cops' unmarked car. In the cold backseat, soon warmed by hidden joy, I stared out the window, watching the lights of downtown Los Angeles flash across the glass. I was too tired to care about those towering buildings.

I finally allowed myself to feel the exhaustion of the last several days. The sleep I had lost by sitting upright in plastic chairs surrounded by people and intercoms that kept me nervously awake now piled up on me and made my eyes heavy. Still, I tried to keep myself awake in order to see where I was being taken. Leaning my head against the window and dozing off, I finally lay my body across the seat and slept the rest of the way to McLaren Hall.

CHAPTER 9

McLaren Hall

Inside the Gates

I SLEEPWALKED THROUGH THE whole receiving process at McLaren Hall, not awaking fully until I was given a bath inside its closed gates. In the silent wee hours of the night I was taken into an open dormitory where two rows of perhaps forty beds, most of them filled with sleeping boys, stretched from one end to the other. Still exhausted, I lay down on mine.

It seemed as though I had just fallen asleep when all the dormitory lights came on. A counselor stood in the middle of the aisle, rallying everyone to get up. In a loud voice, he reminded us all to make our beds, and then he herded us into a locker-room and shower area. Everyone but me seemed to know what they were doing. I was still half asleep as I followed along. Other kids showed me where to ask for a toothbrush and toiletries. They pointed me to the laundry room where a boy handed me clothes and a pair of sneakers. We all wore the same size khaki pants and sweatshirts; I only had to ask for my shoe size.

We filed into the coed dining hall. The girls ate on one side and the boys on the other, five to a table. At my first meal I met Pablo and Sunny, friends for years to come in many institutions. On the San Quentin yard Pablo would hand me a photo of his daughter only moments before being stabbed to death. Sunny would commit suicide in another prison.

We were from ten to twelve years old, sitting around the dining table. The others had their girlfriends blowing kisses at them from across the hall. Pablo and Sunny, too cool and in love to eat, gave me their food. I scraped it onto my plate and kept grubbing. I didn't know I would be able to get extra portions until the head cook announced seconds, but by then I was too full for more.

Pablo, Sunny, and some other boys helped me learn everything I needed to know. They said I'd been right not to tell anyone my name, but now that I was there I wasn't at risk of being returned to the Duponts. Once my social worker found out where I was, they said, he would visit and try to convince me to go back. But he couldn't force me to return.

I only had to briefly describe life at the Duponts' before Pablo and Sunny were filling in the blanks like they had been there themselves. My tales of being beaten and slapped around didn't shock them or anyone else at McLaren Hall. Only when I talked about the Prockses were they surprised. They couldn't believe that I'd been in such a loving foster home. They always wanted to hear more about the Prockses, as if I affirmed for everyone that such a home could exist. I came to feel differently about people, depending on what they wanted to hear. I didn't like the people who just wanted to hear about the terrible things that had happened to me. But the friends who wanted to bask in my fondest memories of the Prockses made me feel special, inviting me into my own sense of knowing a right from a wrong.

Mr. Higgins came to visit almost two weeks later. We sat in a small office facing each other. At first, he just assumed that he would be returning me to the Duponts. I said I wouldn't go. He stated flatly that he would be returning me. When I said I'd run away again, he threatened me with juvenile hall.

"I'm not goin' no fucking anywhere," I replied with my head down, not flustered by his threat. "You let those people hurt me, and I am not going back there. Not now, not ever again!"

Mr. Higgins was shocked. He had never before heard me curse or speak out against him. He stared at me as if he was trying to piece it all together. The more puzzled he looked, the angrier I became. Silently, I had begun to blame him and him alone for taking me away from the Prockses. It was his fault that I had been placed with the Duponts. And I hated him for never believing me all those times I'd tried to tell him what was happening to me. Because of him, Mamie and Dennis hadn't believed me either. So I blamed him for everything there was.

As if he had read my mind, Mr. Higgins apologized for how hard it had been at the Duponts'. He asked if I thought another foster home, one of my choosing, might work. His apology and care filled my eyes with tears. I wasn't angry, only hurting to be heard. I wanted him to know what I felt. I wanted him to believe me.

We agreed that I wouldn't go back to the Duponts, and that I would not be placed in another foster home unless I told him I wanted to do that. Until then, I would remain at McLaren Hall.

I knew what Mr. Higgins thought: sooner or later I would be begging him to take me out of McLaren. In his eyes, it was much worse than a loving foster home. What Mr. Higgins didn't know— and neither did I—was how quickly I would adjust to being locked up, how soon I would feel safe and protected. I would never want to risk another foster home, especially after everything Pablo and Sunny had told me. I was finding myself in the dream that Arnie had described on the Duponts' roof.

From my first day at McLaren Hall, I felt free from the wrath of the Duponts. But I was growing an attitude that said, "If they took me away from the Prockses, the only people who ever really knew how to love me, then I'll take myself out of their rotten system by staying right where I am."

A Sense of Belonging

I FOUND A LOT to like about McLaren Hall. Going to school every day was fun. I liked the teachers, whose style made me feel like I had an older sibling looking over my shoulder in the classroom. Unlike my teachers in elementary school, they talked and dressed like educated hippies, the women in long dresses that looked like they had splattered paint all over them, the men with leather straps tied around their foreheads. These people always had time to be more than just teachers. We all needed their attention because of our troubled lives, from the pain of missing our parents to the trauma of having been abused and neglected. We couldn't help but bring these troubles with us into the classroom. They would cry when we told them what had happened to us. Then it was up to us to cheer them up.

One day as we were doing our bookwork, a teacher suddenly asked us to help him remove all the desks and chairs from the center of the classroom. Then he sat us all down in a circle, brought out his guitar, and sang songs. We recognized the lyrics—the poems and stories we ourselves had written! After that I wrote more, searching dictionaries for new words to express myself. Every day we walked out of class believing that what we did mattered.

In the big auditorium, volunteers, mostly retired actors and dancers, taught drama and dance. While none of us wanted to be actors or dancers, we trampled each other's heels to get into this, the only coed class at McLaren. There were only a few volunteers to supervise us. Separating us into groups, some taught dance while others helped us remember our *Romeo and Juliet* lines. Many of us used this opportunity to slip out with our girlfriends. The auditorium's secret hiding places—back-room offices, closets, and storage rooms—were perfect for making out. Here I was introduced to sex.

Most of the girls were older than me and knew things I hadn't imagined. I worried which would be worse: being laughed out of the dorm by Pablo, Sunny, and all my other know-it-all buddies for asking a question that showed that I'd never been with a girl, or sneaking into a room and letting the girl find out everything I didn't know. For a while this seemed to me to be a life-or-death question that took away my appetite.

Then one day a girl named Brandy, seeing how shy I was, took me by the hand and pulled me off the stage and into a closet, where we were almost caught kissing and grinding. After that there were many other trips into the closet. Brandy taught me a lot about sex. To my surprise, she said she had learned what she knew from her uncle.

But my best times at McLaren Hall were playing sports. Whether it was basketball, football, baseball, track, or volleyball, on the field was where I wanted to be. The staff and counselors too were serious about sports. After we competed against other dormitories, the best athletes were selected to form an all-McLaren team that played in a league with other institutions, including other boys' homes and ranches and even special units that housed wards of the state not classified as juvenile delinquents.

I tried hard to make those all-McLaren teams, and when I succeeded I felt like one of the favored. I enjoyed being coached. I liked having someone in my face who would tell me what I needed to do in order to improve and who would also ask, "What the hell were you thinking out there, Masters?" whenever I made a mistake. That same someone would be the first to hug me and cheer me on when I played well. I craved this kind of attention.

The rivalries ran deep between the staff at McLaren and those at other boys' homes. Often the staff placed bets, with the losing counselors paying up from their own pockets. An institutional game was not just a game, it was a high-stakes game for titles, reputations, and bragging rights. The night before the games my teammates and I would fold our jerseys and place them under our pillows so they'd be neatly creased in the morning. The entire population of McLaren Hall, including the girls, would catch that pregame fever.

Because we were locked in and the other boys' homes were free of fences, the big games were held on our field. All the McLaren Hall kids came to the games. I had never before felt such a sense of belonging. McLaren was a world where I fit in. Whenever I came off the field, whether we won or lost, I felt there was no better place than McLaren Hall.

Every day I grew angrier with the Duponts. Sometimes I stared down at my hands in a panic at how close I had come to losing my fingers, feeling the hatred swell inside me. Running away was the best thing I had ever done for myself. My only regret was that I hadn't done it sooner.

One day twelve of us who had earned the privilege were taken to a theater. A few kids figured that this would be a perfect opportunity to run away. They tried to convince me to join them, but I couldn't understand why anyone would want to run away from McLaren. I wanted to be adopted by McLaren. I needed that fence only for protection. Completely dumbfounded, I watched my friends scatter. What were they running from? Where were they going?

Arnie had not told me that I would develop such deep bonds of friendship at McLaren. He hadn't told me I would run into other kids who shared my past. At public school I had been ashamed of being a foster child. But since all of us at McLaren Hall had suffered some kind of abuse, neglect, or abandonment, we had nothing to hide from one another. This was reflected in our relationships. We had no desire to take a scalpel and cut deep inside one another, trying to figure out what was wrong.

A Best Friend

ONE OF MY BEST friends was Fred, whose father had tried to kill him by setting him on fire. Fred would scream aloud off and on during the night, waking us all up. As I lay there trying to go back to sleep I would sometimes hear Fred muffling his screams with his pillow to keep from disturbing us again.

In the morning nobody ever teased Fred about his screams. The way he suffered at night was a serious matter, something we could relate to. Each of us felt that we could have been Fred, so we treated him the way we would have liked to be treated. None of us knew what trouble from our own past might expose itself in our sleep, so we looked to one another for examples. Someone who could snore through anything was the envy of the dormitory: the peaceful sound of snoring was comforting, like a bedtime story. It always helped me sleep.

No one was more thankful than I not to have experienced what Fred had been through. Every time I looked at the dry white scars on his arms and legs and the spots on his neck and face, I would quietly touch my own body and feel lucky. There had been adults in my life who could have left such marks on me. I felt blessed that I'd been spared.

One day after Fred had just returned from a visit with his mother, he and I were alone in the dormitory. As he was changing into his football jersey his eyes welled up with tears; he turned away so that I wouldn't see the drip of emotion. He didn't want me to know what his pain looked like. My heart told me that Fred's reasons for not showing himself had become part of the pain of his life experience.

Because he'd turned away, I was looking at Fred's back, marked with burn scars that looked like dried lava pushed up against itself. I had never seen anything quite so gruesome before. The burns had left little of his natural dark skin. The exposed, healed flesh revealed all the reasons that we heard Fred's scared screams deep into the night. Seeing it made me sad.

Fred finally turned to me, wiping his eyes, and said, "Man, I just can't stand it. It just makes me sad for all of you who don't have a mother who comes to visit." My mouth dropped open in awe. Compared to Fred, I wasn't as lucky as I had thought. Remembering how I had just felt looking at his scars, I thought, *How could he say that?* I was trying to get to the place where he was coming from. I'd never heard a voice like this before, or had someone say words like this to me. It was Fred's compassion speaking.

It was like Fred and I had each become a mirror for the other's heart. That day on the field, for the first time, I played as hard with Fred as I did with anyone else. Game on—*bam!* With a snap of the football, my hardest block got enough of Fred to put him on the ground. The whole squad looked on in shock: we'd agreed that we would go light on Fred. Now I wanted them to know that this dude was for real. He didn't need or want our damn pity.

We all watched Fred get up, dusting himself off. No pity, no pity! In the next practice drill, everyone was shocked again—this time at Fred's blindsiding block that landed me on my back, staring up at the sky. I didn't know it was Fred who had done it until he helped me to my feet.

Those blocks made Fred and me the very best of friends. We walked home to our dormitory together that day, crossing the football field. No one who watched us—boys and girls, teachers and counselors—had ever thought Fred could be more than a person half gone by fire, but now they saw him as whole. And me, I never thought a best friend could be as good as Fred.

Growing Up Fast

To my disappointment, it turned out that McLaren Hall was only a place where they put kids until they could find something more permanent. Mr. Higgins's visits quickly became trips to look at foster homes, homes I rejected miles before I set eyes on them, and not just because I wished to stay at McLaren Hall; I had lost all trust in Mr. Higgins. Every time he spoke highly about a possible foster home, it only echoed what he once had said about the Duponts.

I was growing up fast, and Mr. Higgins couldn't see it. I was becoming institutionalized right under his nose, but he thought I was still the Jarvis he had first met sitting on Mamie's lap, bobbing my head "yes" to his every word.

Whenever we arrived at a foster home, I always looked at the faces of the other kids. The moment they were called into the living room was the most important part of my visit. If they seemed scared to get close to the parents or looked nervous and tried to stay still yet flinched at the slightest movement, they were saying, *Fool! Don't come here! This place ain't nothin' nice!*

I always looked over at Mr. Higgins and wondered why he couldn't see the fear on these kids' faces. Sadly, he'd never seen my own fear at the Duponts' either. No matter what, he would just keep chatting with the parents. I felt sorry for the children I met in these dark-lit homes. After every visit, I left with a piece of their fear, a reminder of my own experience.

We visited other homes where the kids would run into the room with full smiles across their faces, playful and happy to show their personalities. They stayed close to their foster parents, wary of strangers, and would even ask for things like junk food or permission to sleep over at a friend's house, knowing this was a good chance to get what they wanted. When the children's faces said, *It's cool here!* the homes were harder to reject. Still, when it came down to choosing between them and McLaren Hall, I chose McLaren Hall every time.

What troubled me most was being able to see things that Mr. Higgins couldn't. I knew it was his job to trust foster parents. I knew he was concerned for my well-being and wanted the very best for me. But I needed him to see more than I could see, to be more aware of things unknown to me. I needed him to protect me, to be my social worker. He honestly believed that all the foster homes were good, but I knew differently.

After nearly a year of visiting foster homes, other social workers got involved in my case. When I knew for sure that something was about to happen, I paid attention to the rumors about a place called Boys Town of the Desert. Most of my friends at McLaren had gone on to Boys Town, including Pablo, Sunny, and recently Fred. Since none of them had bounced back to McLaren with bad reports, as many of the kids would, I figured Boys Town was worth a chance. I asked Mr. Higgins if I could be placed there.

I could see the relief on Mr. Higgins's face: there was somewhere I wanted to go. In no time he and I were back on the freeway, taking a one-way trip to Boys Town of the Desert. The occasion was marked by Mr. Higgins allowing me to turn on the car radio for the first time. And he stopped at McDonald's and treated me to burgers and all the fries I wanted, even offering me his own for good measure.

CHAPTER 10

Boys Town

The Ladder of Merit

ARRIVING AT BOYS TOWN of the Desert felt like being lost in the mountains of nowhere. I had never been in a place that was so hidden away. It was so secluded that it seemed like a town unto itself. Nestled in a valley of rolling hills, it consisted of a huge chow hall, a school area, and administrative buildings overlooking a small cluster of cottages. It could have been a summer camp.

On my first day Mr. Higgins took me to the dean's office. The dean introduced me to my new home with a long list of warnings: no fighting, no stealing, no running away, no skipping school, no glue-sniffing, no drugs, and no setting fires. His list led me to believe that other boys had gotten into trouble for all these things. I didn't even know what some of them meant. Did kids really set fires? Did they really do drugs here? And what exactly was glue-sniffing? Any of these offenses would add more time to my stay at Boys Town.

I was confused by the idea that I would get more time for violating the rules. I thought I was being placed at Boys Town permanently. How could I get more time? In order to stay here, I would have to act up and get into trouble. None of this made sense to me, and I didn't have the nerve to ask where I would go if I stayed out of trouble.

After saying good-bye to Mr. Higgins and finding my assigned cottage, I started to feel my own way through Boys Town, learning what I needed to know from the boys who were already there.

Each cottage was large enough for ten or fifteen kids, with five or six bedrooms and a large living room area for recreational purposes. Each cottage had its own counselor who lived with the boys.

I immediately liked how the counselors treated us. Though we were all young—ages nine through fifteen—we were allowed to smoke cigarettes and drink coffee. We were also expected to take care of ourselves. I felt comfortable with this. I knew how to take care of myself; I had even taken care of my siblings. There were structured programs in place that made each kid responsible for specific jobs in the cottage. I quickly fit into these programs, just as I had at McLaren Hall.

The in-house counselor kept a check on us with a merit ladder system that included everything from who made his bed best to who completed his weekly chores first. At the end of each week the system determined our allowances and eligibility for certain privileges. Our scores were posted on a board in the recreation room.

As soon as I arrived I began to make my way up in the merit system. Unlike other boys who rebelled against being told what to do, I liked having structure, a system to follow. I considered making my bed, passing inspections, and doing my chores a part of my life.

I quickly connected with all the sport activities, spending my time on the basketball court, baseball diamond, and football field. There I began to see my old friends from McLaren Hall. But this led to conflict.

From the moment I arrived the boys in my cottage told me how they hated the boys in other cottages. Because of events that had occurred before I got there, I couldn't be seen talking to my good friends Pablo and Sunny. Pablo and Sunny hardly even looked in my direction when our cottages played sports against each other.

A few days after I arrived I had seen Pablo in the chow hall. With food tray in hand, I walked over to him sitting with his friends and sat down across the table. We laughed with surprise at seeing each other. We had exchanged only a few happy words when someone at the table asked which cottage I was in. I didn't even remember the name, so I described where it was located. Then they all shouted, "You can't sit here. We don't let our enemies eat with us." "Pablo, tell this dude to leave," they said, turning to Pablo with real anger in their eyes.

I looked at Pablo. Were they playing a joke on a newcomer? Seconds passed.

"Man, Jarvis," said Pablo, sadly, "you can't sit here with us. You have to go sit with your own cottage." Seeing the pain in his eyes, I knew it was not a joke. I slowly got up and went over to eat my dinner with my cottage. But for the rest of the evening they all ostracized me. I had ignored the rule of not speaking to anyone from an "enemy" cottage. I felt miserable. That night while I slept, someone squeezed a tube of toothpaste into my hair. I had to use scissors to cut it out in the morning, cutting my hair short so I didn't have patches missing. Only after they were sure I hadn't reported the incident did my bunkmates begin talking to me again.

I was determined to find out who had put toothpaste in my hair. Until then, I was keeping a brand-new tube of Crest wrapped in a cloth in the bottom of my dresser. I was going to get him back. But the longer I waited to find out, the more impressed I was that nobody told me who did it. Even when there was a big feud in the cottage, nobody would say who put the toothpaste in my hair. I took this to mean that I would have an issue either with everyone in the cottage or with no one at all; that I could be part of the group or totally ostracized. Even if I didn't like it, I was warned.

It didn't take long to realize that there were very few of us wards of the state placed at Boys Town. Most of the kids living here were the youngest offenders in the juvenile justice system—purse-snatchers, shoplifters, bike thieves, and, worst of all, kids who boasted of killing dogs, cats, and other animals with knives before setting them on fire. These juvenile delinquents were homesick. They had calendars hanging above their beds, and each morning they crossed out another day. They counted the months, weeks—even hours—until they could go home to their parents.

With a point system that granted an early release based on good behavior, I felt like the odd boy out. Many times my name reached the top of the merit ladder, indicating that I would be next to go home. I always had to figure out how to move my name back to the bottom, for I had no home to go to. I never told anyone that I was a ward of the state. The other kids were scratching the door to be let out. I didn't want them to know my dirty little secret.

The worst times were when the others cheered for me because my name was at the top of the list: I was next to be released. Before my secret could be exposed, I'd do something disruptive like throwing a chair through a window or breaking into the counselor's bedroom and stealing his watch, which I would leave on my bunk so that I'd be caught. Then, losing my credits and privileges, I'd fall back down to the bottom of the ladder.

The truth is I had been living on borrowed time. Since landing at the Duponts', I had ceased to be the boy I'd been growing into—the boy who knew and cared about himself. Instead, I was once again a hurt child who needed more help than just love could provide. For all the affection and care in Mamie's and Dennis's strong arms, for all the power of sports to draw me into the world, at Boys Town I saw vivid memories chasing after me. The pain and suffering of the child—especially all the fear I'd felt in being left alone with my sisters—caught up with the boy and made me a ghost.

After a short-lived attempt to be as I had been in all the other places, I was now hanging out sniffing glue with other kids as if we were taking LSD. Instead of playing sports, I began acting out. I was constantly looking for trouble, stealing and escaping up into the hills. Most of all, I was wanting people to hear me say, "I need you to help me, please." I was never able to give in to asking them outright.

After a few of these cycles, I developed a reputation for being crazy, as I'd thrown my release date right out the window with the chair. I began to hang out with other boys who couldn't go a week without getting into a fight or sniffing glue up in the hills. I vowed never again to reach the top of that list. The pain of not having a home was in my face. I wanted to break everything. I used my anger to numb the hurt.

Up in the mountains, with our brains fried by glue, my friends and I sometimes played Russian roulette with an old miner's pistol. It was not that I wanted to kill myself; I wanted to live. But I also wanted to know that if things got too bad, I had an option. If I wanted to take my life at any time, I could do it.

Soon I was spending most of my days hanging out in the mountains. Pablo and Sunny began sneaking out of their cottages to join us. Some of the boys heard about an old miner who was willing to sell us booze. We put our allowances together and gave it all— about twenty dollars—to the miner, who lived several miles down the hill in a junk trailer. In exchange, he gave us a big bottle of his homemade brew. Perched around a campfire, we passed the bottle around. Some of us fell out drunk as we emptied it.

These were my best times at Boys Town. Just sitting by a warm fire with no worries, knowing that no one could find us, laughing— by definition that would be a good time for anyone anywhere, but especially for kids like us. The campfire was the only place where, no matter what our cottage or the color of our skin or whether others considered us tough or weak, we were all the same. Our drunkenness made us so. We laughed at ourselves and at what we were doing. But most of all we laughed because there was nobody there to stop us. There was always some guy whose way of laughing seemed funnier than anything else. The sound of that hyena among us would have us rolling around and slamming our hands down on the ground. In tears, we would beg that boy to stop laughing.

Sitting around the campfire was our class trip. No one could take these times away from us, when we were so drunk that we needed to hold on to each other's tiny bodies as we staggered out of the mountains back to Boys Town. No one who was there will ever forget those moments.

We were smart enough to know that even before uncorking the bottle of booze we were in trouble. To participate meant you didn't care. I had forgotten all about the merit ladder and the point system. In a strange way, I began to appreciate myself more by breaking the rules. I was putting myself in charge of why I was not going home, so having no home didn't hurt the way pain does when you have no control.

I liked being at Boys Town, but I was never able to just be who I was in a system that rewarded good behavior with a one-way ticket home. Once, I had been the new kid who wanted only to play sports and do my schoolwork and chores in exchange for being the first one out on the sports field. Now, to keep my hurt and shame under control, I was known as a screwup by my cottage counselors, and as cool and crazy by friends. The big secret was that, no matter how it had appeared on the surface, I had always needed help, and I failed to get it. The complexity of my stay at Boys Town was the turning point of my whole life.

The Great Escape

IT MIGHT HAVE BEEN over a jug of booze while we were up in the hills that Pablo and I and some others decided to run away from Boys Town. Everyone else was homesick, desperately wanting to get home to their families; I was the only one whose reason for running was just to have fun. Everyone was saying, "Yeah, let's do it, you guys!" Unlike my escape from the Duponts' abuse, this time I was only following the crowd.

There was no punishment I feared. To lose good-time credits meant nothing. As a ward of the state, if I got caught, the worst that could happen was being sent back to McLaren Hall. Everyone else had more to lose: getting caught would mean starting their sentence all over. They might even get additional time or be locked behind a fence in juvenile hall. The escape plan took on a serious cast that I pretended to share with the others.

We decided to stay together only until we made it to town. We would then break up into smaller groups. Pablo and I decided to stick together. That night we followed Allen, the oldest, who said he knew the safest way to get to the Greyhound station. Fleeing across miles of open fields in pitch darkness, we found ourselves up in the hills and then back down in the fields.

"Hey, Allen. Man, where are we?" someone asked, breathing hard as we plowed forward through brush.

"Shit! He don't know. He can't admit we're lost," said another.

"Are we really lost, Allen? Are we?" someone else piped up.

"Hell, yeah, we're lost! He don't know where we are," voices grumbled back and forth as we trucked across the field.

"Is that true, Allen? Are we really lost?"

Allen replied by starting to run again. Not wanting to be left stranded in the middle of nowhere, we all stopped whining and ran to stay on his heels.

When we came out of the fields and onto a highway, we were happy. Soon we saw cross streets with cars and trucks, and then the downtown area of Beaumont. Now in more optimistic spirits, we each blamed and pointed to someone else, but no one in particular, for not believing in Allen. As planned, we broke into groups of twos and threes and went our separate ways.

Pablo and I hung around near a gas station next to the freeway. We didn't want to try sneaking onto a Greyhound like the others; we thought we'd get caught. Instead, we decided to bum a ride from the gas station to the next town over and then sneak onto a Greyhound to Los Angeles.

We studied the people driving up for gas. Pablo was Puerto Rican and I was black, and Beaumont, California, was a small, all-white town. We knew that the best people to approach for a ride would be people who looked less like the town types and more like the hippie types—and in 1973 there were many of those.

But as we continued to hang out at the gas station, our hopes faded by the hour. At last, as daylight brought more cars into the station, a colorful, banged-up Volkswagen bus pulled up. Seeing peace-sign stickers on its fenders, a white dove painted on the side, and yellow, red, and orange flowers on its hood, we knew we'd found our ride. Two couples, both white, got out and stretched. The driver went around to gas the van. Uncertain who should do the talking, we both stepped out from behind the filling station and simultaneously asked him for a ride.

"Sure, why not?" he said. "If y'all are headed to L.A., we can take you all the way. Hey, just jump on in!" He had a southern twang that didn't seem to match his beads and hip-hugging clothes. With his tinted wire-framed eyeglasses and long black hair, he almost looked like John Lennon.

When he hung up the nozzle and walked over to pay the station attendant, Pablo and I exchanged a glance that said, *Hell, why not?* and got into the van.

Toking It Up

SLIDING THE SIDE DOOR shut, I saw that the back of the van had no seats. A mattress covered the floor, and half a dozen pillows lay scattered about. A second man sitting in the passenger seat began chitchatting with Pablo. Two women, blondes in their early twenties, sat in the back with Pablo and me. One curled up in a blanket as if she were going back to sleep. The other woman, wearing a long psychedelic dress and sitting cross-legged with a shoe box across her lap, kept her head down, preoccupied with rolling what I thought were cigarettes. By the time "John Lennon" got behind the wheel, reefer permeated the air. As we drove out of the gas station I was already feeling the effect of the marijuana smoke.

Pablo kept nudging me, his eyes nearly popping out. He seemed to be saying, *Man, you see what she's doing? That's weed, the real deal, marijuana!* I elbowed him to quit nudging me. The woman leaned forward, still in her guru pose. Without a word, she offered me the reefer. For a split second I stared at the burning joint. As a tail of smoke floated up to my nose Pablo reached over me in a wild stretch and took it away. Still holding her breath, the woman smiled. Seconds passed before she tilted back her head and softly exhaled a thin cloud of smoke.

"So, what are you guys' names?" she asked in a slow, almost dizzy southern accent.

"Who, me?" I pointed my finger at myself. "My name is Hen— . . . mine is Henry—"

"Your name ain't no Henry," said Pablo, interrupting. "He's Jay, and I'm Pablo."

Pablo and I had agreed that we weren't going to tell anyone our real names. I wondered if it was the pot that made him change his mind.

"Why ain't you guys in school?" she asked.

"'Cause we just ran away," said Pablo, as he inhaled with a loud sucking sound.

"So, what are you guys' names?" I asked.

"Well, that's Annie there," she pointed to the woman sleeping, "and I'm Carolyn. But just call me Crystal, and you can call her Moon. And that's John and Richie in the front."

"So, you guys are runaways, eh?" piped up John. "Man, that's cool. Far out! Hey, we can all dig that. Were you guys in some kind of camp or something?"

"Nah, we were only in a boys' home," said Pablo, exhaling and adding to the cloud of smoke around us.

I didn't think Pablo knew how to smoke pot, but he seemed to fall right into the groove. I was beginning to feel like the odd one out when he tapped my shoulder and passed me the joint.

I studied the burning joint in my hand, now just a butt. I didn't have to look up to know Crystal was staring at me. Not wanting Pablo to seem more grown up, I brought the joint to my lips and took a great big toke, inhaling until the butt began to burn my fingers. With my lungs filled to the brim and trying to hold it all in, I felt a dangerous itch in my throat. I began coughing as if I were trying to put out a fire burning in my chest, choking until my eyes felt half unglued from their sockets. All the while John, Pablo, and Richie were laughing.

"Hey, Jay! Hey, are you okay? Are you all right back there?" asked John. Now that I was feeling a buzz from the pot, his accent made me chuckle.

"Yeah, I think so," I said with that slight coughing itch in my throat. It was the first time I had smoked pot. When I finally raised my head, I saw that Moon was now sitting up. She looked hung over, or perhaps just tired. She used her fingers to comb her long hair. The others began asking Pablo and me questions in a friendly tone: How old are you? Are you from L.A.? I began to like them as they described how they had packed up and left Kentucky to go to San Francisco.

John, Richie, Crystal, and Moon were everything I had imagined hippies to be. Crystal and Moon smoked pot like a smoker smokes cigarettes. They both wrote in their diaries, and then Moon played her guitar, singing from the pages of hers. Her songs were sad, very folklike, reflecting a longing for peace and love in a world that had no inkling what it was doing to itself. Up until this time I had never heard songs so up close, personal, and meaningful. When I had heard music on the radio, I had felt distant from the lyrics, only tuning in to the beat. But Moon's songs were different. They spoke to the ear that heard the world crying out. It was like we were all going to die really soon. After listening to Moon sing from her diary, I never heard another song quite the same way.

Dumpster Diving

I THOUGHT ABOUT TELLING Pablo that I wasn't going to get out in L.A. with him; I would go to San Francisco with the van. The more I got to know these people, the more they felt like a dream come true. I liked who they were and how they looked at life. They seemed only to want to find freedom, to seek greater peace. But I kept falling back into the fear that, without Pablo, nothing I envisioned was likely to happen. He was my road dog. We weren't going anywhere without each other.

Pablo didn't make a real connection with anyone in the van. Beneath his smiles, he saw them only as a ride. His trust was cautious, while mine continued to grow. John, Richie, Crystal, and Moon felt like family to me. But Pablo thought I'd lost my mind when I whispered that we should go all the way to San Francisco. It worried him that I had foolishly abandoned our plan. I began to doubt my desire to stay with the hippies. It made me seem even crazier than Pablo told me I was, and to be overheard telling me how crazy I was made Pablo nervous.

The only time John gave Pablo and me a real scare was when we turned off the freeway and drove right on past several gas stations. Our routine had been to stop at a filling station as soon as we took an exit. Now we were afraid to ask where exactly we were going, since that would have signaled that something felt wrong. But Pablo started inching toward the side door, and I planned to be right on his heels if he bailed out of the van. Then John pulled into a Safeway parking lot. We slowly drove around to the back of the store. What was going on? Were John and Richie staking the place out? We came to a stop, and they jumped out of the van, saying they'd be right back. In fear, Pablo and I just stared at each other. We looked over at Crystal and Moon to see if they knew something, but if they did, clearly it was no big deal.

After a few minutes Pablo slid the door open and got out of the van. A smile spread across his face as he waved me out so I could see Richie standing in the middle of a big Dumpster, handing things to John, who was putting them into a box. We ran over to see that they had found apples, oranges, and baskets of strawberries. No way were they actually going to eat this stuff out of the Dumpster! John grinned, grabbed two oranges from the box, and tossed one to me and one to Pablo. We closely inspected the fruit, but we couldn't find one thing wrong with it. In no time we were peeling our oranges and eating them like they had just fallen from a tree. Then Pablo leaned into another Dumpster and pulled out a bunch of pastries, still in unopened boxes. We ended up with almost three full boxes of fruit, doughnuts, pies, and cookies.

John stopped at a filling station where we washed the fruit before getting back on the freeway. We feasted on strawberries. Pablo chose only the ones that weren't bruised, but I didn't care. I had eaten worse pieces of fruit in the days when I had stolen fruit from people's trees. I also remembered Mamie saying, "God made dirt. Dirt don't hurt." I ate strawberries all the way into the city of Los Angeles.

When we neared downtown L.A., I still secretly wanted to go with John and the others all the way to San Francisco. I never stopped asking: What if? What if Arnie were where they were going? What if my whole life were to change in San Francisco? I kept picturing the beautiful Golden Gate Bridge postcards that I had seen in the gift shop in the L.A. Greyhound station when I was on the run from the Duponts. If I had not been with Pablo, my road dog to the end, I would have stayed in the van. But around the campfire Pablo and I had already traveled all the continents of the world together. I couldn't leave him now.

CHAPTER 11

Off the Road and On

Pablo's Mother

SOMEWHERE IN LOS ANGELES we thanked John and Richie, Crystal and Moon, and I sadly followed Pablo out of the van onto a busy street. I felt lost when my new friends drove away. Night was fast approaching. I looked up at the street sign. We were on a long-worded street.

"Pablo," I said, "where are we going now? Shoot! We could have gone to San Francisco! Man, why didn't you want to stay with them?"

"'Cause we can go live with my mama," he said as we walked down Hollywood Boulevard.

"Yo' mama? You have a mama?" I asked, stunned. He had never once said anything to me about his mother. Because he had been in McLaren Hall too, I had just figured that he, like me, had no trace of his mother's whereabouts. So now we were looking for his mother? Why his, not mine? I grabbed him by his coat and kept him from taking another step: "Your mother?! Do you know where she is? Where she lives?"

"Yeah, yeah, I know," said Pablo. "She don't stay all that far from here."

"Nah, man," I said, "you just want us to look for your mother. That's all. We could just as well look for mine."

"That ain't true," said Pablo, looking around. "I remember this street, Hollywood Boulevard."

"No, you don't. You ain't never been on this street before." We stood on a busy sidewalk with passersby watching. It was only after Pablo reminded me that he had asked John to let us out on this street that I tagged along. I still didn't think he had a clue where we were going, but I walked with my road dog all the same.

Night fell as we trudged down Hollywood Boulevard. After a few miles the office buildings and smiling faces of people coming and going were replaced by drunken winos sitting on the sidewalk and homeless people shuffling along haplessly, pushing all their worldly goods in shopping carts. Prostitutes stood on every street corner and approached the cars that pulled over to the curb. The farther we walked, the worse conditions became.

"Pablo, man. We're lost! I knew you'd get us lost out here," I complained. "Shoot! I don't know why we didn't go to San Francisco."

"No, we ain't," said Pablo. "You see right there?" He pointed across the street to an old hotel. "I told you we ain't lost! You see, now do you believe me? Do you believe me now?" he kept asking, excited.

"Do your mother live in there? Pablo, is that where she live at?" I asked, chasing after him as he crossed the street. We ran into the hotel lobby. Pablo knew exactly where the old elevator was. We had to close a gate and pull the door shut before pushing the button that would take us up. When we opened up the elevator, kids were playing up and down a narrow hallway, their ragged clothes practically falling off them. They were playing with trucks that had no wheels and dolls with missing limbs. The stench of urine and cigarette smoke hovered in the air. The paint was peeling off the walls, and the carpet was moldy, full of holes.

Many of the doors to the rooms stood open. As Pablo and I walked down the long dark hallway I couldn't help but look inside every room. People were lying next to ashtrays in clouds of smoke. They all had a television set turned on. I sensed a hopeless plague of despair. The doors seemed to be left open so the apartments could air out—to keep the cramped stench fanning out into the hallway— or perhaps only so parents could keep track of their kids.

At the end of the hall Pablo knocked on a door. When no one answered, he tried to open it, but it was locked. He found a clothes hanger and rankled the wire along the doorjamb. It was giving him difficulty. I wondered when he had last seen his mother and whether she still lived here. I hoped she did, and I hoped she didn't. I hoped we weren't breaking into someone's pad, and I hoped that Pablo would get to see his mother again.

Just when Pablo was about to give up, the sound of a woman's voice, shouting, came through the open window at the end of the hall. He stood up, dropped the clothes hanger, and sprinted down the hallway. I had to jump over the kids to keep up with him. We ran down the back stairs and out behind the hotel. Pablo found his mother sitting in a car with a man. They were arguing. I stayed in the shadows while Pablo leaned through the open window and embraced his mom. It was the first time I had ever seen him cry. I knew he could speak Spanish, but now he even cried in Spanish as he and his mother found a way to hold each other. She was so loaded that she wasn't able to get out of the car. He had to help her stand. The man was shouting about money. Enraged, he began to get out too. Pablo's mother reached down into her bosom, pulled out some bills, and slapped them right into his face. "Take your fucking money, you son of a bitch! I got my boy with me now. You ain't shit!" She tried to kick at the car tire but only managed to flip him off as he drove away.

Struggling to keep his mother from falling, Pablo called me over to help. We half-carried her up to the third floor, her arms slung over our shoulders. Pablo opened the front door with his mother's key, and I laid her down on the couch in the front room. As I turned on the kitchen light to get her some water, there was a loud buzz like the sound of bees. Cockroaches scampered everywhere. A rat was eating off a plate of food on the kitchen counter. Seeing me, it stood up on its hind legs like a kangaroo and started waving its paws in front of its face as if challenging me to a fight. I jetted straight out of the kitchen. Without telling Pablo what I had seen, I said, "You go get the water!"

Either Pablo didn't see the rat or it didn't bother him. He returned with a cup of water for his mother. She looked more sick than drunk. It was the heroin. By now I had noticed on the table the burned spoons, the thin rubber strap, and all the other paraphernalia I remembered from my early childhood. But the telltale sign was how Pablo's mother lay almost lifeless on the couch, oblivious to the world around her. I related to that most of all. My own mother had laid exactly the same way while Birdy would brush her hair, the rest of us watching and waiting. In Pablo's mother I saw my own. Even though I wasn't yet eleven years old, I wished that I could find my own mother and care for her. I wanted to protect her from whatever caused her to do this to herself.

That night we stayed in the front room with all the lights on, watching Pablo's mother sleep on one couch as we slouched at the opposite ends of the other. Knowing the rat was still around, I dozed fitfully, jumping out of sleep at every twitch of sound. If the rat could get up onto the kitchen counter, it could certainly make it onto the couch. I didn't want to be surprised.

The next morning when Pablo's mother woke up, she thought we were both sleeping. From under half-closed lids I watched her make her way into the doorless bedroom. From my place on the couch I had a direct view as she moved restlessly about the room before sitting on the naked mattress. Hunched over, she lit a whole book of matches and used the flame to heat a spoon. She baked the heroin for several seconds before blowing out the matches. Then she stuck the needle into the spoon and slowly drew up the liquid.

She blew on her thumb like she was blowing up a balloon until the veins swelled up in her neck. Then she spanked the side of her neck several times and pushed a vein up with her thumb to make it bulge. She was real rough with herself. With her other hand, she scooted the needle into her vein, drew blood into the needle, and then injected it back in with the heroin. She barely had time to pull the needle out before she rolled over into a fetal position. The way she slowly wiped her face with the palms of her hands brought back my earliest memories. My mother had rubbed her face with her hands in exactly the same way. I saw Pablo go into the bedroom. For several seconds he stared down at his mother lying on the bed.

Time stretched out. Pablo looked around the room, and then, as if he had lost all reason, he shouted, "Let's go, let's go!" and ran past me and out the door. As we walked along the sidewalk, the silence of his hurt and anger unbroken, a police car suddenly drove up alongside.

"Why aren't you boys in school?" asked the cop.

"We . . . we going now," said Pablo, trying to stay calm. I kept my mouth shut to keep the stuttering from coming out.

"In this direction?" asked the other cop. "What school do you boys go to?"

"What school?"

"Yes! What is the name of your school, son?" he asked sternly.

In my mind I was telling Pablo, *I'm right behind you.*

Pablo stuttered, pointed, and took off running as fast as he could. With me on his heels, we dashed through some apartment complexes and came out into a back alley. We ran and ran, hopping fences and knocking over trash cans. When we were certain we had gotten away, we ran out of an alley at the exact moment the police car turned into it. We all hit the brakes just in time to avoid our being plastered across their windshield.

The police handcuffed Pablo and me together in the backseat, but our small wrists kept slipping out of the cuffs. They asked us our names and where we lived. When we wouldn't answer, they decided to take us to the station. Still thinking about Pablo's mother, we forgot we were handcuffed in the backseat of a police car. Reality couldn't overcome the impact of finding her so strung out. I could feel Pablo struggling with whether he could go on loving his mother. And as I sat handcuffed next to him I knew I no longer wanted to look for mine—I had already found her in Pablo's. Mr. Higgins and the others had been right in trying to protect me from what Pablo and I had just encountered.

Seeing Pablo's mother living as she did—taken advantage of by men and so addicted to heroin that her need for the drug outranked her love for her son—had completely changed me. My most precious hopes had been swallowed by what I had seen in that room. Pablo did not have to tell me about the hurt and pain that kept him as silent as a mannequin. The day's events had taken so much out of us that when one of the cops threatened to throw us in jail if we didn't say where we lived, neither of us spoke.

Wrapped in My T-Shirt

AT THE POLICE STATION they split us up. I didn't know it, but I wasn't going to see Pablo again until we ran into each other in another boys' home. Alone now, I sat on the floor with my back resting against the locked door. I wanted out of there so bad. It was the first time I'd ever been locked up in a room that I couldn't get out of.

I curled up with my knees inside my T-shirt and tried to rock myself to sleep. On the other side of the door I heard the chatter of voices. Ringing telephones kept waking me up. Curled up on the concrete floor, I could see from under the door the black shoes of people walking by, their keys jingling. Counting their shadowy steps, I fell back to sleep.

For hours I dozed and woke and dozed again. The silence of that room engulfed my mind and sickened me with despair. Whenever

I opened my eyes, I felt the floor's concrete coldness. My loneliness made one hour of isolation feel like ten. Occasionally I got up and walked around, but I always returned to watching at the bottom of the door for the steps that would bring my release.

I had fallen asleep again when the door finally opened. Standing above me were two white counselors from Boys Town. It was as if two big brothers had mysteriously appeared to rescue me. One of them knelt to lift me off the floor. How long had I been kept isolated? Was I all right? The other counselor kept shouting in the jailer's face.

The jailer snapped and yelled, "You goddamned nigger lover! You just take him and get out!"

The sudden outburst grabbed everyone's attention, including some cops who were standing around the front hall. A chilly, deafening silence froze us all. I could see the big red-faced jailer clenching his fists. In that moment I understood why people called cops "pigs." The jailer looked just like a pig. This discovery outweighed the insult of the racial slur.

The counselors from Boys Town escorted me from the jail, past the booking desk and the cluster of all-white police officers. When I was almost out the open door, I jumped in the air and flipped the jailer off. The crowd of cops clapped, cheering, "Way to go! You tell that son of a bitch, son!" I guess they liked a little boy with so much gumption. On the trip back to Boys Town, I fell asleep in the backseat somewhere in the middle of the counselors warning me not to run away again.

When I returned to Boys Town, I was at a loss. The program meant little to me. Everyone was trying to get home to their parents—I could not get around it. Even the screwups yearned to go home. And though I was always happy for them, I was not one of them. There was nothing at Boys Town for me to cling to, and I started looking beyond the gate.

At Home on the Greyhound

WITHIN A WEEK OF my return, I went hiking up in the mountains behind Boys Town. I had not been up in the mountains long before I found myself on a dirt road. Walking the road for miles, I came to a paved street that led me into downtown Beaumont.

I was sitting on the curb, emptying the dirt from my sneakers, when a Greyhound bus pulled into the station across the street. I hurried to put my sneakers back on and ran into the bus station. Stretching to see the woman at the counter, I asked the price of a bus ticket to Los Angeles.

"Son, are you a runaway? You need to wait right there," she said, picking up the telephone.

At that I panicked and bolted out the door. Without looking back, I kept running back to Boys Town. When I was more than halfway there, the school van pulled up beside me; a counselor ordered me to get in. I didn't know how much trouble I was in. "You don't ask for a ticket in a bus station," he said, "and not be trying to go someplace."

When we arrived at Boys Town, he escorted me straight to the dean's office. The dean stood up behind his desk and angrily pointed his finger at me: "I want you to return to your cottage and pack up all your shit, because you're out of Boys Town, young man!"

When I stood up to leave, the dean called his secretary. As soon as she stepped into his office I stole the wallet from her purse. Instead of collecting my things from the cottage, I took off in the opposite direction, fumbling through the wallet as I ran, tossing out the driver's license, snapshots, and receipts, and keeping only the money. I was too angry to feel sorry for what I was doing.

Within hours I was back in Beaumont. Knowing that the Greyhound station was being monitored inside and out, I hid at a nearby gas station. As the night wore on I grew cold. I found a rusty hanger and used it to break into what looked like a junk car behind the gas station, wiggling it through the slightly open window to lift the lock. Curling into a ball in the backseat, my knees inside my sweatshirt, I tried to sleep the freezing night away. When that didn't work, I climbed into the front seat and fooled around with the radio. To my surprise, it came on. Then I played with the heating knobs and the heat came on as well. Hidden by the frost on the windows, I lay in the front seat with my arms wrapped tightly around my knees, listening to Carole King singing "So Far Away." It was as if she could see me in that moment. I fought hard to keep my eyes dry. Later the Temptations sang "Runaway Child, Running Wild." It was scary, how clearly the song depicted me. Its lyrics were right there:

> *Runaway child, running wild,*
> *Better go back home, where you belong.*
> *You're lost in this great big city.*
> *(Go back home where you belong.)*
> *Not one familiar face—ain't it a pity.*
> *(Go back home where you belong.)*
> *Mama, mama, please come see about me. . . .*
> *But she's much too far away—she can't hear a word you say.*
> *I want my mama.*
> *You're frightened and confused.*
> *Which way will you choose.*

I lay there crying long after the song was over. I was asleep when a voice saying "What the hell?!?" sprang me from my dreams.

"Boy, you are in my car," said the man at the open door. My eyes cleared to see the only other black person I had ever come across in Beaumont. "Whatcha doin' in my car, boy? Is you crazy?" he asked as he scratched his beard with bewilderment. He was dressed in a dark blue mechanic's jumpsuit. I had no answer, no reason even to clear my throat. All I could see was the light of morning on him.

"Boy, you been here with my car radio on all night?"

"Yeah," I mumbled, sadly.

"With my heat on too?"

"Uh-huh . . . only for a little, though," I offered, looking out at him.

He looked at me as if I were one sad case, then walked around the car and opened the trunk. I scooted across the front seat and got out, ready to flee in case he was planning to put me in the trunk. Instead, he removed his jumpsuit, rolled it up, and stowed it in the trunk. Something told me I ought to apologize for breaking into his car. I was about to utter the words "I'm sorry" when he looked at me and said, "You're one of those Boys Town boys, ain't you? You got a name?"

"Uh-huh. Jarvis," I said, watching him.

"I'm Bubba. What, you ran away or somethin'?"

"Yeah, yesterday, Bubba," I said, shivering in the freezing morning air.

"Them white folks wasn't treatin' you right, huh?"

"Not all of them," I said.

"So now, I guess," he said, getting into his car, "you want a ride, huh?"

I stared at him, wondering if he meant well or not. I had grown so cold from the frost of the morning.

"Well, you can get in if you want to." He looked over at me, waiting. "Or keep your tail standing there. It don't matter me none!" I didn't move, and he slammed his door.

When I heard the car starting up, I ran around to the passenger side and got in.

"Now I can't take you far," he said, driving out in front of the filling station, "but where you tryin' to get to?"

"Los Angeles?" I mumbled.

"Los Angeles? Boy, you know how far that is?" he said, slamming on the brakes. "I'm not even going that way, son. You got some money?"

"Uh-huh . . ."

"Then why you don't catch a bus or something? The Grey-hound stop is right over there."

" 'Cause they'll call the people at Boys Town and tell them."

A minute passed.

"Well, here's what we goin' to do," he said, scratching his beard. "I'm goin' to take you over to Banning—that's the next town over. They have a Greyhound bus stop too. If need be, I'll go in wit' you and getcha a ticket so you can get back to your kinfolks, okay? Is that all right with you?"

"Uh-huh," I said, wondering now how much money from the secretary's purse I had in my pocket. I had never counted it.

In my few days back at Boys Town, I'd been happy to sleep in a real bed again. Now I was already back on the run. Getting captured had a different meaning now. I knew I was in trouble. I thought I could even go to juvenile hall for what I had done.

On the way to Banning, Bubba told me about two other black kids who had run away from Boys Town many years before. He said the counselors had sicced dogs on them behind the filling station where he worked. "It sickened me," he said. That's why he wanted to help.

At the bus station, Bubba bought me a bus ticket to L.A. with the money I gave him. He told me to keep the rest, about thirty-five dollars, for when I got to the city. He gave me his telephone number and told me to call him when I arrived.

With a few hours to wait, I walked down the main street. I drifted into a store and bought a small transistor radio. Then I boarded the bus. I was on my way to L.A.

Holding the radio close to my ear, with my face pressed against the glass, I looked out at the hills and the endless bare lands in the distance. Time flew by as I listened to the music, mostly folk rock. I felt freer than ever. Scenes crossed the glass frame of my window like a movie reel: a mountaintop, a wild golden poppy field, cows grazing in the distance.

The pace had slowed enough for me to take hold of myself. Sitting quietly, I revisited the life I had had with the Prockses. I thought about my mother and my siblings and tried to imagine what they were doing inside those moments. I felt closer to them as these reflections flickered across the movie screen in my head and into my heart.

Whenever the bus stopped, I got off and roamed around. Alone in Riverside or San Bernardino, I bought candies to refill my pockets. I always tried to find a seat on the bus where I could be alone, with nobody asking me questions. With the companionship of my radio, I just wanted to disappear from everyone, to be in charge of myself. Ever since leaving the Prockses', I had felt cast out from any sense of normalcy. I had suffered so much at all the other places, but I could see now that they were just holding stations. As I was on my own, the turbulence in my mind had begun to settle. Now I wanted to keep being alone so I could get used to it.

When the bus finally pulled into the Los Angeles Greyhound station, I didn't want to get off. I was determined not to spend the night in the terminal—I had already done everything there was to do in that place. So when I saw another bus that said PALM SPRINGS, I made my move. I had become good at sneaking onto buses. A black family was boarding the bus, and I walked alongside them. As we climbed the steps I asked the parents, "Will we make it there tonight?" so the driver would assume I was with them. Soon I was happily on my way to Palm Springs.

I liked being on the road. I had shelter and something to do. I could sleep, wake up warm and safe, listen to my radio, and sit on the porch steps in my mind, gazing at everything passing by. I hoped it would take hours—the whole day and all night—to get there.

I traveled up and down the state. Sometimes I spent a whole day in a town like San Bernardino, walking for miles. For food I dug into Dumpsters behind supermarkets or doughnut shops as I had learned from the hippies. I stole clothes from Salvation Army stores, simply exchanging my filthy clothes for clean ones with no questions asked. Whenever I needed money, I stole from the March of Dimes baskets in supermarkets. Whenever I spent the night away from a bus station, I slept in a Laundromat or looked for the first unlocked car on a dealer's lot. There was always at least one. I'd wake up and be gone early in the morning. The longer I stayed out on my own, the more I knew it was not just Boys Town I had run away from, but the whole system. Alone on the bus, I felt safe. Traveling was all.

I kept this up for a while before I got caught sneaking onto a bus without a ticket. When I found myself back at McLaren Hall, all I wanted was to get away as fast as possible from this once-favorite place. After that, I ran away so many times. I landed in boys' home after boys' home, and when they all failed to keep me from running, I was again thrown back into foster care. In some foster homes I didn't last a whole day; in others I stole from the refrigerators before leaving, and sometimes before we even reached the next foster home I'd jump out of Mr. Higgins's car and disappear for weeks before ending up again at McLaren Hall. No longer could anyone say I had nowhere to go. I had found a home on the Greyhound.

I began to recognize
my own hurt and pain,
and all the sufferings of others,
as I rested my head against the window
of the Greyhound bus.
Rolling down the highway
opened my mind.
I could see clearly.
Ideas, thoughts,
and songs from my transistor radio,
came to me as if staged
at exactly the right moment.
Life was perfect and free.

CHAPTER 12

Becoming a Man

The Academy

JUST WHEN IT SEEMED there was finally nowhere that would accept me, the Valley Boys Academy opened. The staff of this former military school dressed like drill sergeants. They told me on my first day that their objective was to instill discipline and manhood. If I was weak, I had no business in their new boys' home.

I stood at attention with Mr. Higgins beside me. Since I'd always wanted to have a structure, I knew this was the place for me. I wanted to be trained and disciplined, to earn the right to belong. No boys' home had ever told me that it was a privilege to be there. I felt pumped up by the challenge of becoming a man—a man with the courage, strength, discipline, and determination that these look-alike drill sergeants were looking for. Excited, I promised Mr. Higgins that I would never run away again if I would only be allowed to stay. All I wanted was the chance to be accepted in my own right.

The academy was located across the town of Beaumont from Boys Town and had even taller mountains in its background. With only about twenty kids, it was the smallest of all the boys' homes I'd landed in. We all lived in one building, where the recreation room, offices, kitchen, and dining hall were also located. The dormitory had two rows of steel-spring beds with an aisle between them.

As one of only a handful of kids in residence during the opening days of the academy, I was excited about proving that I had what it took to belong there. I quickly made friends with everyone. Some, like Troy and Scotty, had also been kicked out of Boys Town. We hadn't known one another there, but our shared experiences bonded us as veterans. When we discovered that we were about the same age—eleven and twelve—we had even more reason to be best buddies. As we watched new kids arriving at the academy each day, the three of us just became closer, whispering to one another about what we saw unfolding.

At first the programs weren't in place and there wasn't much to do. But in a few weeks we began to feel the iron-fisted regimentation of the academy. When the dormitory was more than half full, we were suddenly awakened at four o'clock in the morning. Mr. Calhoun, the head counselor, rolled an empty metal garbage can down the center aisle and screamed at the top of his lungs: "Rise and shine! Asses up, boots on!" He angrily turned over the bunks of any kids who were slow to be up and standing at attention. "Time to be men!" he shouted.

I messed up in the first days of this new regime. I went over to help Josh, whose bunk had been turned over on top of him. I was bending over and lifting the bunk frame off of him when Mr. Calhoun's boot came up behind me and sent me crashing into the brick wall. I wasn't badly hurt, but I was slow to get up. Mr. Calhoun stood in the middle of the aisle addressing the whole dormitory. "Listen up, gentlemen! When I reveille your asses up in the morning, it doesn't mean going over to your grandmother and helping her out of bed. It means standing at the foot of your bunks at attention. Do I make myself clear? 'Cause if there is something you meatballs don't understand, I promise you, you will! And for all of you weak-minded individuals who can't get your dumb asses out of the bunk"—he looked directly at Josh—"you will no longer have a bunk. You will be sleeping on the floor until you earn that right."

Mr. Calhoun marched out of the dormitory, leaving us stunned. With no time to discuss what had just happened, we scrambled to get dressed and raced outside to line up double for our morning exercise. It was still dark when we started our morning jog.

Within two weeks we went from running one mile to three around the field in front of the academy. Mr. Calhoun always stood in the middle of the field, staring out at us. When he heard any of us talking, he would yell, "Thanks to Mike, we now have another mile to run." We would all hiss in anger, not only because someone had just made us run an extra mile, but also at the nerve of Mr. Calhoun for using the word "we" when he was just standing there like a fat Christmas tree.

Once we set our pace, I really liked running around the track, but the extra mile would mean a shorter shower and colder breakfast before we reported to the recreation room, which was also our classroom. Our sympathetic teacher would look over the class, see half of us sleeping, and say, "This is so insane." We always thought she understood our agonies, even though she only commuted to the academy.

By the time the academy was full, half the kids were trying to get out. They hated the forced exercise, the verbal abuse, and the staff's new habit of using some boys to beat up others if they didn't conform. Within a short time the academy had turned into a kind of gladiator school. A few students were in their teens, but most of us were younger.

A Test of Courage

AT THE BEGINNING I didn't see the academy's approach as wrong. To me, it wasn't wrong to be awakened at 4:00 A.M. by a trash can bouncing down the dorm's center aisle, or for sleeping boys to have their bunks turned on top of them. Not even after Josh lost bunk privileges and had to sleep on the floor for several weeks did I notice that something was wrong. Even if I'd been the one sleeping on the floor, I'd have considered it another challenge of becoming a "real man." My eyes were clouded by my need to prove that I could handle anything. No longer driven by a desire to be "crazy" or "cool," I wanted to earn the right to be accepted. I saw the academy as a kind of exclusive brotherhood that accepted only a few boys, and I wanted to be among them.

I thought it was part of the training when a counselor would set out a six-pack of Coca-Cola on a table in front of us, asking which of us believed we could win it. From the hands that shot up in the air, he would select two boys. He'd stand them next to each other and ask them each to hold out one arm. Pressing their bare forearms together, he would drop a lighted cigarette in the crack between them. The boy who didn't flinch would win the six-pack. When a boy kept a burning cigarette on his skin for long seconds at a time, we cheered him on. The winners were held in high esteem—the heroes of the hour.

I cringed as I watched how others kept from flinching, wishing I could be like them. But whenever I tried, the smell of my burning flesh made me jerk away. The way others gritted their teeth and raised high on tiptoe as their skin began to burn made me think of when I first arrived, when I was told that if I was too weak, I didn't deserve to be there. This thought obscured all the wrongs I was seeing. My desire to be in the fraternity completely overwhelmed my common sense. When I saw the cruelty and deception at play, I did not compare it to the atmosphere of Boys Town, as if deep down inside a voice was learning to say, *It's all the same!*

With the staff's permission, several groups of boys gave "blanket parties" to anyone who fell short in toughness. They would throw a blanket over a sleeping boy's head, then stomp him and beat him with bars of soap in socks until a staff member told them to "quit the horseplay." But it was never horseplay. Blanket parties were torture.

The night before I had been awakened by the screaming voice of a boy receiving such a party. I thought someone was being beaten to death.

A few months later I woke in the night to see three boys throwing blankets over Josh as he slept on the floor. The blankets muffled his screams as he kicked and tried to break free. The boys were all bigger than Josh. I could hear them beating him as they dragged him out of the dormitory and down the hall toward the recreation room. I lay on my bunk, trying to make sense of this. We all knew Josh had asthma and couldn't keep up on our three-mile run. He would often have an asthma attack after the first mile or so.

I crept down the hallway to see where they had taken Josh. Two counselors were whispering to one of the boys. I was afraid of being seen, but just before I returned to my bunk the counselors got a glimpse of me, enough to know who had been spying.

Back on my bunk, I lay awake the whole night, certain they would do me as they had Josh. I replayed the rumors that boys who'd given the staff problems, or had been deemed weak, were being dragged outside in the middle of the night, beaten, tied to trees, and left until morning. In that moment I realized these rumors might be true.

Not long after I had seen Josh dragged out of the dormitory, he returned. He lay back down on the floor where his bunk had once been, curled into a ball, rocking himself to sleep. There was not a sound, only that twitching rocking motion.

Soon the three other boys came back into the dormitory, each of them carrying a brown paper bag filled with candy bars and doughnuts. They sat on their bunks eating, then stowed the leftovers in their lockers. I wondered if they knew I'd been in the hallway. I kept waiting for them to look over in my direction, to see if I was asleep.

Hours later, when the boom of the trash can woke us up, I told Troy and Scotty what I'd seen while they'd slept. I pointed out the three boys who'd thrown the blankets over Josh and dragged him away. At first they couldn't believe it. They said that if something like that had actually happened, they would have heard it. But when one of those boys left his locker open and I showed Troy and Scotty the candy wrappers, they believed me.

The Circle

ONE MORNING AS WE stood around huffing and puffing after our run, Calhoun told us to form a circle. Bewildered, we did as we were told. Calhoun stood in the middle and slowly looked around, fixing his eyes on each of us. Then he returned his eyes to me. "Listen up, everyone," he said. "Whenever I ask you to form a circle, you will know I have a problem. This circle is going to be where we iron out our problems. So, Jarvis," he said, pointing and waving for me to come to him, "you can step inside this circle, right here next to me."

I stepped into the circle and stood beside Calhoun. I thought it had something to do with the running—I felt I had been better at running long distance than anyone else. I was fantasizing his announcing that I would lead our runs every morning when he told Leroy to come inside the circle. When Leroy stepped forward, I recognized him as one of the boys who had dragged Josh out of the dorm. He was a little bigger than me and had a mean face.

"Now, gentlemen, I got three packs of cigarettes, either Camels or Kools," Calhoun announced to everyone. He pulled the cigarettes out of his pocket for everyone to see. "These packs of cigarettes will be given to those of you who can pick the winner between Leroy here on my right and Jarvis here on my left."

"What are they going to do? What are they going to do?" the boys asked, jumping up and down with excitement. Even though smoking wasn't permitted, there was not one kid at the academy who hadn't started. It felt like a game show, with everyone guessing what the game would be. I hoped we would race around the track.

"Well, this is what Leroy and Jarvis are going to do," said Calhoun. "They're going to do what every man must do. They're going to do what the Romans had to do, and even before the Romans. They will fight inside this circle and do battle to the finish. They're going to show us who is the man and who is the . . . ? Who is what? C'mon, you all know. Who is . . ."

"The sissy! The sissy!" everyone shouted in one voice. All the boys around the circle clenched their fists, declaring the loser the sissy.

"That's right," said Calhoun. "Who is the man and who is the sissy." He held the cigarettes like a sign over his head.

Everyone began betting who would win. Some said I would, but a lot more kids bet on Leroy. I stood inside the circle and stared out at the frenzy. It began pumping me up, getting me ready to fight. The last thing I wanted was to lose.

Calhoun turned me and Leroy to face each other, standing between us like a boxing referee. "Listen, both of you," he said. "In my circle, there is no biting, no scratching, and most of all, no crying! If I see either of you crying, you will lose your bunk for a whole month. There is nothing wrong with losing, but men don't cry! If either of you cries, not only will you lose your bunk, you will eat, sleep, and walk on your knees! 'Cause real men don't cry. Do I make myself clear?"

"Uh-huh!" we both said.

"Okay then," said Calhoun, "now that we got that straight— Mr. Leroy, what do you plan to do to Mr. Jarvis?"

"I'm goin' to whip his ass!"

"And Jarvis, you heard what Leroy just said, son," said Calhoun. "What are you goin' to do about that?"

"I'm going to kick his ass!"

Bam! Calhoun head-butted us into each other. The clash brought everyone to cheers as they tightened the circle around us. Leroy was much stronger than me; his punches to my face quickly knocked me to the ground. As I struggled to get up, he kicked me in the stomach. The pain of having the wind knocked out of me kept me on the ground, and I lost my motor control. As everyone cheered Leroy on, he kept on punching. Whenever his arms got tired, he stood over me and stomped with all his might. He just kicked and kicked, stomping on my head with the heel of his sneaker while I curled up tightly on the ground. There was no question of winning anymore. My lip was busted and my nose was bleeding, but my pride clung to the only thing I cared about—not to cry and not to say, "I give up." Even with all the pain and embarrassment, I had gotten far worse from Florence Dupont.

After what felt like an eternity, Calhoun finally stopped Leroy. I peeked out from under my arms and saw some faces that feared they were looking down at a dead kid. Others were laughing, calling me "punk" and "sissy" and making motions as if they were spitting on me. Some kids who had bet on me and lost kicked dirt into my face.

Everyone hustled back to the dormitory, and I was left there on the ground. Not even Calhoun stayed, not even Troy and Scotty. When I finally managed to get up, I felt like the loneliest, most beat-up kid on the planet. I wanted to run away again rather than go back into that dormitory to get shamed and picked on some more. But somehow I didn't.

When I finally made it back inside, everyone had already showered and was at the chow hall eating breakfast. Sitting quietly on my bunk, I noticed that my locker had been broken into. All of my things had been stolen. Then I smelled urine. Someone had pissed on my bed. I was sitting right next to it. What was I to do? I got up and stood there frozen, looking from the big wet stain to my empty locker. Then I hurriedly stripped my bed clean, throwing the blanket, sheets, and pillowcases on the floor. I got a clean towel from the laundry room, got into the shower, and scrubbed myself clean. I wanted to be done before everyone returned from the chow hall. I felt bruised and beaten all over.

When I got out of the shower, I looked in the mirror. Both my eyes were puffed up. Surprisingly, my lip felt worse than it looked.

More than the bruises, the mirror showed all the pain I felt at having lost the fight. I felt ashamed of myself for not being more of a fighter. *I'm an athlete*, I kept telling myself. *I play sports. I run track, play basketball, football, and baseball.*

Josh

A FEW MINUTES LATER I heard a loud thump from somewhere in the shower room. I looked around, thinking somebody was trying to creep up from behind to give me a "blanket party." I started carefully looking into each toilet and shower stall. Before opening the last shower stall door, I looked down and saw a pool of blood oozing out, to my horror. Slowly, I pushed open the door. It was Josh. He was sitting on the floor, slumped against the toilet with his knees trembling, almost convulsing. Both of his wrists were slashed, and there was blood all over the place. Wearing only my boxer shorts and T-shirt, I ran as fast as I could to the chow hall to tell Calhoun. He and all the other staff rushed to the shower room.

Everybody started asking me what had happened. When I told them what I had seen and showed them the blood on my soles, everyone in the whole chow hall—even the cook—ran toward the showers. But they never made it. The staff contained us in the recreation room. In minutes we heard a siren speeding up to the building. From the windows we saw Josh carried outside and put into an ambulance that left with sirens blaring.

Calhoun came into the recreation room. "Gentlemen, listen up," he said.

I sat in a chair, trying to wipe the blood off my feet with a wet towel.

Calhoun continued. "An incident took place while the rest of us were eating breakfast. It was Josh. He couldn't take it. He didn't belong here. He tried to embarrass this academy and all of you here. Josh was no man. At fourteen, he was older than most of you, and still, all of you are twice the man that he was.

"Now, earlier today," Calhoun continued, looking at all of us with his arms crossed, "you watched two boys squaring off in the circle. We take pride in the victor. But remember this," he said, looking at me. "It takes a man to choose not to run away from a fight, to hang in there! Josh did not do this. He left this academy in shame. Our latrine has been disgraced. We will never forgive this, nor should we."

Calhoun marched out of the recreation room, followed by the staff. We sat in our chairs, mesmerized. It felt like we were part of an elite fraternity, a secret order. Some boys were mumbling with hatred about how Josh had brought shame on us by cutting his wrists. But I couldn't buy it anymore. I kept seeing Josh slumped over between the toilet and the wall with his knees rattling. Only I had seen the bloodstained razor blade lying on the white tile floor beside him.

Josh's name was never to be uttered again. It was not allowed. After hearing what Calhoun said, most boys now totally despised Josh, and we knew that the same harsh standard would be applied to any of us who failed to live up to the academy's expectations. Soon every boy there would live in fear of not being able to endure life there. For our own survival, we tried to turn ourselves into Calhoun's idea of men.

A few minutes after Calhoun's speech one of the staff ordered me in a loud voice to report to the office. I got dressed and walked there double time. Calhoun and half a dozen other counselors sat in the room, not saying a word. I wondered if they thought that because I had lost the fight I was thinking of cutting my wrists too.

Finally, Calhoun said, "Son, you were the only one who saw Josh. You know the mess he made."

"You mean . . . all the blood?" I asked.

"Yes, the blood! I want you to get a mop and bucket and clean it all up. I don't want anyone else back in the shower room until the entire area is all cleaned up."

"You want me to go right now?" I asked nervously.

"Yeah. But before you go," said Calhoun, rocking back in his chair, "there's one more thing. About the fight earlier today. You and Leroy. There are some among my staff who think you could one day beat Leroy, that you could beat anyone here—in time, with the right discipline and training. What do you say about that?" asked Calhoun.

I said nothing. I sat there looking down at the floor.

"Well, no matter," said Calhoun. "Starting tomorrow, you'll be working with Mr. Buck here. He's going to be your assigned counselor."

"And guess why, son," said Mr. Buck, sitting on the edge of Calhoun's desk. "I've been watching you. You don't quit. I like that. I want to put you in some boxing gloves and train you, to see if I can turn you into a boxing champ one day." He jumped up from the desk. "You run faster and farther than any boy here. And though you're piss for a fighter now, I promise you that if you don't quit— and none of us think you will from what we saw today—you'll end up being the pride of the academy!"

"Well, I wouldn't go that damn far," said Calhoun. "You'll probably show him a thing or two, but the pride of the academy? C'mon, Buck! Aren't you stretching it a bit?" They laughed.

I was then told I could leave. I walked out, uncertain whether I'd been bought or sold. It was as if they hadn't even seen me sitting there.

When I went to the mop room and filled the bucket with water, everything I wished I'd said in the office came out. "Assholes," I muttered. "Let me see you guys fight each other! That's all you people wanna see is a fight, fight and fight." After dipping each foot into the water to clean off the blood, I took the mop and bucket to where I'd found Josh. There was blood everywhere. I tried to mop it up, but the mop spread the gluey blood across the white tile floor like a paintbrush. I had to squeegee the blood into a corner to trap it and then use the mop like a sponge. The water in the bucket quickly turned red.

When I had finally cleaned and disinfected the whole shower area and returned to the dorm, I noticed a new mattress and clean folded linen. I saw that my things had miraculously reappeared in my locker. As I stood by my bunk the boys all hovered around, asking me if Josh was dead. None of us would ever know the truth. Josh's disappearance became a mystery used to intimidate any boy who wanted to leave the academy. When the staff would say, "There is only one way you will ever be allowed to leave this academy," we knew they meant "like Josh."

Gladiator

AFTER THE FIGHT I gradually regained my reputation. But the more I felt accepted, the less I trusted anyone at the academy. I could forgive those who had called me names, broken into my locker, and peed on my bunk, but I wasn't able to forget how in one moment everyone had liked me and in the next they had all hated and despised me. Not even Troy and Scotty had said a single word to me after Leroy beat me up. I didn't understand. It was as if the counselors had played some sort of magic trick to change everyone in a flash.

The other boys hardly mattered to me anymore. Nobody did. Why be friends with anyone when they were only the bows and arrows of Calhoun?

Mr. Buck started keeping me running around the track every morning after all the other boys had been dismissed. His constant shouting, as if he wanted to bite my head off, made the other boys think I'd done something wrong. Why else would I have to run the whole three miles over again? They laughed with derision.

Unlike fat Calhoun, who always stood in the middle of the field while we ran, Mr. Buck was a well-built ex-Marine who ran alongside me. Sometimes he pushed me to run faster; other times he made me run with my arms held out to the side or high above my head. My arms felt heavy as bricks, but he would slap the back of my head if I let them drop. Once when I was holding my arms overhead I felt so much shoulder pain that I stopped short and went down on my knees. Mr. Buck screamed in my ear to get up, but I couldn't. My arms hurt too much. Buck dragged me to the field next to the track and kicked dirt into my face and all over my body, as if his feet were shovels. Then he lifted me off the ground like a rag doll and took me to the chow hall.

When I stumbled into the chow hall covered with dirt, the boys exploded with laughter. They had already showered and were eating breakfast. As I took my seat they laughed even harder. I didn't know which hurt more: my shoulders or the laughter. When I lowered my face closer to my plate so I could scoop the corn-meal up without straining my shoulders, the boys started barking like dogs. Their faces—laughing, fixing their mouths before they barked—printed themselves in a collage in my mind. Afterward, when I ran, when I found myself alone, and even at night in my dreams, I saw the image of everyone laughing and barking at me, and I hated them.

Because I ran an extra three miles every morning, I had permission to get to school late. Soon I realized that if I stayed outdoors running around the track, I didn't have to report to class at all. I ran longer to be alone with myself, holding in my mind thoughts about the mountains in the distance or the birds gliding above me. It was a treat to have these fresh thoughts blow across my mind—much better than being stuffed into a classroom. These laps were the easiest ones to run.

Mr. Buck had other plans for me besides running. From his own home he brought a hundred-pound punching bag and an entire weight-lifting set, converting one of the large vacant rooms at the academy into a workout gym. Then came jump ropes, floor mats, and boxing gloves.

Mr. Buck began by teaching me how to kick the punching bag. He made me kick the bag until I couldn't raise my legs anymore, and when I stopped, he kicked me in the chest, knocking me clear across the room. "How did that feel?" he asked as I lay on the floor, rolling from side to side, gasping for air. "Get up! You get yo' ass up!" he shouted. "No man lies on my floor, only sissies. Get up, get up!" He crouched down and screamed in my face until I dragged myself to my feet. Then he said, "That's what makes you a winner, son. A loser don't know how to get up! You remember that, okay?" Then he patted me on top of the head.

In demonstrating punching and kicking techniques, Mr. Buck attacked the punching bag until sweat flew off his body. Then he held the bag and demanded that I do the same. "Damn it, don't punch like a girl," he yelled. "Punch like a man! See him? Look dead at your enemy. Imagine his face. Hit him! Hit him again! Use your foot! Your foot! Kick him. Hit the face, the face, the face. Now! Kick him in the balls. Now back to the face again. That's right, son! You got him now," he said as I kicked wildly at the bag. "Yeah, you got your enemy now. Don't stop. Kick, kick, kick! Punch, punch, punch! Kick, punch, kick, punch! Good job! Good, good job!"

I bent over, completely out of breath. My arms and legs felt as if they were about to fall off. But now Mr. Buck threw a jump rope over to me. "If I can do it, so can you," he said. "We'll jump rope together."

In a way I hated this workout, but in another way it was like being coached in sports. Like my other coaches, Mr. Buck only wanted me to do better than I thought I could. His belief in my potential and its accompanying demands made me feel special. He had chosen me from all the other boys. It meant a lot for him to call me "son" after I did what he wanted. I began to crave that fatherly response. His thumbs-up sign and nod meant that he was proud of me.

But more than anything else, I saw results. I stopped getting tired. I made loud pounding thuds as I kicked and punched into the bag. After a while Buck didn't need to be in the room to watch me kick and punch. He could sit in his office across the hall and know by the sound whether I was just playing around or whether I was giving it my all. No longer sore, I felt powerfully angry as I imagined doing so much harm to others.

The worst part was the boxing. Buck used the whole room as a boxing ring, knocking me hard to the ground so many times. He gave me many bloody noses and bright bouncing stars to see. With the boxing gloves on, Buck became angry. He fought me as he would fight someone a lot bigger and older. More than showing me how to fight, he was teaching me how to take a beating and not cry. If he saw any trace of tears, he just hit me harder. I would bend over, hiding myself to protect my face, but then Buck would curse and pound me almost as hard as he could. One time Calhoun, standing in the doorway, wondered aloud if Buck had been hitting me "a bit too hard?"

"He's going to learn what hard is," answered Buck, hitting me. "If he don't start fighting back."

At this, Calhoun left. When I heard that door shut, something in me snapped, and I charged at Buck wildly. I was beyond anger. Rushing at him with my head down like a football player, I wrapped my arms around his legs and drove him backward with the force of my adrenaline. As soon as he fell to the floor I tried to swing my fist up into his face. I wanted to hurt him so bad—to mash his face in, gouge my fingers into his eyes, and squeeze out his eyeballs. But the boxing gloves prevented me. All this time, Mr. Buck lay on the floor laughing. "Good job! Good job! This is what I've been waiting to see. Way to go, Jarvis! Way to go, son." He sat up and patted me on the head.

In wrestling and martial arts as well, Mr. Buck purposely unleashed my rage. When I went beyond myself, almost imploding with blackouts of hatred, I received his greatest applause. What Mr. Buck didn't know was that, in spite of his praise, I really did want to turn on him like a mad dog against his master. I had secret fantasies of catching him alone in his office: I'd creep up behind him and bite his neck. While he screamed, I'd rip and pull at his flesh until he died.

I suppose Buck wanted to feed these fantasies; he had reached deep inside me to find viciousness and bring it out. I thought that if I really clamped my teeth onto him, I would hear in his screams the echo of praise. Though I never did follow through with any of my fantasies, they were always present. The seething rage was always there.

CHAPTER 13

Coming Unleashed

Threat and Confidence

VIOLENCE WAS ON MY mind as I ate breakfast in the chow hall one morning. For months I had been getting along with everyone. Though I had barely sat a day in class, the rest of my daily routine kept me running in and out of the dormitory, playing sports and indoor games, and hanging out once again with Troy and Scotty. Often the three of us would go up in the mountains to get away from the incessant bullying.

At breakfast, sitting across the table from Troy, I saw that he had been the victim of a blanket party. His whole face was beaten; his eyes were bloodshot red, his nose and lip were swollen, and he had a nasty bump on the side of his forehead. He was eating out of the side of his mouth. I watched him looking down at his plate, fighting tears while the whole chow hall laughed and teased him.

I gritted my teeth in anger. Their laughter reminded me of how I had felt when Buck had brought me into breakfast after kicking dirt into my face. I stared over at the staff table, knowing that Buck remembered too. Buck looked back at me with an expression that said, *So what are you going to do about it?*

Seconds passed. I ate a little more of my breakfast. The boys were still laughing at Troy. When I looked back up at Buck, our eyes locked. There was no doubt he was telling me to do something. I looked at Leroy sitting several tables away, laughing. I was sure he was one of the boys who had given Troy the blanket party. I had never liked him since our fight, and he had also been involved in Josh's party. Watching how his jokes at Troy's expense had all the boys chuckling, I hated him even more. I looked at Troy again, then over at Mr. Buck. *Go for it! Show that son of a bitch!* Buck's face said, and he flicked his eyes at Leroy. *Go get him. Get him now. Now!*

Leaping to my feet, I ran between the dining tables toward Leroy. He turned to me in time to meet a kick in the face. I knocked him out of his chair, jumped on him, and hammered his face. He was trying to take cover behind his arms when I pulled his steel food tray off the table and beat him over the head with it. I kept on beating and kicking at him until two counselors pulled me off him.

Buck was standing behind me, rubbing my shoulders. "That's what I'm talking about, Jarvis! That was damn good, son!" he whispered into my ear. "Son, you did great! You did great!" He kept rubbing my shoulders like a corner man in a boxing ring.

"So, you want to form the circle?" said Calhoun. "What do you guys say? Should they fight in the circle?"

"Yeah, yeah! Let 'em fight in the circle," the whole chow hall hollered and cheered in unison.

"Well, then," said Calhoun, "let's go outside." He wrapped his arm around Leroy and whispered into his ear, like he was Leroy's personal manager. We all knew that Leroy was Calhoun's favorite. Everything Leroy did to other boys was on the instructions of Calhoun.

Outdoors in the circle, Calhoun continued to pump Leroy up, shaking his shoulders as if instructing him. I looked around for Buck. He was deep in a huddle with all the other staff, taking bets. I could see the money changing hands. Then he sauntered over to whisper in my ear, "Son, you know how much I trust in your ability, right?"

"How much?" I asked.

"Boy, two hundred dollars' worth!" he said, kneeling down on one knee in front of me. "Son, listen, you are going to win. Just do what I taught you. I want to hear that boy scream! If you get him to scream just once, no other big boy will ever want to fight you. You hear that? No other boy! So don't just win—hurt him! Hurt him! Hurt him bad and make him scream, you hear me?" With this mixture of threat and confidence, he stared almost coldly into my eyes.

With Calhoun and Buck out of the circle, Leroy and I stared at each other. I saw the fear in his eyes.

Fighting with Mr. Buck in our workout room, I had always pretended he was Leroy. Now the real Leroy looked so small, not even half the size of Mr. Buck. I was going to hurt him. Mr. Buck didn't have to encourage me. I wanted to destroy that cruel, unforgiving laughter I'd been hearing since the opening of the academy.

At the sound of Calhoun's whistle, we clashed, and in no time I got the best of Leroy. I heard Buck yelling for me to use my knee. When I came down on his head with it, Leroy almost began to cry. I stayed on top of him, kicking and punching. I went crazy—I couldn't stop. In my rage, Leroy felt like Buck. I wanted to hurt him so bad. Pounding and kicking weren't enough—I went at him with my teeth and bit him on the back of his neck. I was trying to take a mouthful of his flesh when he began screaming, "Get him off me! Please, oh please, get him off me!" He flailed wildly to keep me from latching onto him. Buck and Calhoun finally came into the circle and took me away.

With Buck hanging on to my torn T-shirt, I was like a mad dog at the end of a leash. Leroy looked over his shoulder, crying as he crawled out of the circle. Wiping the back of his ear, he came away with blood on his hand. "Man, he's crazy. You guys saw him! He's crazy, man!"

The whole circle of boys just stared at me. This fight had not turned out as they had expected. They felt embarrassed that the academy champion had crawled out of the circle. There was an evil anger on Calhoun's face. He looked around at all the boys, looking for the one to push into the circle to avenge Leroy. But in response to Calhoun's survey, each boy shrank back and hung his head.

"You see 'em, son," Buck whispered in my ear. "They don't want to fight you." He rubbed and thumped my chest. "Look at 'em. They're all scared. Now, if Calhoun don't pick someone else, this is what I want. You see Jesse over there?"

"Yeah, I see him," I huffed, still catching my breath. Jesse was Leroy's best friend.

"He is not to leave this field," said Buck. "I want you to attack—you hear me? Attack Jesse!" He squeezed my shoulders, getting me ready for the charge.

When Calhoun reluctantly announced there was not going to be any more fighting and told us to return to the dormitory, Mr. Buck released his hands from my shoulders—my signal. I took off after Jesse and landed a flying kick to the center of his back. The other boys ran scared to get out of the way, calling for Calhoun. I was on top of Jesse, lifting and slamming his head into the pavement with both hands when Calhoun booted me hard. "Boy! It's over. You won. The fighting is over for today." He turned and walked toward the dorm.

I got up off the ground. As Calhoun walked away I rushed toward him, attacking with all my might. I was on his back, trying to bite his neck, when he shook me off. Suddenly I found myself flat on my back staring up at his red face, cold blue eyes, and stained yellow teeth. He was choking me hard with both hands. I kicked and scratched my nails into his hairy forearms, fighting for air, as I felt the life being squeezed from me. I heard Buck's panicked voice shouting at Calhoun to let go, that he was going to kill me. Then Buck jumped on Calhoun, desperately trying to loosen his hands from around my neck.

Shoveled Away

I WOKE UP ON the floor in the mop room with only one sneaker on. I had no idea how long I had been there. I got up and tried the door. It was locked. I paced around the tiny windowless room, my neck burning. Was there any skin left? It was on fire. Sitting next to the locked door to distract myself from the pain, I thought about my fight with Leroy. It felt like someone else had controlled my punches, another angry me inside—the same one who had leapt from my seat in the chow hall and attacked Leroy in a rush of hatred. It was such a strange feeling. I could have cracked his head wide open with the steel food tray. I felt scared. *Why did I do that?* I asked myself. *For Troy!* I justified. It was for Troy, for how he'd been beaten up. At that moment it was my only excuse.

I saw Leroy and me fighting in the circle and realized I'd been fighting Buck. It was as if I'd turned on him like a wild dog. It now seemed impossible that I'd done this. I felt glad I hadn't attacked Mr. Buck when I had had those fantasies. I told myself I was going to run away the moment the mop room door opened.

Daydreaming, I saw myself back on the Greyhound bus. I longed to peer out that window again, alone with my radio, traveling from town to town, sitting close to my true self. All the fighting seemed to be for nothing. There were no big thrills in beating up Leroy; I felt no different winning than losing. All I wanted was to leave the academy. Now that I had a plan, sitting on the floor in the locked mop room was bearable. I would not stay at the academy a minute longer than necessary.

I was somewhere on the road, looking out the bus window, when somebody tapped on the door. "Who's that?" I asked, putting my ear down against the cold floor.

"It's me, Scotty," he whispered, sliding two cigarettes and a book of matches under the door. "That's all I can do for now," he said in a low voice. "I'll try to get you more later."

"Who put me in this mop room?" I asked, lying flat on the floor and talking through the crack under the door. "When they going to let me out?"

"Shit, dude! Man, I don't know," he said. "The cops were here!"

"'Cause of me?"

"I don't think so. They were in Calhoun's office. Before they came, though, right after you beat the shit out of Leroy—Jesse too—fat Calhoun called all of us into the rec room."

"For what?"

"They said people were coming to interview us about Josh."

"Josh?"

"Yeah, yeah. Josh. Remember? He cut his wrists?" His voice was hurried. "They told us a story, a fuckin' story to tell the cops, you know? Some bullshit about how we always been seein' the staff trying to help Josh, you know?"

"Are they still here—the cops?"

"I think so. Man, I'm not for sure, though," said Scotty with panic in his voice. "Hey, I got to go, man, before they catch me here talkin' to you."

"Wait, wait, Scotty," I pleaded, almost kissing the floor next to the door. "Why did they put me in this mop room? Just tell me who put me here before you leave, okay?"

There was a pause.

"Well, I helped 'em," said Scotty with a sad hesitation in his voice. "They just freaked out when they heard the cops were coming. They didn't know what to do, you know? They told me and Troy to carry you inside and put you in there. Shit, man! You were totally out. Mr. Calhoun thought he was going to be arrested! Man, they all freakin' out, big time!"

"Hey, I gotta talk to these people!" I said. "Are they still here?"

"They won't let you. That's why we put you back here."

"Who said that? Calhoun?"

"Man, they all did! All the fuckin' staff! They all fuckin' freakin' out, man! Hey, I gotta go! I'm goin' now," he said in a rush. I saw the bottoms of his shoes disappear from the other side of the door.

I sat up, more scared than ever. I lit one of the cigarettes and puffed hard, thinking over everything Scotty had said. Would Calhoun kill me to keep me from talking to the authorities?

I had seen so many bad and terrible things at the academy: what had happened to Josh, the blanket parties, the staged fist fighting with the staff betting on the outcomes, and other cruelties—like forcing us to kneel for hours or dragging boys out of the dorm at night and tying them to trees as punishment for less than snoring. Then there were the rattlesnakes—about a half dozen—they had thrown into the dormitory, to teach us how to work together. We had only so much time to round up and kill them as they slithered around under our bunks.

I had not yet seen a line that Calhoun wouldn't step over. He seemed capable of doing whatever it took to cover up the truth about life at the academy. My being locked in the mop room said as much. If I started kicking the door, even with only one shoe, it would make a lot of noise, but enough to get the visiting authorities' attention? Were they even still here? Perhaps Calhoun himself would answer the call, and I'd get myself a blanket party or worse. I lit the second cigarette and puffed nervously.

After another hour or so, Calhoun and Buck unlocked the door and squeezed into the room with me.

"Listen, son," said Buck, "we're having problems here at the academy. And while we're going to let you out, you are not to talk to anyone about anything—none of the things that have taken place here—"

" 'Cause if you do," interrupted Calhoun, his face red, "let's just say you'll regret your every word!"

"I won't say anything," I said, staring up at both of them. I thought: *I won't because I'm runnin' away.* I'll be gone tonight! I held this thought in secret and watched their eyes study my answer. Satisfied that I wouldn't talk, they waved for me to get up from the floor.

Bracing myself, I stood and walked between them through the mop room's narrow door, heading straight to the dormitory.

Cruelty Exposed

WHEN WE REACHED THE dormitory, several beds and their lockers had been stripped and emptied clean. The folded mattresses meant that some boys were suddenly no longer at the academy.

Everyone else was sitting around quietly on their bunks. One by one they began making their way over to me. With smiles on their faces, they surrounded me, lying and cheering and telling me how they had always thought I would beat Leroy. Some brought over treats from inside their lockers—I had become their new champion. In a way, it felt pretty cool to see the bullies kissing up to me. I stared into the eyes of boys who, not long before, had called me names, teased me, and pretended to spit on me. Now they were all gathering around and giving me whatever they thought I wanted. Even Jesse, who I'd jumped on outside the circle, offered me packs of cigarettes. How could everyone be my tormentor and then, just like that, become my admirer? Somewhere inside I knew they could go back to disliking me in a flash.

I left the mop room with every intention of running away the following morning. But when morning arrived, the whole program had suddenly changed, and I thought differently. There was no wake-up call, no three-mile run, no lines. The change scattered us in a wandering maze. Without the compass of the clock or the shouting of the staff, we weren't sure where we were supposed to be. Although nobody threw a trash can down the dormitory aisle at 4:00 A.M., our automatic timers had most of us lying awake, waiting for the lights to come on. When they didn't, we got up on our own and roamed around in the dark dorm as if in a forest, lost unto ourselves. We didn't even know if we needed permission to turn on the lights.

We were all up and dressed, hanging around talking to each other while the sun eased across the windows, and still no staff came into the dorm.

Nobody knew why several boys had left the day before. We suspected that during their interviews with the visiting authorities they'd said that they wanted to leave. My friend Troy was gone. That made sense. His whole face had been swollen that morning at breakfast. The authorities would have seen what I had seen in the chow hall. Leroy was gone too. The boys said he had wanted to leave. They watched from the window and saw him get into the backseat of one of the visitors' cars.

Nobody really understood what the authorities were looking for. They asked each boy they interviewed different questions about particular incidents. Some boys were asked about Josh slashing his wrists, others about the snakes thrown into the dorm, others about the tree tying, and still others about the blanket parties. It never dawned on us that all these questions tied into one central question: were there cruelties, physical abuse, and torture taking place at the academy? We couldn't see it, partly because we had accepted it, and partly because so often kids were abused not just by staff but by other kids.

When the sunlight came through the dormitory windows, we had already been talking to one another for hours, the first time we'd ever sat around and talked like that. For almost six months we had lived close, and yet we were prepared to treat one another according to Calhoun's orchestrations. We'd been divided, which made us capable of dehumanizing each other and doing terrible things without thought.

So when two counselors finally entered the dormitory late that morning, we felt like we'd just met. Before we were able to hustle back to our bunk areas and stand at attention like soldiers, one of the counselors, Mr. Mosley, stood just inside the doorway and announced breakfast. He said we were all expected to participate in school immediately following breakfast. Then he left. We stared at one another. We didn't know how to respond or what to make of no shouting, no morning inspection, no outdoor exercise. We hardly knew how to leave the dormitory without being told to march in a single-file line to the chow hall. After breakfast we sat in our classroom barely able to concentrate, constantly looking around for clues as to what was going on.

For the next few weeks the staff were mysteriously nice to us, though we continued to flinch whenever a counselor approached. Every day a new rumor would float around the dorm: they were going to take us up in the mountains and kill us; they were waiting to poison us—someone had seen a bottle with a skull-and-crossbones on the label. We believed these horror stories. After all, we knew the cruelties that had already taken place. A select handful of boys told us horrible things they had been forced to do for the staff, like sexually assaulting the weakest boy, urinating on other boys while they slept, and crawling under their bunks at night with lighters, trying to set one on fire before the smell could wake us all up. Now these same boys were running away from the academy, disappearing from under our eyes. The abuse these few boys could expose in detail had us thinking they were being killed in order to destroy the evidence. This belief reinforced our fear of getting caught trying to run away, never to be found again.

Two New Brothers

ONE DAY, WITHOUT GIVING any reason, Mr. Mosley told me to shelve my schoolbooks. I was to report to Calhoun at the main office; I wouldn't be returning to class that day. All the boys sat in their chairs, their gaze pounding against my heart. I knew they imagined they were seeing me for the last time. It was now my turn to disappear from the academy.

When I got to the main office and saw my Mr. Higgins talking to Calhoun, I just about jumped into his lap. I had been praying for his appearance ever since being let out of the mop room. There was no way that Mr. Higgins would leave the academy without me; I was going to be in that passenger seat, one way or another, beside him.

When they asked me to sit down, I refused. Calhoun rocked back in his chair with a big threatening smile on his face. This looked like a bad sign to me. Had he been lying to Mr. Higgins? Way too often I had walked into the living rooms of foster homes to see lies wrapped in smiles just like his.

"I don't want to sit down," I said, standing in the doorway. "Can I just talk to you, Mr. Higgins? Outside, in private?"

"Well, we can do that," he said. "But later, okay? Right now I think we should all three talk."

"About what? I don't want to stay here no more!" I said. I was afraid to enter the office and get caught in an invisible web. Once I walked in, I might never walk out. "And nobody's gonna make me either!"

"Son, that's why your social worker is here," said Calhoun. "We've found another place that we think you might like."

"I won't be staying? I'll be leaving?"

"Yeah, we're here to work it out," said Calhoun. "If you can just take a seat, son."

I walked into the office and took a seat right next to the door. I didn't trust either of them. I was ready to spring right out of my seat and run.

"Son," said Calhoun, "you and the other boys are probably aware that the academy will be shutting its doors—"

"Why? What happened?" I interrupted, wanting to hear his explanation. I was thinking that I would show Mr. Higgins the marks still showing on my neck from Calhoun's hands.

"You know why!" said Calhoun, his face turning red. "You know exactly why!"

I looked over at Mr. Higgins. I wanted him to see the anger on Calhoun's face. But he had his face down, reading a file while he picked his nose.

"So, Jarvis," said Mr. Higgins, closing the file on his lap, "since my office was informed that the academy was closing—about three or four weeks ago—I've been in constant contact with Mr. Calhoun here. The last thing we wanted was to have no place to send you but McLaren Hall. So I've been talking to your family."

"My mother?" I asked.

"No, others you probably don't remember."

"Who? Who?"

"Well, did you know you have two big brothers?"

"No, I just have a baby brother."

"You also have two big brothers—Tommy and Robbie."

"No, I don't!" I said.

"Oh, yes! Yes, you do!" said Mr. Higgins, smiling.

"Would you like to meet your brothers?" asked Calhoun.

"When?"

"How about now?" said Calhoun. "If they were to walk through that door, what would you say to them?" Confused, I looked over at Mr. Higgins. I wanted to see if they were joking. There was no trace of any big brothers in my memory. Uncles, yes, but big brothers?

"Is it true, Mr. Higgins?"

"Well, Jarvis, would you like to meet them?"

"Now?"

"Yes, right now!" Mr. Higgins stood up and walked over to the door.

"Yeah, I guess so," I said, as Mr. Higgins stepped outside the office. I almost hoped they were lying to me. Part of me didn't want to meet two big brothers I'd never heard of. I wasn't ready.

A few minutes later Mr. Higgins walked back into the office with two well-dressed young black men. They looked down at me. "Hey, little bro, we're your brothers. Remember us?" They stood me up and embraced me. "We're your brothers, Jay!"

I knew I'd seen their faces before, perhaps while visiting my grandmother. I had seen them there.

My oldest brother, Tommy, hugged me while Robbie stood close by. Then Robbie hugged me too. When I wrapped my arms around them, I knew they really were my brothers. I felt a strange new happiness. It was almost too much: part of me wanted to run from the office, but the other part never wanted to leave my big brothers.

For such a long time I had been my own protector. I'd had no one else to depend on, and my experiences had aged me beyond my years. Now, in the presence of these new big brothers, I felt myself shrinking to size again. It felt good to fit inside this little body, to be a little brother to someone like Tommy or Robbie.

When my brothers and Mr. Higgins left, I stared out the window into their promise. Their visit had been brief, just long enough to make plans for me to leave the academy and be placed permanently with my family. But my brothers assured me they were coming back. "Even if we have to break you out of here," Robbie had secretly whispered on his way out. I clung to this as if I had given them my last drops of trust. The car drove away in slow motion as I placed my hands on the window and watched all my hopes go with them, leaving me there with only a promise.

CHAPTER 14

Home to Memories

The House on the Hill

A COUPLE OF WEEKS after my brothers' surprise visit to the academy, I was in the front seat of Mr. Higgins's car, looking out the window, headed to my aunt Barbaree's apartment in Harbor City for a weeklong visit with my relatives before being placed with them. I instantly knew that I had been here before. The apartment building was still the same color.

I remembered my grandmother, how I used to climb onto her bed, and how she always kept a bowl of fruit on a table beside her. When we finally got out of the car, I even saw the window to my grandmother's bedroom. Without Mr. Higgins telling me which apartment my aunt lived in, I led him right to the front door.

When my aunt Barbaree opened the door, I saw the face of the person who had cared for my grandmother. I had always thought of her as the "toy lady," because she had given Charlene and me lots of toys. It turned out that she had worked at Toys R Us at that time.

When Barbaree saw me, tears ran down her face. We hugged each other. "Child, do you remember me?" she sobbed.

"Yeah, you're the toy lady," I said to the laughter of a fat man sitting on the couch. I hadn't noticed him there.

"Yeah, Barbaree," said the man. "That boy does remember you! All those damn toys you kept bringing to the house."

"And you see what them toys did too!" said Barbaree, joyfully wiping her tears. "They helped my nephew remember his aunt Barbaree! Ain't that right, Jay?" She smiled. Not until that moment did I know that Barbaree was my auntie.

I looked around the tiny living room. So many things had remained frozen in time. The photographs on the walls, the placement of the couches, even the old sewing machine I used to play with brought back memories. It felt like so long ago.

While Mr. Higgins and Barbaree sat talking on the couch, I went over and sat next to the fat man. "Boy, you know who I am?" he asked. He had an unshaven, mountain-man look. By now I wasn't easily scared, but I pretended to be, since he was giving me a mean stare. Still, I saw love in his face.

"My uncle?" I guessed.

"Yeah, that's right! Your big bad uncle to you, though! You could ask your mama. She'll tell you I'm her oldest brother, Dewitt."

I smiled.

"Boy, what the hell you laughing at?" he asked, interrupting Mr. Higgins's and Barbaree's discussion. Everyone was now looking at me.

"You ain't big! You fat!" I said, as Dewitt grabbed me in horseplay. Even as he held me in a headlock, I knew he was expressing his joy in having me there. In that instant, he became my favorite uncle.

When I asked Dewitt where Tommy and Robbie were, he secretly placed a finger over his lips as if to say, *Not now,* but to wait until Mr. Higgins left. Then he signaled that they were in one of the bedrooms. I didn't understand the reason for all the secrecy, but I was game for it. I talked to Dewitt as if I had known him my entire life.

When Mr. Higgins finished speaking to Barbaree, we all walked him out to his car. He made me promise that I would stay there until the end of the week, when he would pick me up and take me back to the academy. I had already told Mr. Higgins my misgivings about returning to the academy. He'd assured me that the academy would be closing soon; he was trying to place me permanently with my family. He persuaded me to cooperate by returning to the academy one last time while final arrangements were being made.

As we watched Mr. Higgins drive off, I heard Dewitt mumbling, "Barbaree, we ain't goin' to give this boy back. He's ours— this boy is ours!" We walked back inside the house.

Getting High

I WATCHED DEWITT knock several times on the bedroom door before it opened and my two big brothers appeared. Happy to see me again, they invited me into their room, where on the floor lay several pounds of marijuana scattered on top of newspapers.

"If y'all get this boy high," hollered Dewitt from the living room, "I'm goin' to kick your asses. Y'all don't have no business with all that damn weed in dis house any damn way!"

"Say, Dewitt," Tommy called from the bedroom, "ain't nobody tryin' to get him high. What you talkin' about?"

"Yeah, Dewitt," Robbie echoed. "Ain't nobody tryin' to get little Jay high." He lit a joint and passed it to me. "We know better than that, don't we, Jay?"

I inhaled and immediately began choking and coughing.

"All right, you two! I can hear that boy coughing back there," shouted Dewitt. "Y'all think I'm playin', huh?"

"Nah. That ain't Jay smoking. He's coughing from the contact smoke, that's all."

My brothers and I burst out laughing.

"All right, let me find my damn gun," yelled Dewitt. "I'm goin' to shoot me some asses up!"

"What does he mean, Tommy?" I asked. "He ain't really goin' to shoot us, is he?"

"Hell, yeah!" said Robbie. "Hurry, go lock the door!"

I ran to lock the bedroom door as Tommy and Robbie rushed to open the window. I thought they were trying to let air in, but they were trying to climb out, laughing. Dewitt began pounding on the door.

"Open dis goddamn door." Dewitt banged. He threw all four hundred pounds of his weight against the door, and it flew open before Tommy had completely escaped. Dewitt lifted his BB gun and began firing, shooting Tommy several times in the butt before he managed to fall out of the window.

Standing in the middle of the room with my hands raised as if under arrest, I kept my eyes on Dewitt waving his pistol. *He's crazy, crazy,* I kept thinking nervously.

"Now, nephew, I told them! Didn't I tell those fools?" he said, looking straight at me.

"Yeah, you told them, Dewitt. You did tell them," I said with my hands still up in the air.

"Now, boy, I'm goin' to ask you one thing—and only one thing," said Dewitt. "Did you smoke any of that weed?"

"Nope! I did not, Dewitt. I swear I didn't." I tried keeping a straight face.

"Are you sure?"

"Yeah, I'm sure, Dewitt."

"Are you lyin' to me, boy?"

"No, Dewitt. I'm telling you, I didn't. I didn't smoke any, man! That's for real!"

"Well, what's dat between your fingers then?" He used the barrel of the pistol to point to one of my hands that was still raised over my head. I looked up. A trail of smoke drifted from the still-burning joint between my fingers. I stared up at the smoke. It was the funniest thing I had ever seen.

"Dewitt, I swear, I don't know who put dat there!" I was able to say before the high from smoking just about knocked me over laughing.

Pow! Pow! Dewitt shot me twice in the leg. The sting of the BBs propelled me onto the bed. "Damn, Dewitt! What you do that for?" I asked, clutching my leg.

"Boy, it ain't funny no more, huh?" said Dewitt. "Shit, I ought to pop you one mo' time." He chuckled, pointing the pistol at me. Then, reaching into his back pocket, he pulled out a tiny paper bag. "Here, put some of that stuff in dis here bag," he ordered, tossing the bag over to me.

"What, the weed?" I asked, rubbing the area where I'd been shot.

"Yeah, the weed, boy! Put some o' dat weed in de bag," he ordered, aiming the pistol at me. "Hurry! Hurry up before your crazy-ass brothers get back!"

I filled the bag with weed and gave it to Dewitt.

"And if you tell 'em I got it," Dewitt threatened, "I'm goin' to pop your ass again!"

"Man, I ain't goin' to tell 'em—"

"You best not!" said Dewitt. "And if I was you, I'd get a handful, steal you some while you can." His stomach bounced up and down as he chuckled. " 'Cause your brothers—jus' wait, you'll see— is stingy. It ain't a word for how stingy they both is!"

Then Dewitt left the room.

I felt like I had just been robbed at gunpoint. I hadn't been with my relatives more than a couple of hours before I had smoked weed, witnessed my two oldest brothers jumping out of a window, and been shot twice by my uncle. It was more fun than I had ever imagined. In spite of the burning sting of the BBs, there was something about Uncle Dewitt that I liked.

I found Dewitt outside that night, smoking weed by the fence behind the building. I waited until he finished before asking him about my mother. "Jay, your mother tried her best to protect you and all her kids," said Dewitt. "They had to put her in a mental hospital after she lost you. She damn near died there, wanting you guys back. Yeah, I know your mama made mistakes—hell, she's been doing dat her whole life! But, boy, don't you ever let nobody tell you that your mama didn't love you! I know 'cause I had to take care of her for a long time—we all did—after they took you guys away. She must've tried to kill herself a dozen times—all because she didn't think she could live without you kids." Although I blocked out the idea of suicide, Dewitt's words proved what I had always known—that my mother really loved me.

"Now, don't get me wrong," said Dewitt, lighting up the dark with a cigarette. "Your mama is crazy! She's more crazier than bed bugs. I've seen Venus cut men with straight razors in a way that she jus' had to be crazy. That's right." Dewitt leaned on the fence.

In Harbor City

ALMOST ALL OF MY mother's siblings lived within a few miles of each other. My cousin Ricky, known as Boo-Boo, showed me around the neighborhood. He was only a few months older than me; we instantly became inseparable. Boo-Boo took me to visit all my relatives, giving me the chance to feel so much love. By the week's end, I had met all my uncles and aunts as well as a whole village of cousins on my mother's side of the family. They remembered me as a small child and wept, wishing they could have cared for my siblings and me before we were taken away by the state.

I felt at home with my family. They all wanted me to stay with them, so each night I slept on the couch at a different relative's house. Although none had room to put me up permanently, more than anything my family desperately wanted me back, out of the foster care system. They especially didn't want me to return to the academy with its cruelties. They cursed and cried that they could have done better, if only someone had sought them out instead of putting me in places like the academy. I actually had to convince my relatives to let me return as promised. I told them that I would run away if, for any reason, I wasn't going to be permanently placed with them.

By this time I had known Mr. Higgins for what seemed like my whole life—since I was seven or eight years old. He would never have shown me how to find my relatives if there'd been any doubt about my living with them. I didn't say so to them, but Mr. Higgins knew me better than they did.

So after only two weeks, I was back in Harbor City, permanently placed with my relatives. I'd told Mr. Higgins I wanted to stay with my cousins Boo-Boo and Little Ronnie at Aunt Nadine's house. With my favorite aunt, Barbaree, I could laugh and have fun, but Aunt Nadine was raising two boys of her own and had created a good environment for that. As much as I enjoyed hanging out with my big brothers and Uncle Dewitt at Aunt Barbaree's, Nadine's place felt like a home.

But for some reason I was placed with Aunt Barbaree. Originally my grandmother's, the house on the hill had been my family's nerve center for many years. There was never a dull moment. Loud music was always playing. People brought their newest albums for all to hear, and they danced the latest steps. Folks hung out, and many others bunched up, smoking weed nonstop. From a block away, you could smell Barbaree's southern fried cooking. Uncles Calvin and Big Ronnie—the mechanics for the whole neighborhood—had the latest tools, and everyone came to work on their cars and motorcycles there. My uncles not only repaired cars but also worked on televisions, stereos, and anything else that needed fixing.

People were always dropping by. Some were childhood friends of my mother's. Others said they had seen her just weeks before. I didn't ask anyone where she was because, after seeing Pablo's mother, I was afraid to find mine in the same state, shooting up on a pee-stained mattress, caring more about dope than about me.

Not all the visitors were blood relatives, but they felt like they were. They had memories of changing my diapers, finding my siblings and me alone, and many other moments we had shared. I didn't remember all these people, but they remembered me.

Suspended from School

NO SOONER DID I enroll in Normount Elementary to complete the sixth grade than I got suspended.

I had not been in a real school for several years. From the very first day, the schoolwork had been too hard for me. I couldn't keep up. I was too embarrassed to admit that I didn't know how to read or do the math that the rest of the class was doing. I had already seen how my teacher, Mr. Quigley, made a laughingstock of the students who made mistakes. "Perhaps we need to get Mr. Jones a second-grade book so he can read to all of us," Mr. Quigley would rail when a kid mispronounced a few words. "You may now take your seat, Mr. Jones. No, wait," he would add, "perhaps you belong in the sandbox! Can anybody tell Mr. Jones where the sandbox is, for the kids who read like Mr. Jones?" And the whole classroom would laugh.

I had been warned about Mr. Quigley. Stories floated outside on the recreation field and around the table at lunchtime. Everyone in class was afraid of him. I tried to fit in by fearing him, as all my friends did. I didn't want to seem abnormal, made braver by my years inside institutions.

Mr. Quigley kept catching me not paying attention. When this happened, I'd put my head down on my desk as we'd been told to do. This time, in front of the whole class, he wondered if I had the brain cells of a human or not. I kept my head down. Fitting in was important to me. From the first moment I'd felt as if I had outgrown everyone sitting there. I had even outgrown the chairs. I wanted to keep my past well hidden from everyone in class, especially the girls, who'd been checking me out, the only new boy they'd seen since first grade.

But the next day in class, when I didn't know the answer to a question, Mr. Quigley snatched some papers out of my hand, rolled them up, and began tapping me on the top of the head with them. Rage rose up in me and slapped the papers clean out of his hand.

"Oh! We have a Bruce Lee in class!" Mr. Quigley announced as he jumped into a karate stance. The whole classroom burst out laughing. In my mind, I silently begged him to leave me alone— please, not me—trying to show that I was scared of him. When he walked back to his desk and turned to the chalkboard, I actually thought he might have heard my plea. With his back to us, my friends sympathetically began picking up the papers that had fallen around their chairs. But Mr. Quigley turned around and shouted at them to leave all the papers where they were.

"Mr. Masters will be picking up the papers during recess," he said to the class. I didn't mind. I was wrong for slapping the papers out of his hand. But when he described how I would be down on my knees picking up the papers as a metaphor for something else he was trying to explain to the class, I knew that I wasn't going to pick up those papers. The surer I became that I wouldn't do it, the more Mr. Quigley found opportunities to refer to me on my knees during recess. Watching him with fierce hatred, I began counting the times he said it.

My rage made me lose count. When he'd turned back to the chalkboard, I leapt from my seat and ran forward, jumping onto his desk at just the moment he pivoted around to face the class. In one full motion, I kicked him in the face as hard as a football punter kicking a field goal. He never saw it coming. He flew back against the chalkboard and slid down the wall. Blood gushing from his nose, he moaned and crawled toward the alarm button. I was afraid to turn and look at the other kids, but I could hear them gasping in shock.

When Mr. Quigley had reached the button, I jumped down from the desk and bent down over him so he could see my face, as if to say, *How does that feel? Not good, huh?* as Buck had done to me.

Then I walked to the principal's office and told him what I'd done and why. I said I'd do it again if Quigley kept abusing me in class.

By now I had become a kid whom I secretly hated. I had no response to conflict except violence. I envied other kids their ability to walk away from confrontations. I wanted to ask them, "How did you do that?" as if they had just done a back flip.

The principal listened to me. He thought I was exaggerating until Mr. Quigley stumbled in, wearing only his bloodstained T-shirt and holding his dress shirt to his nose. "My God, Henry, what in the world happened?" the principal screamed in a panicked voice.

"That son of a bitch right there socked me in the face—that's what happened," Mr. Quigley mumbled. He was tipping his head back, trying to keep the shirt pressed against his nose.

"No, I didn't. That's a lie!" I said. I walked right up to him. "I kicked you in the face!"

"You what?"

"I said I didn't sock you in the face! I kicked you!"

The principal couldn't believe my nerve in standing so close and correcting one of his teachers.

I knew I was in trouble, but at least I no longer had to pretend I was afraid. I wanted to show Mr. Quigley that I wasn't like his other kids; I had never been frightened. At the academy I had grown accustomed to being beaten by the counselors. I wanted Quigley to get so mad that he would snap and punch me, sock me, or whatever he wanted to do. I wanted him to hit me hard so he'd feel we were even; I wanted him to see that I could take as well as give. Then I wanted us both to return to class. Where I'd been, I'd learned that getting even brings mutual respect. That's what I wanted for Quigley and me.

But Mr. Quigley didn't snap; he just stood there tipping his head back. It wasn't supposed to happen like this. Why wasn't he jumping on me? I knew I deserved it; I was ready. I wanted to get it over with. The counselors at the academy would have ripped right into me, but the principal and Quigley did nothing. Not to receive a retaliatory burst of violence made things worse. Quigley's groans weren't the reaction I'd been bracing for. Something else needed to happen.

The vice principal escorted me to the school infirmary while the principal sorted out what to do. I was playing with the scale when the hall monitor came in and handed me an envelope addressed to Aunt Barbaree. Then he escorted me to the front gate and told me to go home.

On my way home I opened the envelope. It was a notice of suspension. Sitting on the curb between two parked cars, I sounded out the big words that I knew described the reasons. I was able to figure most of it out before I got home and gave the letter to Aunt Angie, who was married to Uncle Calvin. Anger steaming from her face, she called Dewitt and Calvin and Barbaree and some visiting friends into the living room and read the letter out loud. It said that following my attack on Quigley, he had restrained me in a full nelson.

I tried to tell Angie that Mr. Quigley hadn't touched me; nothing like what the letter described had taken place. It was no use. The grown-ups went on arguing and talking over each other: the nerve of a white teacher to put their nephew in a full nelson! With so much noise, it was impossible to figure out why Quigley had lied. All I wanted was to get outside where I could hear myself think. Before I reached the front door, Angie grabbed me. Shaking me hard, she screamed, "Jay, don't you ever, ever let anybody—I mean nobody—put their damn fuckin' hands on you!" I felt her spit on my cheek.

"Nobody did, Angie," I mumbled.

"Jay, the next time that fool teacher Mr. Quigley, or whatever the fuck his name is, touches you . . ." She knelt down and took something out of her sock. "Here! Take this!" She handed me a push-up box cutter. "I want you to cut his ass! You cut him clear across his damn face. Do you hear me? Do you?"

"Yeah, I hear you," I said, looking at the box cutter in my hand. "But, Angie," I tried again to say, "I kicked him . . . Quigley, in the face. . . ."

"Angie, he don't even know how to use that thing!" Dewitt said.

"Yes, he do," said Angie. "Jay, the next motherfucker who puts their hands on you at that school, you cut the shit out of 'em. You hear me?"

"Yeah, I hear you, Angie," I said again. I wiped my face and walked out the front door with the box cutter in my hand. Sensing everyone looking at me from the window, I practiced swinging it at the air and imagining the bloody mess it could make. I knew from what Dewitt had said that my mother kept one, with no qualms about using it, but I liked my fists better. A few blocks away, I dropped the box cutter in a garbage can. Looking down at it shining among the banana peels, I knew there was no way I could ever cut anyone.

Muddy Shoe

LATER THAT DAY, WHEN I heard my lunch money jingling in my pocket, I walked down to Bob's Liquor Store. I liked talking with the "crazies" who hung out in the parking lot. Most of them were Vietnam veterans who were recently home and already living off the bottle, drinking booze like water. They were like elders to me. One day I had asked a neighborhood friend why everybody called them crazy. He said, "Just look at 'em, the way their eyes want to cut you into tiny little pieces." I did, staring back like my eyes could cut *them* into tiny pieces. One of them smiled and gave me a peace sign. "Do you know him?" my friend asked while we were in the store. "No, but I bet they know all my uncles," I bragged.

The one who had given me that peace sign we called Muddy Shoe. Now drinking outside the liquor store, he was wearing his worn-out army green overcoat, a camouflage cap, and old army boots so molded to his feet that you could see the shape of the corns if you stared long enough. When he asked me why I wasn't in school, I sat down and told him the whole story. He asked if I still had the box cutter. I told him I'd dropped it in the garbage bin.

"Come here," he said. Then he grabbed me, almost lifting me off the ground. He frisked all my pockets, then my shoes.

"Man, I told you I threw it away," I said.

"Well, I'm just making sure you did," said Muddy Shoe. "Boy, if I ever find out you still have that box cutter, yo' ass is mine! You hear me?" He took a long nasty swig from his bottle, wiping his mouth on the sleeve of his coat.

"My mama had one," I said, seeking a response. It was my only regret about having thrown the box cutter away.

"Shit! Your mama is grown! She's a grown woman!"

I stared at my sneakers and said nothing.

"So, am I right? Am I right or not?" asked Muddy Shoe, squinching up his face as he took another swig.

"Yeah, you right, you right," I said, feeling better about throwing it away.

"Okay, then. Sit your rabbit-ass down," said Muddy Shoe. "I still haven't told you about Minh-Khai. Now that was a beaucoup bad, bad, bad-ass bitch! She ran a whorehouse right on the outskirts of Hanoi." He looked up and down the street, checking for passing cop cars, and then secretly slipped me his bottle. "Go on ahead, take you a swig, boy! Go an' get cha' some, boy! You deserve it today." He grinned, showing the dirty rust of his teeth. "Go on! Grow some hair on dat chest of yours! You did somethin' good, throwing dat fool box cutter away."

I wiped off the mouth of the bottle with my shirt and took a big swallow. My whole body quivered, feeling the heat of the booze climbing into my nose. It was nasty, oh, so nasty! It stunk like brewed sardine juice.

"Pass it on back," he said, taking the bottle and drinking it all the way down with a gurgle. "Now, back to Minh-Khai," he said with a loud belch, beginning one more of the Vietnam tales I loved hearing. Almost from the first days of living with my relatives I'd listened to these stories in the parking lot. Muddy Shoe and I sat in front of Bob's Liquor Store that whole day.

I was a long way from sitting on the red porch with Mamie reading me astronaut stories. It seemed like the more I tried to return to that innocent life, the more the child in me fizzled out. But I couldn't quite ever forget the stars that Mamie had lit up in my heart. Throughout my childhood, what stayed bright were the people who cared about me.

CHAPTER 15

Taking On the World Together

Venus

ONE TIME WHEN I was outside playing at Aunt Barbaree's, my mother unexpectedly dropped by. When my aunt called to me that my mother was there, I ran as fast as I could to find her in the living room with Dewitt and Calvin, who were showing her how to kick-box and handle the butcher knife she was holding. Relatives and friends were watching her kick high into the air with the knife in one hand and a cigarette in the other. I couldn't believe it. Instead of giving me a hug when she saw me flying through the front door, she went around the room telling everybody, "I told you so," collecting dollar bills under threat of the knife. It turned out that she'd bet everyone I'd come running the moment I knew she was there.

Now she rolled the money up, knelt down, and stuffed it in my pocket. Then I got my kiss. Standing up, she asked, "Which one of you all wanna step up? 'Cause me and Jay will kick anybody's ass who wants to fight, including you, Dewitt!" "Now, baby," she said to me, smiling. "You have to get your big uncle Dewitt. Can you whip him?"

"Yeah, I can," I said, dancing around him like a prizefighter all of twelve years old.

"So come on! Bring it on, you bad motherfucker!" she shouted, still waving the knife. The first of her children to return from foster care, I reminded everyone of my mother. The way we took our stance in the middle of the room pretending to be dead serious had everyone rolling in laughter. I felt so proud standing only chest high next to her, as if we were taking on the whole world.

"You see, Jay? They know when I get you by my side, what we can do. Ain't that right?"

"That's right, Mama," I said, with my dukes up. "Come on, Dewitt, let's fight!"

"Okay, baby," she said. "They don't call me Shorty for nothin'! I'm a ba-a-a-d woman! And your uncles know it. I was kickin' their asses back when, and I'll kick their asses now!"

"Sit your crazy ass down, Shorty," said Dewitt, still sitting on the couch. "We've been protectin' you all your crazy damn life." Everyone laughed. "And, Jay, boy—you know your mama ain't goin' to be around tomorrow. What your bad-ass goin' to do then, huh? You too best sit your ass down!"

"I'm goin' with my mama," I said. "That's what I'm goin' to do!" But I knew it wasn't true.

My mother grew serious. "Dewitt," she said, "you better not go messin' with my baby when I'm gone." She turned to me and asked me to put the knife back in the kitchen.

When I returned to the living room, I saw my mother on top of her oldest brother on the couch, scuffling like kids. She had his massive body in a headlock, all four hundred pounds of him. Even as he was telling her to stop messing around, I saw the love between them.

Later that day she took off her shoes and we went out in the middle of the street. People came out of their houses like spectators at a major event to see my mother, barefooted, demanding that I race her down the block. I thought she was crazy for wanting to race me. I was too young, too fast. It wouldn't be fair. I didn't want to look back over my shoulder at my poor ol' mama behind me. But the more I declined, the more insistent she became. So I decided that instead of trying to win, I would just run by her side and however fast she ran, I'd be there, escorting her down the block.

I heard, "On your mark! Get set! Go!" and suddenly she took off. I tried to catch up, but fell farther back instead. Seeing how fast she could run was blowing me away. I could only think about what my friends would say if she won. The teasing I'd hear at every neighborhood playground kept me running as fast as I could. But she was way too fast. When I saw her standing at the corner waiting for me, I realized that I couldn't have beaten her even if I'd wanted. Did her speed have something to do with her running barefooted? I could find no other explanation.

When my mother said good-bye, I could tell that she'd truly been home. I was going to miss her more than ever, but being with relatives made a difference. With a hug, she walked out of my world and back into her own. According to her siblings, it was a world that had taken her beyond anyone's control. Yet they extended understanding and sympathy to her in so many ways, including trying to raise me, a ward of the court who had already been institutionalized.

I kept hearing lots of stories about Mama's life. They weren't all good, but no matter how many times my relatives called her "crazy," these kitchen-table stories helped fill in the gaps about her. My mother had grown up a tomboy whose brothers taught her how to fight. For a while they were always protecting her and beating up her boyfriends, but once they showed her how to use a box cutter, she didn't need their help anymore.

"There was one time," Dewitt told me, "when your crazy-ass mama and I was at this joint in Long Beach—right around the time you were born. And there was this fool who snatched your mama up, you know, trying to manhandle her. He lifted her onto the bar and tried to open her blouse—boy, now what he tried to do dat for . . ."

"What happen? What happen, Dewitt?" I asked.

"Well, your mama slice him with a straight razor. Whack! She cut him clean, from one side of his face to the other! I had to get her off him 'cause if I didn't we was sho' goin' to jail dat night! That's for sure! She's crazy all right." Dewitt ground the butt of his cigarette into the concrete. "But ain't nobody who knows your mama, Jay, can ever say she didn't love you kids."

When social workers used words like "neglected," "abandoned," or "abused" to describe my early years, they never seemed to give my mother's suffering a thought. As a child, I felt like I alone knew what those words really meant. I never shared with anyone my memories of hearing Mama being stomped by my father or seeing her lying in a pool of blood. I saw her as a victim who always struggled back to her feet. Her protective instinct overshadowed any neglect I had felt.

Time after time, staring into my mother's eyes, I had seen real suffering. Whenever the social workers separated us, the suffering and fierce love that I had witnessed only brought me closer to her. I spent few of my growing-up years around her, and yet she knew me well. She could see right through to me, as if we had never been separated. No one else seemed to understand our deep connection.

Barely Alive

"Jay, your mama is dead."

I'd come home to find Barbaree's living room filled with aunts, uncles, brothers, and cousins.

"Where is she? Is she in the room?" I asked. Although they said the word "dead," I heard something else. They must have meant my mother was here someplace.

"No, Jay!" said the voice. "Your mama is dead . . . she is dead, Jay!"

Seconds went by. I couldn't see whose face was talking. So many were staring at me. I blinked, trying to wake from this nightmare.

Suddenly I saw people rising from their seats, approaching me like monsters. I closed my eyes and started fighting all of them. As I swung my fists into Uncle Dewitt's huge stomach, I felt him put his arms around me and heard him say, "Let it go, get it all out." His stomach muffled the sound of my cries and hid me from the others. Dewitt told them to stay back; I would be all right.

With everyone standing in a circle around us, I just stood there crying and crying, wanting Dewitt to keep holding me. I hated myself for crying, but the harder I tried to stop, the more I cried. The tears felt like melted lead. It hurt to realize that I wasn't as strong as a man was supposed to be. I was already thirteen, and I thought my crying years were behind me.

While Dewitt was still holding me, my cousin Angie came running out of a bedroom yelling, "She's alive! She's still alive! Jay, your mama is alive!"

Everyone began talking at once. Dewitt told them to shut up so Angie could tell us what she'd just found out from the other relatives who were at the hospital: my mother had been gang-raped and beaten, dumped in an alley, shot seven times, and left for dead. A witness who'd watched a car drive up the alley and seen the bright flame of every shot had found and recognized my mother. It was he who'd started the rumor that she was dead.

The doctors didn't know if she was going to live; she had suffered several serious bullet wounds and lost a lot of blood. In the meantime, the rumors of her death had spread quickly throughout the whole family. That was why everyone was gathered at Barbaree's: they'd wanted to tell me the news before I heard it on the streets.

Now Angie was speaking directly to me. My mother was in critical condition, but the doctors were giving her a good chance of pulling through. Uncle Dewitt shook me and told me to wipe my face. He knew my mother, how strong she was. If those bullets didn't kill her right away, they weren't going to kill her at all.

It wasn't what my uncle was saying but how he said it that made me believe him. My family's shock now turned to hope. The news that she was dead had vanished. I was convinced that my mother would live.

Everyone started swapping stories about how tough my mother was. If anybody could survive being shot seven times at close range, it was Cynthia, Shorty, Lady Day, Venus—they had many names for my mother.

That night I finally got to the hospital to see her. All of us—my uncles and aunts, brothers and cousins—stood quietly around her bed in a darkened room filled with the sound of medical equipment at work: an IV drip, a heart monitor, and a machine that seemed to be helping her breathe. Every so often an alarm would go off; a nurse would rush into the room to check a machine and make an adjustment to the mask on Mama's face or one of the tubes running in and out of her body. Because of all the equipment, I was afraid to touch her; if I broke something, she might die.

I watched her hand resting on the side of the bed. She didn't move. Other family members were trying to speak with her. Leaning over the bed, they whispered her name, "Cynthia, can you hear me?"

The more they tried to communicate with her, the more my attention was drawn to her hand. If only her fingers would tell me she knew I was there. It would be our secret. It was how she could tell me she was all right, without anyone else needing to know. Looking at her hand, I remembered the time she had reached out and gripped mine, even though she had been horribly beaten.

I waited for my mother's hand to touch me now, my mind begging her to let even a finger tell me that she knew I was there for her again. When the nurse came in and said we had to leave so my mother could get some rest, I couldn't give up wanting her to know I was there. When someone touched my shoulder, trying gently to lead me away from my mother's side, it felt like they were trying to rip us apart. I gripped the bed rail. I wasn't going anywhere.

"No, no, *no!*" I yelled.

Slowly my mother's hand began to move. Lifting it to the bed rail, she softly pried open my hand and brought our hands together on the bed. A flood of tears ran down my cheeks. I looked at my mother's hand lying on top of mine. When she slipped her fingers between mine, I knew that she knew I was there, even though her eyes stayed closed. Her fingers spoke without words.

In the following weeks, I hitchhiked to the hospital to visit my mother. It was too hard to wait for an uncle to get off work or an aunt to finish what she was doing, only to be left with broken promises. But my mother kept my heart from hardening against my relatives. She always listened to me curse them out. She swore that as soon as she was strong enough to get out of bed, she and I were going to kick some asses. She told me how I would grab Dewitt's legs and jump on his back and kick his ass for not visiting her. In this way, she made light of my anger.

After my mother was well enough to be transferred to another part of the hospital, you almost needed a ticket to get in to see her. Loads of people from all walks of life crowded into her hospital room. There were men friends, those old-time drunks and addicts. There was a steady stream of prostitutes, professional con artists, street peddlers, and homeless people going in and out. Even other patients were wheeling their chairs into her room. All you could hear was laughter.

Each night was a party. They had a few bottles stashed away, but for the most part the crowd wasn't there to get drunk. Something else—I'm not sure exactly what—turned my mother's hospital room into a gathering place. I saw the traces of her life in everyone who came and went.

One day, standing in the doorway watching everyone laughing with her, I felt left out. Then my mother said to all those visitors, "Hey, you guys—time to go. I'm goin' to spend some time with my boy." When they left, she said to me, "What you waiting on? Come on over here!" I jumped onto the bed beside her. She asked, "What you wanna watch?"

"Anything with sports," I said.

She found a baseball game, and we settled against the pillows. With a teasing tug at the bill of my baseball cap, she asked, "You happy now?"

CHAPTER 16

The California Youth Authority

Following Family Footsteps

LONG BEFORE PITBULLS WERE trained to fight in the back alleys, the hidden pit yards, and the open fields where audiences and owners laid down their bets before unleashing the madness of the killing dogs, it was youngsters like me who fought for the profit of our older brothers and uncles. Pitbulls came later to take our places.

I was torn apart because my brothers, whom I loved and admired, exploited my experiences at the academy by making me their very own prizefighter. Their profiting from my pain hurt me more than anything. They had me fighting other youngsters my age, the little brothers of their friends. I fought and bled in the back alleys. Whenever I lost, which was rare, they called me "a little punk," and I bled even more.

Although I sometimes hated my brothers, it was easier to hate the fighting: rolling around punching each other along the noisy fences with the garbage cans crashing over, the cheering, the scuffles, the yells. Finally the cops would come and scatter us in every direction.

I never had anything against the other boys whose heads I was trying to smash on the ground while the crowd hollered, "Get him, kill him!" The crowd's voice would rise whenever blood sprayed onto our faces and clothes. To make things worse, we who fought each other became friends, calling each other "homeboy" and ditching school to go fishing at Harbor Lake. We avoided our older brothers as best we could.

Some mornings half a dozen of us would jet across town on our bikes, up into the hills, where we would make ramps and challenge one another to jumps until school got out. Then we'd ride back home to get our fishing poles or baseball mitts and head over to Harbor Park.

We often went directly from these activities to staring at one another sadly as everyone gathered around us in the back alley. Our older brothers would stand behind us massaging our shoulders, getting us ready to attack each other like dogs. We weren't able to stand up to them; we knew if we refused to fight we would suffer in worse ways.

At the same time, we each in our own way started imitating our brothers' activities. I followed my closest brother, Tommy, into the neighborhood gang. My friend Jumbug, who had the same birthday as me, followed his older brother by becoming a heroin user. It was the same for my friend Marcus, who sold weed from his brother's bedroom window; Charlie Mo started holding up stores with his brother Donald. Even the youngest among us, eleven-year-old Little James, climbed through impossible windows to burglarize homes, stores, and factories, then peddled his stolen merchandise with his crazy uncles.

Hershey

BECAUSE I WAS ALREADY on probation for a series of minor offenses—from smoking pot at school to skipping school to joyriding in stolen cars—my chances with the juvenile courts started to run thin. When I was fifteen, they finally ran out. Within days of getting caught beating up another kid and taking his watch, I crashed into a garage after stealing a car. Finally I was sentenced to the California Youth Authority, which was like a state prison for incorrigible youth offenders, the very last stop before they graduated to the adult prison system.

I entered the CYA more hurt and angry than I had ever been. I hated it. I felt thrown away and abandoned. I got into one fight after another, with both other wards and the counselors. After many escape attempts and transfers from one state facility to another, I eventually ended up at O. H. Close, a Youth Authority institution in northern California. There, after several fistfights, I slowed down enough for one counselor, Hershey, to take a special interest in me. I was then placed on his caseload.

At first glance, Hershey was like all the rest of the counselors I'd encountered. I didn't trust him. My intent was to wear him down, to cause more havoc than he had ever had to deal with. But before long I realized that ol' Hershey wasn't like the others. For one thing, he had more patience than I'd expected. He didn't react to my attempts to get his goat. Instead, he was friendly. He seemed to want to get to know me, and he encouraged me to cultivate my interests.

Hershey's kindness began to break through my hard shield and untangle many years of hurt and unflinching anger. I learned that I could never assume that Hershey would do anything that I'd learned to expect from other counselors.

There were times that I'd be called back to my cottage from school because Hershey had said that he needed to speak to me. Not knowing why, I'd walk into the cottage dayroom to see him sitting among the rows of chairs in front of the television, watching cartoons. He'd hear me coming, and without even looking around he'd ask me to take a seat next to him. For a while we'd both sit there, looking at the cartoons on the big screen. Then I'd idly ask

Hershey what I was doing there instead of in school. "Hell, that's what the teacher says you wanna do—watch cartoons, eh?"

"Huh?" I'd mumble.

"Yeah, that you prefer doin' nothing!"

"Nah, it ain't like that, Hershey," I'd say.

"Hmm. So who do you like?" Hershey would ask. "Bugs Bunny? Road Runner? Tom and Jerry? Who?"

"Man, can I go?" I'd ask, thinking, *What kind of counselor is this? What's his damn trip? This dude is jus' as crazy as me—probably more so! He couldn't care less what I do!*

"Go where?" he'd ask.

"Man, back to school. To class!"

"You sure," Hershey would ask, staring up at the TV, "you don't want to sit here and watch some Tom and Jerry?"

"Yeah, I'm sure! Can I just go, eh?"

"Yeah, uh-huh. I'll see you later," he'd say, not looking back, as if he didn't care either way.

I would always return to class. Besides wondering if Hershey was really crazy or just manipulating me, I always felt like he was somehow making an important point. Rather than put me under pressure, he was allowing me the space to make my own choices. He acted the same way when we went over the many pages in my case file. Instead of concluding that I was a hopeless case to just mechanically push through the system, he went out of his way to ask questions about what had happened: "Why did you run away from Boys Town?" "What happened at the academy?" He was curious about my destructive behavior.

As a result, I ended up pouring out my whole life story to Hershey. He helped me see that my behavior came from my habit of expecting the worst to happen. I was locked into a self-fulfilling prophecy. If I couldn't break the pattern, it would be only a matter of time before I was once again behind one high fence or another.

More than anyone else in my life, Hershey was like a father to me. Our relationship made me feel that I had no right ever to give up on myself, because he showed me that I could appreciate who I was. With his confidence, I began to feel less like a ghost and more like a real person. I no longer assumed I would naturally fail at everything. I began to take school, and myself, seriously enough to earn a diploma—if only barely.

But when I walked out the gates of O. H. Close, I proceeded to blow the chance that my encounter with Hershey had given me.

CHAPTER 17

My Mother's Dream

All Together

THE FIRST FEW MONTHS after being released from the CYA and paroled to a group home in Stockton, I was working two jobs: dishwashing at a shopping mall restaurant and learning the welding trade across town. With pockets full of state-paid and -issued tickets, I rode buses from here to there and back again to the group home.

Every morning I stepped out of the house and into the wide-open freedom of my release. I no longer had anyone looking over my shoulder telling me what to do. I was on my own.

While I was adjusting to being free from the California Youth Authority, I exchanged phone calls almost daily with my family down in L.A. County. It was a dream come true to find out that my siblings, who had by now outgrown the foster care system, had reunited with my mother and stepfather Otis, who were no longer in jail or living on the streets. My two eldest brothers had their own apartments nearby. Now my mother and other relatives wanted me to come live with them and be part of the family again. Every time my mother spoke to me about this—often sobbing—I felt the pain of being severed from my family.

Ever since I was first placed in a foster home, my mother had promised me that someday, somehow, she was going to get all of us kids back. We were going to be a family again. Those promises had resonated in me throughout my young life as my mother's dream permeated my own. Someday I wanted to make her dream a reality.

Now I felt the pressure of this dream every time I heard my mother's voice on the telephone. She desperately wanted me to move down to Long Beach to complete her life's promise to me and to my siblings. I was the missing piece. She would plead into the telephone for me to come be with them. As happy as I was to hear my family's voices during these phone calls, I knew it would be an awful mistake to leave this fresh, clean start. I had to keep my life straight and follow my own dream.

My life had taken a dramatic turn from the violence, petty crimes, and gang activity that had kept me bouncing in and out of the juvenile justice system for years. Being with Hershey had taught me that always expecting the worst for myself had kept me from being part of a bigger society. Now I had everything I needed to stay on a straight path. I felt changed. Inside, I wanted to be with this change. The opportunities in Stockton were everything I needed for a successful parole.

Because I was finally believing in myself, I could no longer digest the lies I kept hearing, like the alcohol I was hearing in my mother's and stepfather's voices on the phone. I knew that they were drinking heavily. It bothered me when my two oldest brothers bragged about their drug-dealing operation and promised to make me an equal partner, even though I knew it was their way of saying they loved me and wanted me to have the best the streets could offer. And I knew the old neighborhood wasn't the same: my sisters described the shootings they heard through the night, and how So-and-So had been shot at a party just days before.

I felt torn between the desire to make my mother's dream come true and the fear of ruining my life forever. Whenever I tried to brush aside the harsh realities echoing in my family's voices, a clearer voice from deep inside said it would be wrong to return to Southern California.

Constantly thinking about my family was like having graffiti sprayed on the wall of my mind. Here I was, free from the CYA, but unable to see my mother's face. Finally I decided to get permission from my parole officer for a one-week visit with my family. I figured this would make everyone happy, including me. How much trouble could I get into in a week? I boarded a Greyhound bus and stared out the window as it headed south. No Greyhound had ever felt as frightening.

When I arrived at my mother's apartment, the family—my siblings and most of my aunts and uncles from my mother's side—was waiting for me, laughing with joy. Mama began sobbing so hard she fell to her knees. In these precious moments we all remembered how years of separation had affected us. Some of us began to cry at seeing her happiness in finally having all of her children gathered around her, bringing her back to her feet.

We were all nearly grown now, though our baby brother Dean was barely a teenager. The second youngest, Carlette, was in high school. Seeing one another overwhelmed us with heartfelt joy. We stood in my mother's tiny living room while Mama, wailing, placed her hands on our faces as if tracing lost memories. We had all been pitched into separate orbits, into almost every horror that could be told, yet we remained strung together by the single thread of our mother's dream. Mama had given us this dream to hold on to, and now it had come true.

We embraced. We cried for all the times we'd ever wanted to cry, for all the times we hadn't known how, for all the times we'd needed each other, and for everything we'd suffered to finally be together. Then, to our surprise, we were all laughing in unison, as if someone had pushed a button. In that instant, I knew that this was my family. Tommy and Robbie took me outside on the porch and fired up a joint. As it came my way, I held it between my fingers and briefly considered its hazards before taking a big, long toke. It was good. My sister Birdy joined us, and we all got loaded together, smoking and swapping stories until we were called in for dinner.

The kitchen table was too small for all of us, so we sat around the living room and ate. Mama told story after story of each of us as babies. She told us how Carlette would burst into tears. We watched Mama break down in her memories of Carlette's twin, Carl, who had died from sudden infant death syndrome. Through her tears, Mama was asking all of us to forgive her. We did, as my stepfather Otis held her in his arms, slowly lifting her out of that very dark space.

Tommy and Robbie tried to get me out of the house, but I didn't want to leave right then. When I'd first arrived, they'd again promised to make me an equal partner in their drug operation. They thought this would be the best incentive for me to stay in Long Beach. Before I entered the Youth Authority, this proposal would have appealed to me greatly. In those days, I always wanted to have a seat next to my brothers in the underworld. I wanted to be just like them, especially Tommy—with plenty of money, lots of guns, and a name on the streets that demanded respect, if not fear. My brothers had no reason to believe that I no longer felt this way, and I wasn't eager to tell them otherwise.

I felt ashamed of having lost my identity, of not being a part of my family. Worse, I was afraid of being abandoned by my brothers. Offering to make me an equal partner was their way of wrapping their arms around me and welcoming me home. The rough hustle of the streets was the only way they knew to survive a bitter, hostile, and hopeless reality. I understood this well.

Entering the Underworld

THE FAMILY DECIDED THAT I would sleep at Robbie's apartment, several miles away. It was late at night when we finally got
there. Carrying my luggage inside, I noticed that his place was
filled with brand-new stuff, from television and stereo equipment
to black leather furniture—the kind of things that, in my adoles-
cence, I would have stolen and sold within minutes to the likes of
my brother. Standing in his well-decorated flat, my main thought
was: *Man, if this house were to get raided by the cops tonight, that would be
it! I'd go straight back to CYA!* But I could hardly ask Robbie to show
me someplace else to spend the night.

We settled down on the living room couch and smoked more
weed. While the unwatched TV flickered in front of us, he told
me about everything that had happened during the four years I had
been gone. All the while, I kept getting whiffs of a strange chemical
odor. I didn't know what it was, and the high from the weed made
the smell irritating.

Finally, I turned to Robbie: "Man, what is that nasty-ass shit
I'm smellin'?"

My brother began choking. He took the joint from his lips and
busted out in a loud, coughing laugh.

"Man, what is it, Robbie, or am I just trippin'?" I asked him.

"Nah, nah, you ain't trippin'," said my brother. "I got something
I wanna show you."

He signaled me to follow him. At the back of the apartment,
he opened a door to reveal a tiny secret room, no larger than an
oversize closet. With its black light on, it reminded me of a pho-
tographer's darkroom. When my eyes got used to the dark, I saw a
whole armory—pistols, shotguns, and other weapons I hadn't ever
seen before—and two five-gallon water jugs filled to the top with
the stuff I'd been smelling. The fumes were so strong that they
clung to my clothes.

"What *is* that, Rob?" I asked.

"Young bro, it's called PCP," said Robbie. "And there is millions ready to be made with this shit! Now, bro," he placed his hand on my shoulder, "do you want in? All of this could be ours. Just say you want in, and we can make millions overnight."

When I looked at the handguns, rifles, boxes of bullets, and those huge jugs of PCP, I suddenly saw my whole life ending in a blaze of glory, with only my name left on a movie marquee. For a brief moment I would be revered on the streets, before going straight down into the dust of history.

I surprised myself. Turning to Robbie, our faces only inches apart, I stared dead into his eyes, and years of rage seemed to speak through my words: "Man, I'm serious! Bro, you got to gets me the fuck outta this house! This shit ain't cool for me—not now, not later! That's why I didn't wanna come down here to Long Beach in the first damn place! Man, if it wasn't for Mama I wouldn't be sweatin' this shit. 'Cause, bro, none of this shit is cool for me. No, not no more. And don't tell me it is, 'cause none of y'all done my years! And I ain't talking about no foster home shit either! And if you thinking I'm scared—I ain't!"

"Yeah, you is," Robbie was mumbling. "That place done got you scared. Boy, those ol' white folks done got you not even likin' us any mo', Jay. You don't want be wit' us anymore, huh?"

I exploded. "Man, Robbie! I'll beat the holy shit out of you, here and now! Man, who in the fuck you think you're talkin' to?" I felt my left hand balling into a tight fist.

Standing in the doorway, I stared into my brother's eyes. I was only a half-second from attacking him. Memories were rising to the surface of my mind: How Robbie used to beat me up or make me fight other kids. How he used to make me drink booze so he and his friends could laugh when I vomited. The times he would put me at the front of our criminal activities, making me the one most likely to get caught. Rage was smoldering inside me like burning coal, tempering my closed fist. We stood there, facing each other.

"Man, Robbie, I w-will b-beat yo' bitch-ass right here," I stammered, wishing he'd say anything, just something, to make me lunge forward.

But he didn't. My outburst took the wind out of his sails. My brother always believed me to be crazy. The more he shrank in front of me, the more I felt like exhibit A backing up that belief.

I felt trapped. The decision to come to Long Beach had not really been mine. It was based on what everybody else wanted and on what I'd been trying to believe. Now invisible forces were ripping at me, pulling me back. For the first time in my life, I knew it was not good to be with my family. Not knowing how to get out, I began to implode.

Robbie backed off. I figured he decided it wasn't worth it for us to fight. But the following morning he said he had just been "protecting his merchandise." Getting into a ruckus might have brought an unwanted visit by the cops.

Our near-skirmish started us talking, and in the days that followed we tried to understand each other better. Robbie was beginning to see the possibility that I would be the one in our family to make something of himself, like a talented athlete who escapes the ghetto.

Once he took this view, he kept encouraging me—usually with a joint dangling from his lips and a beer in hand—to become whatever I wanted to be. I'm pretty sure he thought I was crazily chasing after a pipe dream when I told him I wanted to become a welder, but at least he didn't laugh at me openly. For the rest of my stay, he said whatever was necessary in order for us to get along.

The whole family did the same thing, avoiding conflict regarding my mother's drinking. I couldn't stand seeing how much she was drinking, yet not one of us dared voice our concern. It shames me to admit that even I would bring her cognac, wanting to surprise her as well as to feel the warm squeeze of her hugs in the days before I left to go back up north.

CHAPTER 18

Wake-up Call

A Drive into Memories

FOR SIX DAYS I stayed in Long Beach, the town of my earliest childhood memories, where my siblings and I had been taken from my mother. On my last day there, I asked my brother for his car. I wanted to visit Harbor City, several towns away, before leaving to go back up north. It was my old stomping ground, my gang turf, where I had driven my aunts and uncles crazy. It was in Harbor City that I had graduated into the life of a juvenile delinquent, professional shoplifter, petty weed dealer, house burglar, and car thief before finally being sent to the California Youth Authority.

I hadn't been back to Harbor City for over four years. I took Robbie's keys and headed onto the Pacific Coast Highway, turning off into the projects. Driving past graffiti-covered walls, I saw my name still there, which made me smile. How many nights had I shaken a can of paint and plastered graffiti onto whatever brick wall of a canvas I could find?

I slowed down to case out all the old hideouts: the places where we used to slingshot house windows and the junkyard fields where we rode our minibikes and fought with BB guns that my uncle Calvin had bought us at Kmart, terrorizing the folks who peeped out from behind their curtains. We'd watch the cops they called stop at their front porches and then patrol the streets, looking for us.

As I parked across the street from Aunt Nadine's apartment complex, I noticed some kids, barely teenagers, playing in a field that I had played in. I watched as they jumped out of hiding and threw rocks at the house on the corner—the same house my friends and I used to pelt with rocks. Neighborhood folklore had it that the people in that house ate children.

The kids dashed back between holes in the wooden fence to vanish into the alley. Within minutes they returned, sneaking back into the open field like a pack of hyenas armed with rocks, inching cautiously toward their target. I put the car in neutral. When the kids stood up to throw, I slammed my foot down on the gas, making a rough sound like that of a cop car about to give chase. They dashed like frightened deer back into the alley.

I wanted to see if those kids were as street-smart as I had been when I was their age. If so, they would all be coming out of the alley a couple of blocks away. So I drove over there, swinging into the alley and cutting them all off.

A dozen kids were huffing and puffing, trying to catch their breath. They all raised their hands as if they were under arrest. I looked for the ringleader. As usual, he was the ugliest in the bunch.

"Say, dude," I hollered out the car window, "put your damn hands down and bring your monkey-ass over here. Yeah, you, punk."

He took tiny inch-steps over to the car.

"What you want, then?" he said.

"For you to stop throwing those damn rocks," I said. "That's what I want. Man, that's my grandmother's house y'all throwin' rocks at."

"Nah, man," he said. "Those people ain't yo' grandmother. They done ate my aunt Shirley's baby."

"Who told you that?"

"Aunt Shirley!"

"You say your aunt Shirley—is Murray your uncle?"

"Nah, man, that's my pops. You know him?"

"Yeah, I know him," I said. I didn't tell the kid that I had once changed his diaper. I used to fight with his father, who was close to my brother's age, in the alleys before we became like brothers.

"You just tell Murray that Jay is lookin' for him. Can you do that?"

"Yeah, what I get for it?" he mumbled.

This had to be Murray's son, I thought. Here I am, ordering him to tell his father that some stranger is looking for him to kick his ass, and the kid wants money for delivering the message.

"Well, I tell you what I'll do," I said, reaching into my pocket. "I'm goin' to give you a dollar for the message, and nineteen more dollars for you and your buddies if y'all stop chucking rocks at the house. Then I'm going to give you five more dollars for you to make sure nobody else throws rocks at the house. Is that cool?"

"Oh, yeah." He smiled, turning to his friends. "Man, that's way cool!"

"Okay, then." I handed him twenty-five dollars. "If I hear of another rock hitting that house—I'll find you, dude! There is not a hiding place I don't know."

As I drove out of the alley and back to my aunt Nadine's apartment complex, I couldn't help wondering if Gladys still lived in that house. She wasn't exactly my grandmother, as I'd told the kids; we'd become friends after I got caught throwing rocks at her house.

After Aunt Nadine had taken me by the ear to apologize to Gladys, I'd done her chores and errands, and we'd often sit outside on her back porch. Rocking in her chair, her eyes completely closed, cooling herself off with a paper fan, she would tell me story after story about growing up in the Deep South during Jim Crow days. She told me how after her brother was caught stealing cows, he got chased all the way to New York City, where he put on a zoot suit, gold chains, and those pointy shoes we called roach killers. She taught me old hymns from the time of slavery.

I rang the doorbell three times. The door finally opened a crack and someone peeked out. I asked if Gladys was home, but there was no answer, only silence. The door creaked open wider, sounding like it hadn't been opened in years.

Through the screen door I could see a trembling shotgun with both barrels pointed dead into my eyes. I froze, paralyzed by the idea of having my head blasted from my shoulders.

Then a voice rang out. "Boy, didn't I tell you, if I seen any of y'all devilish children comin' back on my property again—what would happen, eh? You think I'm foolin'? God dammit!" the man yelled, as if in these half-seconds he was bracing himself for the kick of the gun before squeezing the trigger.

A woman's voice came suddenly from behind him and said calmly, "Honey, he isn't one of those children. Those children ain't half this boy's size."

I could see the old black man still shaking nervously. The elderly woman stepped in front of him, trying to put herself between the shotgun and me. "Son, who you?" She squinted to see through the screen door.

I was still in shock. Here I was, a parolee standing on the porch of an old couple's home that had been vandalized for who knows how long. They might have called the police a hundred times, and if they shot me to smithereens, who would care?

As I began to breathe again, the woman said: "Son, is you okay?" She followed my eyes, looking over her shoulder and turning to face the man with the gun. "Honey," she said to him, "you givin' this child a bad heart. Now, go on, put that gun you got up. You hear me?" She looked back at me and said: "Son, you can go take a seat on the porch here, if you need to."

"No, no, I'm fine," I said to her. I was slowly coming alive again. We stared at each other. I wanted this to be Gladys—the resemblance was there—but I knew it wasn't. "Does Gladys still live here? You see, ma'am," I said, "I only came by to visit her—that's why I came."

"Oh, Lordy," she said, stepping out onto the porch to take a closer look at me. "Son, Gladys done passed away. Bless her soul. She passed away wanting to see you, boy. You're Jarvis, ain'tcha?"

"Yes, ma'am. I'm Jarvis," I said.

Her hand came up, and her fingers traced over my eyes as if she were blind, even though she wasn't. I'm sure it had to do with something that went as far back as times of slavery. So many of Gladys's stories had been passed down to her through generations.

"I'm Sadie, Gladys's sister. She told me the night she passed for me to keep prayin' for you."

Sadie began crying. I put my arms around her and hugged her. There were only a few people in my life who had meant as much to me as Gladys, and I still needed all of them. Those who had passed didn't disappear from my thoughts. But I needed to leave, so I said good-bye to Sadie.

Bob's Liquor Store

VISITING AUNT NADINE WOULD have to wait. I needed to pull myself back together.

The more I tried not to, the farther I drove into the old neighborhood. But now it didn't look the same. The graffiti on the walls, the empty fields, the alleys, and the narrow streets all looked like one big death trap. To collect my nerves, I pulled over and parked across the street from Bob's Liquor Store. I sat inside the car and nervously chain-smoked, calming myself.

Watching all the poor people going in and out of the liquor store, I began considering what kind of chance my life would have if I were to move back down here. My brother Robbie was probably right—I was too scared to live with my own family. And why? Because I knew what it meant. I had already come close to getting my head blown off.

A homeless man wearing an army coat, his long gray beard down to midchest, pushed his shopping cart in front of the liquor store. *This wino is going to ask every passerby for money*, I thought, and I watched him do just that. He asked and asked, putting out his hand for money and bringing it back empty.

Then suddenly his luck changed. A young man stopped, reached into his pocket, and gave the man money. The beggar looked at the money and brought both of his hands together in a prayerful sign of gratitude. Smiling, he pushed his shopping cart close to the store's front door. He took a rope from the bottom of the cart and tied the other end around a mailbox as if the cart were a horse to tie up before he went inside the saloon. Then he walked into the store. This homeless person was exactly the kind of man my buddies and I used to get to buy us wine. We'd give him enough money for all of us to get drunk.

Why was I back in Harbor City? I had a fresh start at the group home in Stockton. I was still trying to figure it out when the man came out of the liquor store holding a bottle in a brown paper bag. He bent over his cart as if he was looking for something, then walked to the garbage bin and pulled out a newspaper. He sat down on the curb and began folding and folding the paper. I kept wondering why he hadn't started drinking yet—the bottle of wine was tucked inside his coat. He seemed a lot more patient than most winos.

He folded the paper into something like a pirate hat and put it on his head. He took it off, inspected it, put it back on his head, and adjusted it. He seemed to think himself quite the gentleman as he stood up and strolled over to his cart. Finally he took out the bottle of wine, twisting off the cap and wiping the mouth of the bottle with his sleeve. Then he began to guzzle.

I bet against myself that he couldn't drink all the wine in one swallow. Seconds later I lost. The muscles in his throat opened and closed as he drained the bottle empty. Then he peered into it to make doubly sure there was no more wine. I was amazed. I had never seen anyone down a whole bottle of wine in a single drink.

The wino put the empty bottle into his cart and wiped his forehead. Guzzling had brought on a cold sweat. Then something incredible happened. He took off his handmade newspaper hat, bent over, and began vomiting into it. I wanted to turn away, but I couldn't. *He should've known better than to swig a whole bottle of wine*, I said to myself. Now he was throwing up his guts into a paper hat.

When he finally stood upright, still holding the paper hat like a bowl in both hands, he looked as if he was feeling terrible about wasting the wine and ruining his hat. Just as I was beginning to feel sorry for him, he brought the hat up to his face and began drinking his own puke.

Again I saw the muscles guzzling. My stomach turned; I had to throw my arm over my eyes. When I peeked out a moment later, the drunk was chasing after the last drops, shaking the hat, wanting more. I could only lean back into my seat and stare in the opposite direction, trying to figure out why I was there to witness this scene.

It wasn't just the wino anymore. Everything I'd seen that day suddenly felt repulsive. But it wasn't just what I'd seen. It was me. I was struggling with my family wanting me to stay and me not wanting to—but at the same time wanting to stay for my mother's sake. Every sign on the wall said I'd be a fool to stay.

I sat in the car pretending that I didn't know how to read any of the signs. After a while I glanced back in the direction of the wino. He was sitting on the curb, chasing down his puke with an equally nasty can of Carnation milk. I stared as he carefully folded up the soggy hat and stowed it inside his coat pocket.

CHAPTER 19

My Own Worst Enemy

Uncle Dewitt

THE FOLLOWING DAY, RIDING the bus back to the group home in Stockton, I was haunted by the uncompromising image of the wino. I could no longer fool myself about what it would mean to move back with my mother. And I damned myself forever by overriding my good sense, which was telling me how wrong it would be to return.

After arriving at the group home, I went back to work at the restaurant and continued going to trade school to become a welder. Most evenings, if I hadn't worked too hard, I walked several blocks to the University of the Pacific and checked out the athletic events. Sometimes I watched a home game of Pacific taking on another school. On the weekends, I got up early and headed over to the gym to play basketball at the team's practice sessions, where nonstudents were welcome to play with or against the team.

The longer I kept up this schedule, the more I noticed an eerie feeling growing, like not having my own shadow. Although I had a few friends at the restaurant and even a girlfriend at Pacific, I missed my family. I felt isolated and alone, farther from home than ever, yet I had chosen life in Stockton. It was giving me an opportunity I'd never known before. Now that I had it, why was I complaining?

I struggled with this feeling of wanting to be with my family and knowing where it would lead. One part of me might as well have been living in an Alaskan fishing village under the silent gaze of snow-covered mountains, far from the bustling streets and vacant lots of despair and the cities and gang turfs I knew. But by now I had given up on myself. I had to reach very deep inside to find any reason to hold on. This vision of life gave me nothing to aspire to. I wanted to leave this Alaska as soon as possible to return to who I was, to the life I knew, with all its pitfalls.

Southern California felt more real than the life I was trying to create for myself in Stockton. My visit home had loosened my resolve and made me question all the good reasons I'd had for staying in Stockton. In winning a new life, I was losing everything that connected me to my identity. Angrily, my mind stumbled into a rationale for letting go. Like a dope fiend who makes up any excuse to just hang on the street corner, looking for a fix, I decided that I could be a damn fool like the rest of them.

Before long, I wasn't getting to work on time, I had stopped going to trade school, and I was only doing enough not to violate my parole. I knew I was on my way back down south. I went out of my way to find reasons to harden my decision, picking fights at work and at the group home. I sealed the deal by selling my high school diploma to another parolee.

With Hershey's help, I had worked hard to get that diploma. It was my most valued accomplishment. Completing a high school education had been one of the conditions for parole, and it motivated me. But I didn't value it enough to keep it. When I handed it over, the guy who'd bought it said, "Man, you can always say you lost this copy and get another one." I responded, "Well, it's not going to do anything for me where I'm going. Right now, it can only pay my way to get there." In that instant I knew I would come to regret what I was doing.

I had decided not to tell my mother I was coming home. I didn't want to live with her and buy her alcohol, nor did I want to get too close to my brother's activities and show how scared I was to get involved in whatever he was doing. For now, Aunt Barbaree was the only one who knew I was returning. Barbaree was the one caretaker whose heart had never closed to me. She never stopped putting up with me. Even when I was a small child, she had always had a warm lap and a toy for me. Now she promised she wouldn't tell a soul that I was coming home to stay with her. I'd figure out how to tell my mother later.

The Greyhound took me straight to Long Beach, where I caught the commuter bus to Harbor City. What was I doing back here? When the bus reached Normandie, instead of turning west into the rough parts of the city, it stopped on the corner of Pacific Coast Highway. I was the only passenger left, sitting a couple of seats behind the driver. I could see him staring at me in his rearview mirror. He finally opened the door, still looking back at me, and said, "This is as far as I go."

Surprised, I looked down at the bus schedule in my hand. It showed the last stop as farther down on Normandie.

"Well," I said, "don't your route suppose' to go down . . ."

"Man, I s'pose to do a lot of shit," he replied. "And keepin' my black ass alive is what I'm goin' to do! Now, son, I don't got a lot of time. You gettin' off?"

"Yeah, give me a second. I'm gettin' off."

I was trying to gather my things—two suitcases and a small box—when the driver said, "Son, you know where you goin'?"

"Why you say that?" I was still struggling with my luggage.

" 'Cause you sure don't look like you know," he answered, "with all that stuff you got there. I seen folks get killed for less."

"Well, the schedule said you suppose' to stop on 253rd and Normandie."

"My ass!" said the driver angrily. "Them white folks who make up dis schedule—you let them get shot at day in, day out! *Then* tell me what the schedule say, okay?"

"Well, I don't know. I'm just goin' back home." Holding on to my luggage, I stepped off the bus.

When the bus door shut behind me, I turned around to see this crazy driver firing up a yellow-papered joint hanging from his lips. Then he drove off.

As I walked down Normandie, I kept looking over my shoulder. It was late in the evening. The thought of what that driver had said about seeing folks "getting killed for less" began to strike my nerves. Were those footsteps I heard behind me? The farther I walked, the more moving shadows I saw. I began to feel like prey. The shadows were kids following me. They hid between houses and apartment buildings and peeked out from behind bushes, dashing into open space only to cross a street or alley. After a while the kids trickled out from hiding. There had to be at least a dozen boys and girls, each as dirty-kneed as the next. Giggling, they followed only a few feet behind me. I thought one of them might offer to help with my luggage and then run off into the alleys with my stuff. But instead, they lagged behind, following me all the way to Barbaree's front door.

When Auntie opened the door, wearing her apron and holding a broom, she called each and every one of the kids by name, saying, "Scoot your tails and fannies on home!" Then she dropped her broom and rushed to give me a big hug. While she held me, she whispered, "Jay, your mama is goin' to kill me if I don't tell her you're here."

"What she goin' to do that for, Auntie?"

"'Cause she still crazy as ever," she answered, and we both laughed.

Barbaree brought me into the kitchen and turned on the light. "Now come over here in this light," she said, "so I can take a good look at my nephew. Boy, you still look like that daddy of yours. When you last seen him?"

"I haven't."

"That's good! You know, your uncle Calvin almost killed your daddy when he beat up your mama like that. Y'all was just babies, just tiny things." My aunt became visibly upset with her own recollections. "But come on, boy, let's not talk about that! Let's talk about my nephew being home with me. You hungry?" she asked, wiping her face.

A voice from the back room called out, "Yeah, that ugly-ass boy is hungry! Feed him and call his mama to come pick his ass up! He don't need bein' here!"

I recognized my uncle's voice. "Hey, Dewitt, you fat-ass jalopy," I hollered. "*You* bring your fat ass out here!" I laughed, and I could hear Uncle Dewitt laughing too.

I had always clung to my mother's older brother Dewitt, by far the baddest, craziest male figure on that side of the family. Just hearing his voice reminded me of the time when I had first stayed with Aunt Barbaree, when I was around twelve or thirteen. He was as strong as an ox, but I would hit him as hard as I could and then run circles around him.

One time Dewitt caught me with his pocketknife and sliced my arm—a mark I still wear. Another time, right before I went into the Youth Authority, my friend Madboy and I, along with some other friends, stole his six-pack of beer, laughing and flipping him off while we strolled down the street. Dewitt got out his .30-30 Winchester, stood out in the middle of the street in broad daylight, and shot at us from two blocks away. Although he was shooting to scare, not to hit, we weren't so sure, and we scattered and dove into bushes as his rifle tore a hole in the air.

Everyone in the neighborhood wanted an uncle like Dewitt. His weapons would always catch up with our bad asses, even if he could not. So when I went into the back room to pay my respects to my favorite uncle and saw Dewitt lying on his stomach watching television, it felt natural to take hold of his foot and try my best to pull all four hundred pounds of him off the bed.

"Come on, get your fat ass up," I said, gritting my teeth and yanking with all my might.

"All right, you bad-ass boy!" said Dewitt, looking back over his shoulder at me. "Don't have me go lookin' under this mattress to find something for your young ass!"

"You ain't going to do shit!" I hollered, still unable to budge him. "Yeah, I got your big fat ass now. You can't do nothing to me."

Just when I said this, Dewitt bent his knee. Then he suddenly kicked his leg back out—like a lion flicking his paw at a pestering cub—and knocked me clear across the bedroom and into the wall. *Bam!* Auntie yelled from the kitchen, "Don't y'all tear up my house with all that damn playing around back there!"

"You see, Dewitt," I said, getting up off the floor, "I just got home, man, and you already got me in trouble."

"I ain't got you in no trouble," he mumbled. He had not moved a single inch as he lay there staring at the television screen. "Hell, you come back here with your bad ass, messing with me. I ain't done nothin'."

"What you mean you ain't done nothin'?" I said. "You damn near broke my back!"

The next day Dewitt sat me down and told me not to hang out with my old friends.

"What old friends?"

"You know who I'm talkin' about, Jay," he said. "I'm warnin' you, nephew, 'cause we don't want to see you locked up again, you know?" Then he put me in a headlock and let his horseplay say what his words couldn't.

Madboy Marcus

MARCUS AND I HAD grown up together sharing pretty much the same road from grade school to the time Uncle Dewitt shot at us for stealing his beer. We'd both been to reform school, and we'd been forced to fight each other in the alleys by our older brothers. Then we'd become gang members and gotten into more serious trouble that took us to the California Youth Authority only a few months apart. I went in for auto theft and taking another kid's watch as well as other serious and not-so-serious offenses that had mounted up; he went in for joyriding in a drive-by shooting of a rival gang. Now we were both back in Harbor City as parolees. Once again, we were like brothers, hanging out every day and night.

Marcus still looked the same, like he was keeping sour pieces of hard candy locked in his jaws. Even as a kid he never smiled but always wore a serious frown. Marcus's mother was very strict, and he would get into trouble if he stayed out too late at night.

One night a bunch of us kids dropped Marcus off before going home ourselves. It was past his curfew, and his mother caught him trying to climb through his bedroom window. When all the lights in his house came on, we knew he was busted.

We snuck around the house and stood under the open kitchen window. We listened as Marcus made his case to his mother. We had to cover our mouths to keep from laughing.

"And don't you be lookin' at me like you're mad, got the devil blood in you," his mother shouted, grabbing a skillet out of the kitchen sink. "You mad, boy? Well, goddamn it, I'm mad too!" She began whipping him first with the skillet, then with the coffee pot extension cord. We listened from under the kitchen window. As the pots and pans from the kitchen counter crashed to the floor, the neighbors started turning on their lights.

Between "ouches," Marcus pleaded, "I'm sorry, Mama! I won't do it again. I swear, Mama, I won't! I'm sorry, Mama!" We heard the cord tearing at Marcus and dropped to our knees laughing. We knew if Marcus had heard any one of us getting it as bad as he was, he'd be laughing just as hard. The next day Marcus got plenty of teasing and imitations of his mother scowling at him while she whipped him. That's when we all started calling him "Madboy," and the name stuck.

Blowing It

IT HAD BEEN ALMOST four years since I'd hung out with Madboy. We were walking around the Harbor City projects with nothing in particular on our minds. We'd run out of cigarettes and went to get a few packs at the USA gas station across the street from the projects.

While I was at the vending machine, Madboy tried to con the attendant into buying a joint for a few dollars so that he and I could buy some chips as well as cigarettes. We had the munchies from all the pot we'd been smoking and we hadn't eaten anything all day.

But the attendant—one of those beach-bum surfers who only worked there to support not working at all—wanted Madboy to give him the joint before he handed over the money. It dawned on me that Madboy *was* planning to take the guy's money and not give up the joint. As the attendant grew more suspicious, I began showing off, trying to impress Madboy.

"Go ahead, man, give the guy the joint," I said.

"Yeah, but how do I know he ain't no cop?" Madboy said, turning to me. "This dude could be a cop!"

"Hey, dude, dude yourself!" The attendant was offended. "I'm no fucking cop! Ask your brothers in the projects. Just ask them about me, about Surf!"

"Nah, Madboy," I said, half smiling, "he ain't no cop." I nudged his shoulder, a signal to chill out. I had a plan. "Say, man, we know you ain't no cop. Hell, Surf, I'm so sure about you being on the up-and-up that we're going to smoke a joint with you right here and now. Say, Madboy, fire up that joint. Let's get Surf high!"

From the corner of my eye I watched Madboy staring at me the way he always stared at people. I could tell he was angry. He wondered what I was doing, and why I had called him by his known name if I was planning something illegal. I wanted to show Madboy just how smart I could be. I looked back at him, my eyes asking him to trust me.

"Go ahead, fire up that joint. That is, if Surf ain't afraid of losing his job. Are you, Surf?" I watched Madboy take out his lighter and light the joint.

"Not me, dude!" said Surf, flabbergasted at my question. "This fuckin' job stinks, totally stinks! Dude, I only work here so my mom and dad don't fuckin' kick me out of the fuckin' house."

"Is that the only reason?" I asked.

"Well, not really," he said, as Madboy passed him the joint. "It also pays for going surfing and . . ." He looked down at the joint, then quickly around to see if any passing cars could see him. Then he took a big, unflinching toke, as if to show how much he didn't care. Exhaling, he chuckled. ". . . and gettin' stoned at night."

With a cloud of smoke hovering in the air, the three of us started laughing. We smoked and smoked, rolling one joint after another.

I started to like Surf, who talked with a slow, dragging slur, like one of those surfers you meet only on the beach or on TV ("Gro-o-o-o-o-vy"). He was unlike anyone I'd ever met before. He innocently droned on and on, describing the crisis that was his life. Madboy and I looked at each other in disbelief: Surf's world was crashing down on him because his girlfriend wanted to call it quits, somebody had stolen his album collection, and his motorcycle needed new tires. This was a world very far removed from the conditions just across the street in the projects. Only if I had still lived in Stockton could I have imagined the luxury of having the problems that Surf described.

When I suggested to Surf that there was a way he could make more money, he was all ears. "What would happen," I asked, "if at a certain time somebody would stick you up, but before they did, you had a chance to take a share of the loot to keep for yourself?"

"But I would still have to call the cops," he said.

"Yeah, but what if your descriptions were all wrong? I mean, if they were black, couldn't you say they were white? If they were short and fat, that they were tall and skinny?"

Surf looked startled. Then he threw his long blond hair over his shoulder and smiled from ear to ear. "Hey, dudes, that . . . that's fuckin' . . . oh, man, dude, that's fuckin' far out!"

"Of course," I interrupted, "you'll have to let that person know the best times, when the money is at its most, right?"

"Dude, no problem! You guys wanna know now?"

"Yeah, yeah, how about now?" Madboy asked eagerly. "How much is in there right now?"

"Only a couple hundred bucks or so," answered Surf.

"Shiitt! That's cool. We can take that now," said Madboy.

"Really?" said Surf.

"Hell, yeah," Madboy answered. "And how about those vending machines. You got the keys?"

"Nah, dude."

"Yeah, you do," Madboy insisted.

"Nah, dude." Surf shook his head. "These fucking people don't give me shit!"

"Well, you got two hundred there, right?" Madboy wanted that money. He didn't care about the amount.

"Nah, Surf," I said firmly. "We would only want to do it if there was loot for all of us, you know? And of course, without any guns."

"Hey, dude, what's up with that? Guns . . . I like guns! Dude, just come on over when you see my surfboard like this." Surf went into the cashier's office, grabbed his surfboard, and placed it in the window, under the light. "When you see it in the window like this," he pointed, "that's when it's A-OK, okay?"

We hung around talking about the details. We didn't think of it as a real crime anymore. It felt more like a minor hustle, a scam that carried only the risk of getting from one side of the street to the other. Once we were back in the projects, purposely misidentified by Surf, we would be scot-free—simple—with the money in our pockets.

The first night Madboy and I saw Surf's surfboard in the window, we froze. It seemed too good to be true. We thought it had to be a setup. We watched from inside the projects, looking across the street for cops, for any kind of sting operation waiting to spring a trap on us.

In that moment I thought about what I was doing. Squatting behind a car in the dark, I looked at myself in the driver's mirror. *This shit is wrong! Way wrong*, I said in my thoughts. *Is this what you worked so hard for?* I kept asking. *Is this all you're worth?* I couldn't cross the street into that other life again. I held back, wavering between right and wrong.

Over the next couple days, I went from one end of the spectrum to the other—from impatience for nighttime to reveal the surfboard in the window to resolve without a doubt not to do this job. I was determined to show Madboy just how smart I was. I could easily have said the cops were setting us up, and that would have been the end of it. But my ego wouldn't let go of feeling brilliant to have hatched this scheme. The question of whether it was right or wrong slipped out of my mind without a whisper.

Finally, a week later, Madboy and I crossed the street and held up Surf. Quickly we took the cash and ran back into the projects. The only hitch was that we had to ask Surf not to raise his hands so high. We didn't want any passing cars to see him being robbed.

With money in our pockets from a series of staged stickups at the USA station, we started to do other establishments, from Taco Bells to tiny hamburger stands. We always managed to convince the attendants—people who had grown up with us in Harbor City—to misidentify us in exchange for a share of the loot. The more money we got, the faster we spent it or gave it away. The faster we got rid of it, the sooner we wanted more.

When Surf started leaving less and less in the cash register, we knew he was pocketing it for himself. We actually saw Surf as someone who was stealing from us, as if we owned the gas station. We felt we were the ones being stuck up. Every time this happened we felt more and more pissed off.

We'd only meant to scare Surf straight when we held up a gun and pointed it at his head. But when Surf fell to his knees and started begging for his life, I realized this might have been a big mistake. We went ahead anyway and told him we wanted our full share from the cash register—nothing less, nothing more.

Afterward, I helped him up. For the first time Surf stared at my eyes with something beyond fear in his face. I knew he intended to identify me.

We crossed the street and ran as fast as we could back into the projects. There was a hard pounding in my chest. My heart had stayed in the shadows while I was having my own way, but now it showed how I'd become my own worst enemy. Just like that, I had lost control over my life.

Less than a year later, when I was almost eighteen and tired of hiding, I was arrested walking down a neighborhood street. I was back inside.

CHAPTER 20

Down, Up, and Over

Back in State Clothes

ON THE LONG BUS ride from Los Angeles, the other boys and I—all of us between the ages of fifteen and eighteen—were kept in our seats with wrist and leg restraints that held our hands at our sides and our feet on the floor. After many hours, the bus slowed to the gate of the DeWitt Nelson Youth Authority. This was familiar ground to me. The walls, high fences, and large dormitories were like all the other youth authorities where I'd been kept, and the routines were similar. Rules told me when to wake up every morning, when to eat, when to put on the dingy, worn-out state clothes, and when to do everything else I was expected to do, down to the very minute that the dormitory lights were to be turned out at night. But we were older inmates now, hardened by our years in the gladiator schools of the state system.

I was back in Stockton, but I was no longer free. At night I lay quietly on my own bunk, surrounded by sleeping bodies. I stared up at the ceiling with its clusters of dirty, tear-shaped stains that looked back down, hating the thought of being back behind the fence. I was afraid to close my eyes to face the thoughts that burned inside me. Over and over I traced every step I had taken, trying to unlock how I'd gotten back here again so soon, and for something as awful as armed robbery. I replayed the whole scene backward and forward, again and again, as I stared up at the stained ceiling.

The loud squeaks from the bedsprings of thirty or forty youths shifting in their sleep were like the sound of fingernails raking across a chalkboard. I wanted to get up and tip the nearest bed over—including whoever was sleeping in it. But I never did. It was my own fault that I was here. Lying on my bunk, I remembered the evenings when I'd sat out on the porch with Dennis and listened to the crickets. Now all I heard was my own and others' bedsprings squeaking from restlessness. I was too angry to sleep.

It was freezing cold in the dormitory. I got up to use the bathroom and saw from the clock on the wall that it was past midnight.

The night counselor was sitting at his desk in the office. "Masters, did you raise your hand for permission to use the restroom?" he asked quietly.

"Nope."

"Well, go back to your bunk, lie down, and then, like everyone else, raise your hand and get permission first."

"Are you serious, man? I'm already halfway there. What's the use? This is bullshit, man."

"Well, it may be," he said slowly. "But I'm going to ask you, sir, to go back to your bunk, to get my permission first, sir. It's that easy. We have rules here, sir."

"Hey, you know what?" I said, raising my voice in anger. "I'm goin' to go back. And when I raise my hand, I will be only a fuckin' second from pissin' on your goddamn floor." I was boiling over.

I went back and lay on my bunk. I raised my hand. "Can I use the fuckin' bathroom!" I hollered, almost waking the whole dorm.

"Sir, you sure can," said the night counselor patiently. When I got up and walked by his desk, wearing only underwear, we both stared at each other. "That wasn't so hard, was it, Mr. Masters?"

"Oh, go fuck yourself!" I marched into the restroom. The smell of marijuana was coming from one of the toilet stalls far in the back, and someone was whispering my name. After relieving myself and washing my hands, I looked under the stalls until I found a pair of feet. I went into the adjacent stall, closed the door behind me, and sat on the toilet. I hoped whoever it was would reach under and give me a joint. Instead, he passed me what was left of the joint he'd been smoking.

"Man!" I blurted. "I don't want that—with your damn hands smelling like shit!"

The burst of choking laughter told me it was my homeboy Phil in the adjacent stall. "Man, take the fuckin' joint," he whispered, still laughing. "Ain't nobody back here shitting, fool! I'm getting fucked up, that's what I'm doin'!"

I took the joint and sucked in the smoke. "So how did you know it was me?" I asked, exhaling.

"Bro," Phil whispered, "I heard your crazy ass getting on that damn night man, cursing his ass out! Man, you were loud as fuck, dude!"

"Way in here?" I asked, taking another toke from the joint.

"Man, Jay. Not only me, but everyone! The fuckin' owls, coyotes, and mountain lions could've heard that crazy-ass shit."

Hitting the Fence

AGAINST ALL ODDS, I was in DeWitt Nelson with someone who was actually from Harbor City, a town so small that it hardly existed on anybody's map. Phil and I had grown up together. Despite him being white and me black, we knew practically all the same people. His girlfriend Julie worked at a small hamburger stand that Madboy and I had held up in pretty much the same arrangement as we had with Surf, giving her extra money to visit Phil in Stockton.

The last time we robbed the stand, Julie mentioned that Phil had been hatching an escape plan.

"Tell Phil I said good luck," I said. Then I ran off with the money. Little did I know that soon enough I would be back in DeWitt Nelson myself, sitting barefoot on the toilet in the wee hours of the night, smoking pot with Phil in the adjacent stall.

"Man, Jay," Phil whispered, "I'm gone in the next couple of days. I'm hitting that motherfuckin' fence. Sure you don't want to come, homie?"

Several times Phil had asked me if I wanted to escape with him, and every time I'd said no. This felt like the last chance I had before he would go, with or without me.

"Shit! This fuckin' place is gettin' on my nerves. And I swear, I wanna change my mind, you know? So, Phil, I need to think about it."

"Well, if you do change your mind, I can move up the plan anytime you're ready. Even tomorrow night, when we go to the gym, Jay. 'Cause me, I got this fool willin' to help us for a hundred dollars cash."

"For the both of us?" I asked. "That might only be for you. The guy don't even know about me, right?"

"He'll do it, Jay," Phil said. "I know he will. Don't sweat that."

"And you say it's fail-proof, huh?" I didn't want to know any of the details without committing myself. If I decided not to go and he was caught, I didn't want to be suspected of telling the authorities his plans. "Because, man, if we get caught, who knows where they'll send us next."

"All I can say is, we're out of here! I've been planning this shit a long time. And it's going to work, Jay, I know it is!"

What did I have to lose, really? My attitude was already destined to add more time to my sentence. So far I'd been in fights and cursed out every single counselor. Whether in CYA or as an escapee from CYA, it all added up to the same thing—more time! Having accepted this warped logic, I became fixed on escaping. I would dance to my own rhythm.

It suddenly occurred to me that the night counselor must have noticed I'd been in the restroom for over twenty minutes. "Say, Phil," I interrupted, "I need to get out of here 'cause I know that counselor's waiting on me. But listen, count me in. I'm going!"

"Are you serious?" he mumbled.

"Yeah, I'm serious," I said, flushing the toilet. "I'll be at the gym tomorrow about eight P.M. Cool?"

"Cool!"

On my way back to bed, I stopped where the counselor sat at his desk. I said, "I'm sorry about my behavior. I promise it won't happen again. It'll never happen again."

"That's okay, Mr. Masters," he said calmly. "Your apology is gladly accepted, sir. You get yourself some sleep, okay?"

"Yes, sir," I said, walking over to my bunk. I lay down and turned over into my pillow.

Up and Over

THE NEXT DAY I was at the gym by the time it fell dark. Other than stuffing my address book into my pocket, I'd left the dorm as if I were coming back. I stood by the bleachers, waiting for Phil. At 7:50, in he walked, a bit nervous but holding everything in check. He mingled around the gym before stepping over to where I waited.

Sitting down next to me, he told me the plan: He'd already given Buddy, a prisoner on agricultural detail familiar with the grounds, the hundred dollars to help us climb the fence. There was an area behind the school building where nobody could see us. Once there, the three of us would climb the fence as high as we could. Then we'd climb on Buddy's shoulders to get up and over to the other side. Phil's girlfriend Julie would be waiting by a phone in a Stockton motel room to come pick us up. The only glitch: getting to a pay phone to call her. But that would be a small problem if all else went right.

The plan seemed like a good one. Before we left the gym separately to meet up by the fence, Phil slipped me a tiny piece of paper with Julie's phone number on it in case he got caught and I didn't. He'd already memorized it.

The gym door was open for everyone to come and go as they pleased. When the moment came, we both snuck away unnoticed. There were two full hours before the next head count, when the staff would realize we were missing. The guard outside didn't see us as we slipped across the playing field to the back of the school. Buddy was already there, waiting.

The three of us climbed the cyclone fence behind the building without being spotted. Close to the top, the fencing changed to a fine mesh; we couldn't get a grip. Now Buddy clung hard to the cyclone fence as Phil climbed on his shoulders and went over. Then it was my turn. Buddy lurched upward as I stretched to get myself up to the top. Dropping to the other side, I felt frightened. What if I broke my ankle? But I landed okay.

Avoiding streets and traffic, Phil and I ran through fields and brush until we were miles away from DeWitt Nelson. To our relief, we never heard a hint of a chase. Then we began searching for signs of life—a street, automobile headlights, anything to point us to a pay phone.

Finally, at the edge of a park, we found a phone and called Julie. Taking cover inside a public restroom, we stripped off our state-issued blue shirts and threw them in the trash. We washed our mud-spattered faces and arms at the restroom sink. Then we took off our shoes and socks and washed them too. After that we paced back and forth in our squeaking shoes, listening for the sound of Julie's car, our ride to freedom.

We began to feel safe when Julie had picked us up and we'd put on the fresh clothes she brought. We felt even safer when we'd reached the freeway on-ramp, let the windows down, and headed south to Los Angeles County.

I stared out the car window watching the sights flash by. I felt comfortable, a fugitive nestled in the old familiar pattern of being on the run. I wasn't just running away from my troubles. Ever since I'd left the Prockses, I actually felt safer on the run. I wouldn't have cared if Julie had driven north instead of south. I wasn't bent on returning home. Breaking through those gates and being free was all that mattered. I'd come to love fleeing—the sense of being a tightrope walker suspended in midair. But when you're on a tightrope, it's impossible for anyone to help you. Even the people who had tried their hardest hadn't been able to do anything to change my life.

During those long hours driving south, I never dreamed that the next time on that road would find me in heavy leg irons chained to a seat on the infamous "Gray Goose," the bus that would take me straight to San Quentin State Prison.

Nowhere to Hide, Nowhere to Run

By the time Phil and I arrived back in Los Angeles County, we'd considered everything we thought the authorities might do. Knowing that police rely heavily on neighbors' reports, Julie made us sneak into her apartment complex. We crept up the stairs like burglars and slowly made our way down to the cracked-open door without anyone seeing us.

For three long days we stayed hunkered down. While Julie went off to work at the hamburger stand, Phil and I sat around playing dominos and cards and considered our next move. On the third day I accidentally walked into the bathroom and found Phil hunched over on the toilet seat with a belt tied around his upper arm, his hand balled into a fist and a syringe in his arm.

"Man, what in hell you doin'?" I asked.

"Hold up!" said Phil, staying focused. He kept the needle steady, drawing blood up into the syringe before slowly injecting it back into his arm with the heroin.

I had always remembered myself as that little boy hiding in the hallway as I peeked at a heroin addict through the crack of the bathroom door. Now I was standing cramped inside the bathroom, stuffy with the gray smoke rings circling from Phil's cigarette, watching the back-and-forth play of the syringe as Phil drew the blood up and injected it back several times. Then he pulled out the needle. His face pouring sweat, he was barely able to untie the belt.

"Say, bro," Phil slurred. He used both palms to wipe his face and struggled to his feet with the help of the sink. "Ahh, homeboy, homie," his voice dragged. He was holding on to the sink like a crutch. "You don't fuck wit' dis hop, dis China White. But, man, it's right here if you want some," he slurred, wiping his face again. "Yeah, if you wanna mess with it, you're welcome, homie."

"Nah, I'm cool," I said without a pause. Although heroin had been all around me—too much around—since birth, I had a phobia of needles that had always kept me away from dope. I had no wish to poke a corroded needle into my veins in order to shoot up a substance heated in a filthy spoon.

"You sure?" Phil asked with a drowsy stare. He bent down, gathered all the paraphernalia, and put it back into a black leather shaving kit on the sink.

I wondered whether Julie had gone out and gotten this heroin for him, but since I was their guest, I hadn't asked any questions. The moment Julie had picked us up, she'd kindly offered to take me anyplace I wanted to go. But since her apartment was tucked away in a middle-class suburb in Torrance, far from the ghetto neighborhoods I knew, I felt safe from anyone who might be looking for me. If anything, I was worried about being seen outside in an all-white neighborhood and suspected of being a burglar. I hadn't understood how Julie, who worked at a funky hamburger stand in the ghetto center of Harbor City, had the money it took to live in a beautiful suburban neighborhood.

My mouth dropped open when Phil said that, unrelated to the crime that had put him in DeWitt Nelson, he and Julie were on the run from a biker gang. Phil said he had been in debt behind his drug habits. When his credit was no longer good on the street, he ended up robbing his dope connection, the younger brother of a bike gang leader. He'd had the jones and was desperately in need of a fix. Not only did he botch the robbery, however, but he also panicked and shot his connection to protect his own identity, grabbing all the money and drugs he could find and leaving the guy for dead. He soon discovered that his connection had survived and told his brother that Phil had robbed and tried to kill him. Word spread to the streets. The biker gang was hunting Phil.

"You mean to tell me," I asked, "that this nice pad comes from robbing that cat?"

"Yeah, something like that," said Phil, getting a beer from the fridge.

"Man, are you saying that there's a contract out on your life or something?"

He cracked open the beer and took a long drink. "Yeah, that's pretty much it," he said, looking at me.

"How much is the contract?" I asked. I needed to know.

"Twenty grand!"

"In cash?" I joked. I tried to imagine how that much money would look.

"Man, these fools want my whole family dead!" said Phil. "That's why I couldn't stay in DeWitt, you know? They weren't gonna wait till I got out. They were gonna come after Julie, my whole family—only to get at me, to make them pay for what I and I alone did, y'know? So, I got to get these motherfuckers or else be got myself, y'know? I'd rather they do me in than my whole family. It was me, not them."

"How many are they?"

"Man, there's a whole slew of 'em! But if I can take out dude's big brother, the rest will—"

"The rest will be comin' after yo ass!" I interrupted, pointing out the plain truth.

"Yeah. I have to try, though. I still have to try."

My mind clouded over with fear. "Phil, geez, dude!" I said, nervously scratching my head. "This is some crazy-ass shit you're in!" It all made sense. Julie's tucked-out-of-sight apartment in suburbia proved they were in flight.

The only street bikers I'd ever known were the black ones out in Long Beach. They were scary! They spoke in English when they liked you and in broken Vietnamese—wild, unintelligible words they had learned as soldiers in the jungles—when they were seconds away from killing. The baddest people I knew wouldn't mess with them. Even the roving herd of police cars never stopped to harass them. The thought of a similar group having a contract on Phil's life created instant paranoia in me. Phil was a dead man, so dead that I feared for my own life cooped up in this apartment, especially now that Julie was going back and forth "on errands" for him. The world began to shrink; this suburban apartment felt too confined. We needed to get out into the open, put our ears to the ground, and listen to what was being said on the streets. That way no one could creep up on us.

I assumed that whoever was gunning for Phil was after me as well. Having run away together, we shared the same troubles. And short of being split up by cops chasing at our heels (perhaps never to meet again), as far as we were concerned we would share our fate through thick or thin, good or bad. But being hunted by both cops and bikers, I wasn't about to let Phil keep shooting heroin.

Without question, we had to leave Julie's apartment quickly and invisibly, like the wind. And we had to avoid her being connected to our escape. We couldn't let her become the bikers' target too. I was thinking we should hide out in Harbor City, but Phil had a better idea. We'd go see his close friend in Carson, on the outskirts of the harbor area. Skip was an old street-arms peddler who also owned a tattoo parlor where we could stay for the time being. It seemed perfect—we'd have guns and a fresh place to stay, and instead of just our own two pairs of eyes and ears, there'd be Skip's trusted friends coming in and out of the tattoo shop.

Skip's friends entered through the front door like anyone who came for a tattoo. Then they would secretly slip through a side door and down the narrow hall to the tiny back room where Phil and I stayed hidden. Inside was a thin mattress on the floor and a single-burner hot plate for cooking. Crates of firearms, ammunition, and tattoo supplies lined the back walls.

For almost two weeks this was our cell away from the CYA. At night we ventured out under cover of darkness, each carrying a weapon from Skip's armory. We ended up at house parties and nightclubs in Los Angeles, accompanied by women who were at-tracted to our gun-toting, bad-boy ways. The sex, drugs, and noc-turnal outings didn't loosen the grip of my paranoia. I was always looking over my shoulder, racked with worry, looking for a way we could both back down.

CHAPTER 21

Out of Control

A Miracle

BY NOW I HAD escaped from many institutions and had always been able to avoid capture. I had never felt this anxious, though, like I had to stay awake full-time in order to survive. This was not the simple hide-and-seek I knew. This time people were ready to chase me down, shoot me with bullets, and kill me dead. This reality jolted up and down my spine, especially when I was standing too close to my road dog. While Phil and I felt loyal to each other, neither of us expected to get killed because of the other one.

Seeing how I was putting my life on the line for Phil made me recognize my own sense of self-worth. Yes, Phil and I had a bond: we were from the same neighborhood and had escaped from DeWitt Nelson together. But as we fell into deeper and deeper trouble, we knew that at the end, each of us had to look out for his own survival. All the same, I didn't want to lose my homeboy's back if I got captured and thrown behind bars.

One night Phil and I went to a party. I was standing on the porch when I noticed a car parked across the street. My gut said someone was waiting for us. Turning calmly, I went back in the house, took Phil by the shoulder, and whispered that we'd been set up. Phil sobered up quickly as we walked to the front window and peered into the cold night. I was beginning to think my paranoia had played tricks when at last we saw a movement flicker in the backseat of the parked car—the streetlight reflecting off the rifle barrel of someone lying there.

Phil and I slipped out the back door. As we stood on the porch a mutual anger arose, as if saying, "We're tired of being hunted." This feeling, mixed with all the pot and booze, was all it took for us to abandon any fear we had. We took one look at each other and ran around to the front of the house, our pistols already drawn. Charging at the parked car, we blindly opened fire in a cloud of red and yellow smoke. The car took off, scraping the side of every other vehicle parked down the block. We followed on foot, insanely hoping we'd catch up. But fortunately the car sped away, swerving to dodge our bullets.

The next day we learned that we'd fired bullets into the house the car had been parked in front of. There had been children in the house; bullets had come close to hitting them while they slept. The community was outraged. The first real manhunt for the two of us was on. The police labeled us "armed and dangerous," a euphemism for "shoot to kill." We hadn't been able to trust many people before, but now we had no one to trust except Skip.

We stayed holed up in the tattoo shop, no longer going out even at night. Skip put the word out—even to his closest friends—that we'd skipped town. My old neighborhood in Harbor City was no longer safe. The cops were out in full force, looking for me with a search warrant, breaking down the doors of family and friends. They were even hassling street dealers, thieves, and prostitutes in hopes that they would say, "Fuck this!" and turn me in so they could get back to business. Phil and I were in serious trouble and we knew it.

I thought with horror about what I'd almost done. I imagined the children in the house as my nephews asleep in their bedroom.

I could have killed them. I'd been given a miracle: I didn't have to live with the pain of having killed a child, or anyone in the car either. I couldn't name what I felt; it was beyond regret.

Days stretched into weeks. Boredom made even sleeping tiresome. Lost from my own senses, I needed something, anything, to do. I poked around in Skip's boxes and found the tattoo equipment. I sat down quietly, plugged in a tattoo gun, and set out a bottle of India ink, wondering how much the needle would hurt. The tattoos I'd gotten in juvenile hall had faded. I re-did them now, testing the new ink and needle. The needle didn't hurt. Then I drew new tattoos on my right arm. I was so grateful that none of those bullets had hit a child that I drew praying hands and a cross. Imagining how those children had cried when they were awakened by gunshots, I drew a teardrop beside it.

Then I re-inked the words Harbor City—my home turf. I reflected on how much time I had spent in institutions and drew an hourglass, then a pair of boxing gloves beside it. I'd been a fighter for a long time—and I knew I'd better stay a fighter if I didn't want to be crushed. I saw an image of a prison gun tower. That was my best drawing. I said to myself, *No sense in thinkin' you ain't goin' straight to prison!* I continued until I'd tattooed my whole right arm. I didn't realize at the time that with the ink and needle I'd told the story of my life. Later I asked Phil to tattoo "255th" beneath my eye, something I'd seen on a homeboy lying in his coffin. It was his neighborhood gang, the street he'd lived and died on. It was my street too.

Hiding for days in Skip's back room began to show how strung out my road dog had become. We'd been outside DeWitt Nelson's gates for less than two months and Phil was already hooked. Now that his stash had run out, I saw that his addiction was worse than I'd known. I watched angrily as he shivered with cold sweats and begged Skip or me to go out on the streets to hustle a fix. His pleas fell on deaf ears. We were prepared to watch him kick his habit cold turkey, and we told him so. Pissed off at his deception, I even asked him where the popcorn was for watching the show: him kicking his jones, this heroin addiction that had the power to turn and twist him on his mattress. It never occurred to Skip or me that he would sneak out of the shop to buy a fix.

Phil and I were playing cards. He got up, saying he had to vomit again, and I watched him walk down the hallway to the bathroom. Ten minutes later I was stealing a peek at his cards when Skip hurried in to say that Phil had just been shot. He was lying on the street a few blocks away. I couldn't believe it. I kept staring at his cards. Skip had to be talking about another Phil. Only when he said to hurry up and gather my things and get out before the cops arrived did I begin to think it could be the same Phil. Skip couldn't risk being caught harboring a fugitive or even worse the crates of guns he had in the back room.

"Hey, I'm not leaving without Phil," I kept repeating.

"Fuck, man! Have you been hearing what I been telling you?" He thrust my coat at me. "Here. That stupid fuckin' Phil! Here I am takin' care of him, and he goes out and gets hisself shot! This asshole! They shot his ass just down the street!" He was in a panic. "Hey! You got to go! The cops will be here any fuckin' minute. Go *now!*"

"Who shot him?" I asked, grabbing a few clothes from the pile of laundry on the floor. Should I take a shotgun or not? I already had a pistol tucked in my waistband. I ended up holding the pistol under my coat, sprinting down the dark hall out into the blinding night. With my finger on the trigger, I was ready to do the unthinkable.

The night closed in on me as I entered the alley behind Skip's shop. Fear and adrenaline kept me moving fast, as if I had night vision, though I couldn't see five feet in front of me. I kept the pistol pointed ahead, ready for anyone who got in my way. For all I knew there were armed bikers waiting in the bushes or behind Dumpsters. I ran scared, steadily forward, ready for whoever flinched, whoever could be waiting for me.

I don't know how far I ran before I slowed to a walk. I looked back over my shoulder constantly, making sure I wasn't being followed. I pointed my pistol in the direction of every sound. I hoped that there would be no accidents.

When I finally came out of the alley onto a sleeping residential street, I quickly hot-wired my car of choice and drove away to my brother Tommy's place in Long Beach, the place he always called his "dope shack."

The Dope Shack

STILL BLIND AS TO what had happened to Phil in Carson, I arrived at Tommy's toting two pistols under my coat. Without a cent to my name, I was on the run. My new tattoos were swelling with infection. I couldn't remember when I had last taken a shower. Why hadn't I kept myself behind the gate at DeWitt Nelson?

I was in a downward spiral, half a spin away from being completely out of control. Feeling trapped inside this vortex of violence only increased my adrenaline, yet what I feared most was to come face-to-face with what I was doing. How was I ever going to explain to Tommy all the trouble I'd gotten myself into since my escape?

With some effort, I told Tommy the whole story. Seeing how exhausted I was, he said I could shower, and I didn't hesitate. He offered me his only bed, a lopsided bunk in the back room. I had had better at the Youth Authority.

But I slept well into the next day. When I finally woke up, even before I could rub the sleep from my eyes, Tommy made me a proposition. He said that I could stay there free of charge if I would put protection on him. All I'd have to do was watch his back while he sold heroin from his front door. My job would be to stand behind the door with a shotgun, to be ready in case anyone tried to rip him off, or worse, tried to take him out so they could ransack his place for dope. Knowing Tommy as I did, I suspected there might be a bit more to it than he was choosing to reveal, but he was still my big brother. Backing him up, if nothing else, could help me claim I had escaped from the Youth Authority for a purpose.

Standing behind Tommy's door with a shotgun made me feel important. I was part of the underworld. The sheer weight of the gun initiated a fantasy. Sooner or later I would be shaking hands with the real drug kingpins. They would hear about my reputation all over the state. I'd work my way to the top. I would become a bona-fide gangster.

When Tommy told me to keep our most important possessions packed and to be ready to leave at a moment's notice, "without a second to lose," I asked him why.

" 'Cause, Jay," he said, "we don't know, young bro, when the shit is going to hit the fan, and you might have to blow somebody away, you know? To blow a motherfucker's head straight off, bro! Know what I'm sayin'?"

"Yeah, I think so."

"In this game," Tommy continued, "you ain't goin' to get no respect jus' holdin' a piece! It don't work that way. Only on the day when word hits the motherfuckin' street that you done blown a fool straight to kingdom come," my brother grinned, "*that* day they ain't goin' to be anyone steppin' towards you. They won't be any more jackin', you know?"

"Hell, yeah! I might have to blow a fool away," I answered with hidden nervousness. I hadn't thought it through, what it meant to be a gangster. A dark second passed. *Damn!* I thought to myself. *This stuff is no joke! They really do kill people in order to get a reputation.*

I reflected back on all the dope dealers I'd ever seen with their henchmen around them. They all seemed so cool, friends to everyone, young and old. Did they righteously blow people away for their reps? Did my stepfather Otis blow people away? These thoughts haunted me as I watched Tommy piling stuff under the window next to the fire escape—the leather bag of jewelry he'd been trading for heroin, a new pistol, a pair of good shoes. Then it hit me. All of this packing was in case I had to kill someone! I couldn't believe it. My brother was getting ready for me, of all people, to blow off someone's head.

This bodyguard business was not for me. "No! Sorry! This is not my cup of tea," I mumbled under my breath. But this was my favorite brother. To be there to protect his life was the hand I'd just been dealt. I had to play it out.

So I stood behind Tommy's front door, holding the blue steel of a sawed-off shotgun, listening to the faceless addicts Tommy sold heroin to at ten-minute intervals. Every dope sale challenged me not to piss down a pant leg. He sold everything from twenty-five-dollar balloons—the kind I remembered from childhood—to golf ball–sized sacks that were bigger and more expensive than the balloons. His clientele ranged from the seemingly normal to the totally deranged, from the uptown five-day workers to the homeless cart-pushers. There were sailors on leave in the port of Long Beach, elderly seniors, and even kids on bicycles sent by their parents.

Whenever there was a knock on the door, I'd watch from the peephole, aiming the shotgun right at the buyer's chest. I feared that I would actually have to shoot, spraying blood on the wall across from Tommy.

Almost all Tommy's customers were full of drama. Some came without enough money, swearing on their mother's grave they'd reimburse him as soon as they could. They cried, begged, conned, lied, shouted, cursed, and promised. In response, they received friendly gestures or violent threats, but no heroin. They hadn't a clue that a shotgun was pointed at their chest from behind the door.

"Motherfucker, you know I'll get your damn money," I heard them plead. "Man, Tommy, how long we been knowin' each other, huh?"

A pause, then the voice would continue. "Why you doin' this? Why you goin' to treat me like this, brotha? This is *me*! Don't do me like this—please, please!" The voice would edge close to tears, begging for "just a fix to help me get well."

Other customers, shivering with need, would offer wristwatches, wedding rings, even the pink slips to their cars, as collateral. Sometimes they dug deep into their bosoms or privates for money. When they shifted position, I feared they were going for a weapon. Then my arms would rattle and I'd be close to pulling the trigger. I was determined not to let anyone get the jump on my brother. I knew that if they could, they'd rob him and take him for everything he had.

Frail as they were, they always seemed to be scheming. Their questions scared me: Who was home with Tommy? When was the best time to come by? Would they get a better deal if they copped a thousand dollars' worth of heroin or two? Could they use his shack to shoot up? They might as well have been asking me when Tommy was most vulnerable and how much heroin he had on hand. Friends Tommy had grown up with—people who thought they deserved a special deal—were the ones we distrusted the most.

Day or night, standing behind the door was driving me crazy. I was going to do something awful, I knew it in my bones. I couldn't sleep. I was hanging by a thread, about to go over the edge.

Tommy didn't make things any easier. With my protection, he became more arrogant toward his customers. I finally told him he was setting me up by mistreating people, putting me in a position where eventually I'd have to shoot someone. But because I was there, he kept treating people like trash. He sent his neediest customers away empty-handed. He'd snatch money from them, claiming that they owed him.

One day as I racked a round into the shotgun, I reminded Tommy that I'd recently shot at and missed a parked car, thirty feet away at the most. "I'm letting you know," I said, "there are no guarantees. If you keep playing that bullshit with your customers, I might accidentally blast a hole in your ass instead of them."

"So, what is you sayin'?" Tommy asked. "That you goin' to shoot *me*? Is that what you tryin' to say, Jay?" It had taken only a second for him to become boiling mad. It looked like steam was breaking through his pores.

"N-n-no, I'm just s-s-s-sayin'," I stuttered.

"Then what . . . what you sayin' then, huh?"

"Never mind, never mind, Tommy," I said, breaking away. I was done with it.

In just a few weeks I'd seen so many sick and seemingly dying people—men, women, and young teenagers—all hooked on heroin, begging while they scratched deep into the skin of their arms, ready to do anything to ease their pain.

I had gotten to know people through their voices. I could distinguish the purse-snatchers from the car thieves, the swindlers with the gift of gab from the armed robbers. I knew the car burglars, pickpockets, shoplifters, prostitutes, and street peddlers. I heard all of these voices as I stood behind the door, and there was nothing they wouldn't do to get heroin. I had no illusions about this. In this world, not a soul cared, not Tommy and not his customers. Phil had said as much by his troubles—how he'd lived and how he'd nearly died.

I decided to take matters into my own hands—a big mistake. Tommy had given me some heroin to sell and make some money for myself. But I already had a way of getting money, so instead of selling the heroin, I started giving bits away to the worst cases, those who needed it more than anyone else. Unfortunately, it didn't occur to me that word would hit the streets: heroin was free at Tommy's. Soon the dope fiends started coming around in droves.

When I explained to Tommy what had happened, he went berserk, shooting into the air to chase everyone away. I saw right then and there how desensitized he had become.

An old friend of Tommy's, one he hadn't trusted since the first grade, always said, "All dis here is a dog-eat-dog world." Ol' Bird would grin as he picked at his teeth. "All play is for keeps, and if you snooze, you lose! If you ever get caught slipping, your ass is sliding down into the devil's pit. And better yours than mine!"

CHAPTER 22

Robbin' Hood

Outside the Law

LATE AT NIGHT WHEN I had time off from protecting Tommy, I'd slip down the fire escape, a pistol tucked inside my waistband. I'd started robbing Taco Bells again, up and down Pacific Coast Highway. I knew it was madness but pretended to myself that I didn't care. I'd give the cash register attendants a percentage of the loot in exchange for sending the cops in the wrong direction. Earning minimum wage, and often treated badly by management, the attendants were glad to see me coming.

After the heist I'd steal a car and drive from one side of Long Beach to the other visiting my mother and siblings. They were always happy to see me, but no one liked me to stay too long. They didn't want the cops looking for me to discover their own illegal activities—everything from stolen credit card operations to drugs to stolen property. Everyone lived outside the law—even the grandmothers, who weren't above taking in a stolen washing machine.

I'd give my relatives some Taco Bell cash and drive out to Wilmington to spend time with Uncle Calvin. Then I'd hit Harbor

City, where I felt safest, most at home. I knew this area like a farmer knows his fields.

Sometimes I slept at Mona's place in the projects. Mona was a girlfriend of some years. She was beautiful inside and out. She wore her hair in long braids and dressed modestly. You didn't have to see her temper to know she had one. If we'd had a child together, it would have been beautiful, but she already had a three-year-old son, BJ. Mona would sit smiling on the couch as BJ and I played touch football on the carpet. I suppose I was the closest BJ came to having a father at that time. I never knew who his real father was.

Ever since Mona had met me I was being locked up, and each time I appeared at her front door I was in more trouble than the time before. She took me in, but to protect herself and BJ she would let me stay only briefly, usually at night. Behind closed doors, we made the best of what we had, always with acute awareness that this might be our last time together. These times were so brief that we never had a chance to learn each other's flaws.

A Proposition

WHEN TOMMY RAN OUT of dope and was waiting for the next batch, I'd stay away from his place for a few days. Without their fix, his customers got sick; neighborhood people lay curled up in alleys around the garbage bins looking close to dead. They scratched their arms to bleeding and urinated in their pants. The stench was terrible. I didn't want to be anywhere near that cold scene if Tommy didn't need me.

The other place I stayed in Harbor City was with my closest relatives at Aunt Barbaree's, which was more like home than anyplace else. One day, smoking weed in the back room with some uncles and their friends, I started complaining about how Tommy treated his customers. Who better than these old cats to help me deal with my oldest brother? They knew him even better than I. "Boy," said

Big Ronnie, "you tell him, 'If I ever have to shoot someone 'cause of you, I'm shootin' your ass next!' That's what you tell your brother, Jay! And if he don't like it, you jus' tell him you got it from me, and he can come see me about it!"

"Man, y'all know I can't shoot my own brother," I said.

"Why not?" "Who say so?" "Bullshit!" "Where you get that shit from?" Their many voices rang out as their buckeyes stared at me through a thick cloud of pot smoke.

"Man, y'all is crazy!" I said. "I'm not about to shoot my own damn brother."

"Boy," said Cal in his grumpy voice, "do you think your brother would mess around like that with any of us if we was protectin' his rabbit-ass with that shotgun?"

"I doubt it," I admitted. I couldn't see Tommy acting stupid with any of these old cats standing behind the door for him.

"And you know why he wouldn't?" said Big Ronnie. "'Cause he knows," he stared at me coldly, "I'd shoot his rabbit-ass full of holes! You'd have one dead brother!" He looked down at the joint in his hand, brought it to his lips, and took a deep toke. His inhalation seemed to last forever. Then he fanned the tail of smoke from around his nostrils and passed the smoking hot joint over to me, as if accepting me into his fraternity. They watched as I slowly toked what was left. I thought they were all crazy, and they were!

My uncles' childhood friend Sammy Lee said, "I got a proposition for you, Jay. If you can't deal with Tommy anymore, maybe you'd like to help me on some little jobs I been plannin'. I need someone I can trust." Turning to his friends, he asked, "What do y'all think? Is this boy ready for the big league! Does he have what it takes to be my partner?"

The debate in the tiny smoke-filled bedroom concluded that I'd be perfect for the job. I was happy to finally be free from my troubles with Tommy. I wasn't going to be set up after all. And I would be Sammy's partner! Uncle Cal and Sammy Lee negotiated my split on each heist. Half the proceeds would be mine.

The very next evening I drove Sammy to the pawnshop. I was nervous. To calm me, he kept saying, "It's just business. We're just doing a job." While Sammy walked into the pawnshop, I sat in the car, sweating, with the engine running. Three minutes later he casually walked out. Hopping in the passenger seat, he turned to me with a calm command to drive.

From this one heist, I had more money than I'd ever had before. All the Taco Bell robberies combined hadn't earned me this much. I didn't even know what to do with such a stack—$11,000—other than count and recount it while Sammy and I holed up in a cheap motel. We'd already stopped at the home of his heroin connection, an old friend of my mother's, where Sammy had paid off his debt of thousands and purchased a whole sock of heroin balloons.

Sammy shot up several fixes while I was recounting my loot. As he hunched on the couch in a swaying nod, I realized what he'd meant saying he needed a partner he could trust. In that moment I could have taken him for everything he had. Wads of money hung like pistols from his side pockets, thick saliva dripped from his lips, and a lit cigarette dangled between his fingers, ready to burn him or drop. If I hadn't been there to put it out, fire would have been a real possibility. Sammy Lee was now an easy target for almost anyone on the street, especially with his habit of picking up prostitutes to party with after every successful job.

Why did I keep running into heroin addicts? My brother, uncles, stepfather, and mother—and now my crime partner—all had drug habits.

Right before Sammy ran out of money to support his habit, he would drive the streets, looking for me. Then we'd go on another robbery spree. It didn't take us long to run through the places Sammy had cased out. Soon we had to come up with another list to keep us in front of his addiction.

My story was different. With no bills, no wife, no children, and no drug habits, I had to find something to do with the thousands of dollars I'd made in just a few weeks. I began giving it away, earning the name "the robbin' hood" from local law enforcement. They were waiting for me to grow lax and make another mistake—not so they could catch and arrest me, but so they could kill me.

I also bought used cars for several relatives and a couple of home-boys, friends from the lockups who were out pulling their lives together. Living on minimum wage, they couldn't afford much, and I wanted to help them keep the lights on. I respected them for trying to stay clean. Since I was not, I gave them the money through relatives. I didn't want to cause probation or parole violations.

I also threw a couple of "get high, get drunk" parties for the whole neighborhood, with lots of drugs, alcohol, and loud music blaring from a car as we all danced in the middle of our favorite dead-end street: 255th.

I gave money to poor neighborhood kids, who started following me everywhere. Their parents, who despised me, would alert police to my presence whenever they could. Eventually I won them over by promising them washing machines, paying for rodent extermination, or providing them with cars that ran. Sometimes I bought their kids new school clothes, supplies, and lunch tickets. And of course I was still dishing out money to my own family.

The whole community was now protecting me. I wasn't afraid of ever being captured in Harbor City. But almost overnight I was spending faster than Sammy, and soon I became just as desperate. I didn't have a drug habit, but people were now relying on me for money.

Kmart

THE NIGHT WE WALKED into Kmart to buy some gloves, flash-light batteries, and other tools of our trade, we were spiraling out of control. We had no intention of holding up a store the size of Kmart, but as we stood in line waiting to pay, we saw the store manager moving from one cash register to another collecting sacks of money. Without a word, we finished paying for our goods and got in the car.

"Man, did you see that?" I asked, hoping Sammy's experience would dispel any notion of doing something as wild and crazy as holding up a Kmart. I was expecting him to say, "No way! Get out of here!" Instead, he said calmly, "Listen. If we do this, it has to be right now, while they're collecting the money sacks."

"Are you serious?" I asked. I thought he was just calling my bluff.

"You think I ain't? Are you?" The sweat breaking out across his forehead told me he *was* serious. Sammy was always at his best when he was having a mild jones and thinking about getting all the fixes he wanted. Already feeling the rush, he'd begin sweating early. His eyes would focus instantly when he saw the job ahead.

I stared at the forty-foot front windows of the Kmart entrance. *This gots to be the most crazy-ass moment in my life!* I said to myself, summoning up my courage. How could this be real?

"So, youngster, are you ready?" asked Sammy, sweating more than ever. I didn't blame him; the size of what we were about to do would make anybody sweat. Picking up my sawed-off shotgun from the floor, I took a deep breath as I hid it under my trench coat. I decided to rack a round into the chamber once we were inside. My fear gave way to the anger necessary to get beyond the jitters. I don't even know what I was angry at—I was just angry.

"Now I am! Let's do this shit!" I said. We gave each other one last look before getting out of the car. We moved across the parking lot, spreading farther apart with every stride so as not to be seen together. Inside Kmart, I lost sight of Sammy. Looking for his face in those of the lined-up customers, I suddenly felt my mind change. We had a signal, a nod of the head toward the door, whenever one of us felt uncomfortable. I wanted to call it off, but I couldn't find Sammy.

Just then I heard his familiar cough, the sign that he was about to go ahead. For a second or two I hoped he was just coughing, but then, several registers away, I saw his whole body thrown back by his shotgun's blast. Everyone started screaming, and parts of the ceiling crumbled down. Sammy yelled, "Everybody get down! Get the fuck down!" then—*Boom! Boom!*—more shots rang out as he fired again and again. Customers were dropping their merchandise and running frantically back into the aisles, screaming and pushing others aside, even pulling over shelves. For an instant I felt like one of them. I froze in the midst of the chaos and confusion.

I saw a security officer sneaking up behind Sammy and yanked the shotgun from under my coat. *Boom! Boom!* The shots rang into the air. It was the first time I'd ever fired a shotgun. Each shot knocked me back; I almost fell on the floor. While Sammy kept shouting for everyone to get down, I fired all five rounds. I even reloaded and jumped up onto the counter like something I'd seen on TV. Sammy moved from one register to the next, pawing angrily through the cash registers, spilling money on the floor in his hurry. His hands could only hold so much and he was coughing uncontrollably. The money sacks were all gone—they'd already been collected. The whole scene was a disaster.

By this time Sammy was coughing up his guts. It was definitely time to get out of Kmart. As we backed away, leaving money scattered all over the floor, Sammy's shotgun went off accidentally, exploding a huge front window in a shower of glass. As I stared and watched the glass cave in, my heart and mind also shattered. I was watching my life fall apart.

With pieces of shattered glass on our hair and clothes, navigating through the crowd of terrorized shoppers, we jumped into the car and fled.

Two blocks away we heard sirens. A long line of police cars zoomed past in the direction of Kmart, followed by ambulance after ambulance. My heart pounded and I felt sick to my stomach at what I might have done. I turned off the main highway just so I wouldn't see more ambulances passing. While Sammy kept coughing, I drove on in a trance.

With hardly any money, Sammy and I stayed holed up in a motel until the heat fanned down. The TV news reported that we'd robbed a Brinks truck parked in front of Kmart, making off with hundreds of thousands of dollars. We'd be hunted down "like the animals we were," the police announcement said. We were relieved to hear that nobody had been killed.

Less than a day later there were warrants out for our arrest, charging us with crimes in towns I'd never even heard of. Part of me felt a sense of false fame, as if I had in fact robbed a Brinks truck and gotten away with it. Yet at the same time my heart pounded double time against my chest, screaming in fear.

The fear drove me to seek out my mother. Whenever I would find her, she would be in her own pain, leaning against a doorway on a dark city street or sitting quietly in the back of an apartment building. But no matter what condition she was in, I was still her son, and she feared that the police would shoot and kill me. Although we spent only bursts of time together, it seemed like hours. I thought her every hug would be our last. Pulling strength from deep inside, she'd always find a laugh, a way for both of us to say "Be careful" before we parted.

The Domino Effect

BACK IN THE LIGHT of day, I kept walking the walk and talking the talk, pretending to my neighborhood that I was a big-time criminal as the news said. But in the end I no longer recognized myself. I was scared of who I'd become. I had spun so far out of control that I was lucky finally to be caught.

My entire existence had become focused on avoiding the police. Like a drug trafficker, I kept a CB radio that enabled me to monitor the local patrols, tracking their communication in an effort to steer clear. While the CB radio kept me from being captured many times—sometimes only by seconds—the police were never far away.

Their manhunt kept them posted on rooftops, hiding in garbage bins, disguised as waitresses in local restaurants, and even sitting at bus stops.

I was growing tired. It was finally time to give myself up, but I wasn't ready to admit it. So instead, I grew careless. One day I had chased and threatened at gunpoint a man who owed me money. He happened to be a tenant in the building where my sister Charlene lived.

"You go and get my goddamn money," I had said. "You have one fuckin' hour!"

"Man, I'll get you the money," he said.

"Then go get it," I said, thrusting my hand into my coat in a menacing way. "Go get it!"

When he ran off, it didn't occur to me that he was going to the police.

A couple of hours later I was sitting in Charlene's apartment playing a game of dominoes with a few friends. We heard the action on my radio's police band growing louder and louder, which meant that the police were getting closer and closer. Falling into a quiet shock, we sat there, our faces crossed by fear. What would happen next? If we ran out into the street, we'd be killed. But here? Inside the apartment? How was this going to play out?

I pushed back from the table and stood up. I felt my nephew Donta, who was two or three years old, gripping my leg tightly. As Charlene darted up to take him away, she looked at me through tears. Retreating to the bedroom, I removed all the weapons I was carrying and hid them in the closet.

After that, I didn't have to think about what to do. A voice came through the police bullhorn, ordering me and my friends to open the front door and walk out slowly with our hands up high. Filing out of the building into the police cars' blinding lights, we found ourselves surrounded by onlookers. At the sight of young Donta running toward me, people started screaming, "Don't shoot! Don't shoot!" The police kept their guns on me as I scooped my nephew into my arms, holding him close until Charlene could take him away.

The police had my friends and me bend over the hoods and trunks of their cars while they tried to figure out which one was me. To everyone's surprise, they weren't able to identify me on the spot, so they were examining my tattoos. Then out of nowhere appeared my mother, charging the patrol cars until a policeman held her back. Pointing her finger directly at me, she screamed, "If any of you mess with that boy over there—you see him, his name is Jay— I'll be down there at that jail before you can blink." She bawled out in pain and anger. "You hear me, Jay? You just call me, baby, and I'm telling you all—I'm kickin' ass if you make me go down to that jail! Don't make me go down there!"

The police knew that they had found me.

Sammy Lee was never charged in the Kmart robbery. Someone else was misidentified as the criminal and then wrongly convicted in his place. But I was charged, convicted, and sent to San Quentin, where I remain today. For many years I stared out at what I thought was freedom through a mesh screen and a crack in an old broken window. I would not find myself—and inner freedom—for many more.

CHAPTER 23

San Quentin

Fish in the Tank

WHEN I WALKED THROUGH the gates of San Quentin in 1981, I was nineteen years old. Hearing the door slam behind me, it was hard to imagine that in exchange for the armed robbery, this tiny cement cell would be my home for the next two decades, but that was the card I'd dealt myself.

Even though the cell was small, I wasn't alone—one flip of the light switch revealed clusters of fat cockroaches swirling on the filthy walls and among the random dirtballs on the floor. I almost passed out from the stench of urine sitting in the toilet.

I looked in my "fish kit," a box filled with belongings that the prison issues to each new convict, or "fish." Taking the toothbrush, detergent, and facecloth, I scrubbed my cell from top to bottom. I'd heard that if the power went off, I might be forced to wash my face in the toilet, so I used the military standards I learned at the academy to get it clean. When I felt like I'd be okay even if I had to eat off the floor of my cell, I stopped scrubbing. Then I rolled up wads of wet toilet paper and plugged all the cracks I could find to keep the roaches from coming back.

In order to call San Quentin home, I had to summon up an unbelievable will to survive. Like most new young prisoners, right away I got wrapped up with what the prison system called gang activities. Usually each race in prison hangs out with their own, but the guys my age, no matter what our race, were used to hanging together for a deeper sense of belonging, having found ourselves once again among the only real family we had ever known. But San Quentin was a whole new ball game, and so we had no choice but to seek shelter from the older, more seasoned inmates of our own race. These older prisoners mentored us, showing us ways to survive the ceaseless and senseless violence of San Quentin.

I soon discovered that many inmates had come to San Quentin through places like McLaren Hall, Boys Town, and the CYA. Some of us had been crossing paths since we were six- or seven-year-old snot-nosed peewees pushing up against each other in the recreation dayrooms of the earlier justice systems. I had grown up with some of them, like Pablo, as we moved from one institution to another. Everyone who's passed through such a system has their own personal secrets that reduce everything to "I don't give a fuck," as many of my friends would say. But even so, we all shared memories of what happened at those places. Some of my old friends from the academy still took pride in displaying their scars from the burning-cigarette contests. We would even talk about who had been our favorite counselor there—Calhoun or Buck—and compare notes on the cruelties we'd suffered at their hands.

Those of us who came up through the system had lost touch with our feelings and with any sense of self-esteem. We were at home in San Quentin. We thrived on being hated and feared. We considered a cell our "house." A prison sentence under five years was considered a joke. Almost overnight we became grateful to the academies where we had learned how to sleep on our backs stiff, as if lying in our coffins, to keep from being raped.

The prison system recognized each of us only as a number at a location, but we claimed new names like Bullet, Insane, Killer,

Maniac, Shank, Shotgun, and Snake. These new identities grouped us into intricate social systems with their own power structures and codes. Violence was our culture and our currency.

And the Verdict Is

FOUR YEARS AFTER I entered San Quentin, in 1985, a prison guard was killed. Although the prison authorities suspected that there were many people involved, only three of us, two other inmates and I, were charged with murder and conspiracy to murder. I soon found myself seated in a courtroom facing very serious charges. I knew I was completely innocent and so in some strange way I thrived on the attention these charges brought me. It made me feel important, like I had hit the big times, even though others who knew me well, who grew up with me in the system, knew I wasn't capable of murder. They would shout at me, "Dude, we know you. You might play like you are somebody, but we know better!" But in my ignorance and stupidity, I played in to what was going on around me, believing that in the end I could never be found guilty of something I had had nothing to do with. I acted the role of a hardened criminal as I was transported daily to the courthouse in shackles by armed guards who viewed me in disgust as if I were an animal. And yet, because of the attention directed toward me, as negative as it was, secretly I hoped my innocence would not be rapidly discovered. At the same time, because I had become so detached from myself, as I sat in the courtroom day after day, it was as if I was watching someone else's fate being tried, seeing someone else's face on the evening news.

But as the days and weeks of the trial lingered on, I began to worry. The faces of the jurors grew more grim and blanketed with sadness. I remember feeling sorry for them, for the awful decision that was theirs alone to make. And yet, I was so misplaced inside myself, my mind had separated itself from my head. There was not a tear shed that I can remember as the jury read the verdict. I just kept asking myself, "What in the hell just happened? Did that just happen? Am I supposed to die? When? Now? I couldn't have been that stupid, could I?" The jury found me guilty of conspiracy to murder. The two other inmates were sentenced to life without parole, but I was sentenced to die by lethal injection. In the moment that the sentence was read, my mind flashed back to when I was five years old, standing before another judge, who ordered my removal from my mother's custody in order to save my life. Eighteen years later, this very same judicial system was now ordering my execution.

On Death Row

JUST BEFORE THE TRIAL, in 1988, my mother died of heart failure. I hadn't seen her in many years. Some men don't want their families to see them wearing state clothes in the shit-hole of prison, but every time I glance over at her picture on the wall in my cell, I wish I'd seen my mother's face just once in the visiting room.

Mama died at a point when I felt like I could have begun to talk to her about the experiences I'd had as a child. I wanted to tell her that in spite of our separation, I'd always loved her. In place of everything I ever dreamed of saying to her, I wrote something to be read at her memorial service. For every word I wrote, there were a billion more things in my heart that I wished I could express to her in person.

During the murder trial, I learned things I'd never known about myself, my family, and my past—all at the same time as the jury. Questions I'd never asked my mother—like how long she'd been abused, how long she'd lived on those dark streets, how long she'd been the addict whose illness so deeply pained my siblings and me— were being asked and answered now. As I watched my whole life being displayed on a screen for all to see, I began to feel more curious about who I was and how I'd gone wrong. Was there anything I could do to help myself in prison?

Susan, a private investigator working on my case, sent me books on how to meditate and how to deal with pain and suffering. Like me, she was confronting a lot of things in her past. She was writing and encouraged me to do so as well. Alone with myself, I began to write and the floodgates of memories began to open. I started getting up early to try to calm my mind so I wouldn't panic. Through meditation I learned to slow down and take a few deep breaths, to take everything in, and not to run from the pain but to sit with it, confront it, accept it in a way I never had before.

Since 1990, I have lived on death row, waiting for appeals to be filed and then waiting to hear the outcome of those appeals. Until 2007, I spent all of those years in solitary confinement—or the adjustment center, as it is called—an isolated unit reserved for those people labeled "the worst of the worst." There I had even fewer privileges than "ordinary" death row inmates, who can make phone calls, use pens and typewriters, and listen to tapes. I was allowed only a ballpoint pen filler, a few books, and a television. I left my cell for exercise only for a few hours, three times a week. Having gone through life making one wrong choice after another, on death row I no longer have the power to make even the simplest choices—when to shower, when to exercise, when to see visitors, when to eat, or even when to turn my lights on or off.

Finding Peace

One day, shortly after my death sentence, I started leafing through a Buddhist journal that Susan had sent to me. In it was an article on meditation called "Life in Relation to Death," by a Tibetan Buddhist lama, Chagdud Tulku Rinpoche. His teaching seemed right up my alley, and I wrote him a letter in care of the journal.

I can still remember how blessed I felt when I finally met Chagdud Rinpoche. One of his students, Lisa, responded to the letter I'd written to the journal, sending me a copy of Rinpoche's book *Life in Relation to Death*. She asked if I needed help. I always needed help—I still do—so we began corresponding. After that I would spend hours on end sitting on the floor of my cell reading from the many transcriptions of talks sent to me by her and other practitioners. Lisa eventually began to visit me, and finally she brought Rinpoche to San Quentin.

Rinpoche and I had something in common: he had been a rebellious kid who wasn't born with a silver spoon in his mouth. Now he was a shrewd, feisty guy, a lama who ate beef jerky, got upset, and had jewels of compassion in him. He didn't tell me all this, I just felt it. I thought, *Here's a tough guy who can take me out of prison, even as I remain here. He'll discipline me when I need it and accept me as I am.*

It was difficult to integrate my meditation practice with life on death row. I knew so little that would apply to living a life that reflected the Buddha's ways. As I tried to do it, I could see how I failed all the time. But with Chagdud Rinpoche's encouragement, I hung in there with my meditation practice, and practice has become my best companion.

However, after ten years at San Quentin, I wasn't announcing that I was a Buddhist. Meditation was a quiet activity that I kept secret from my fellow prisoners and the guards; that's how sitting in a cross-legged position in the most peaceful hour of the morning stayed meaningful and pure for me. Prisoners sometimes see other inmates who become practitioners as something of a mystery and tend to look for all their faults rather than trying to understand their purpose in sitting. I didn't want to become one more reason for them to doubt someone's heartfelt efforts in practicing, and at the same time I did not want to feel more isolated than I already was.

Keeping meditation a secret was also a reflection of the questions I entertained in my own mind: Was I *really* a Buddhist? If I was, how would I learn to respond to the violence that was always circling around us at San Quentin? Especially when I took bodhisattva vows through the visiting-room glass in a ceremony with Rinpoche, I wondered if my Buddhist beliefs could cost me my life. The back-bone of the bodhisattva vow is to make the benefit of others my highest priority. Would I be able to do this in San Quentin and still stay alive?

Rinpoche encouraged me to think big and to use my intelli-gence toward "harmlessness, helpfulness, and purity." He reminded me that whether I was in prison or in a mansion by the sea, each moment provides an opportunity to practice these three commit-ments, which are ways of breaking out of the cycle of karma—causes and conditions. He said that if I trained my mind in this way, I would benefit countless beings, which was more important than helping just one. He also told me to end each day by review-ing my actions and to dedicate any virtuous ones to the benefit of others.

Rinpoche instructed me that thoughts—like everything else—come and go like clouds, but they seem so real that we're not able to see the essence of our mind, which is open and brilliant like the sun. He told me that by continuing to practice meditation, I would slowly be able to recognize the cloudlike nature of thoughts, which seem so solid that they block what's really happening. With his advice, I have been able to work with my doubting thoughts and deepen my commitment to the Buddhist path.

I've had lots of time to experiment with the truth of the Bud-dhist teachings. Through my spiritual practice I have learned that taking the view of impermanence—the truth that things are here today and gone tomorrow—helps me whenever I remember to do it. No matter how much trouble I'm having, or how misunderstood I feel, the thought "Nothing lasts" always has the power to bring me back to reality. I've also tried to get in the habit of seeing things with detachment, from my center, not wishing for stuff I want to happen and not pushing away the stuff I don't want to happen. In prison it is especially easy to get attached to the good stuff. Then when the bad stuff comes around, you suffer harder. I need to be able to accept it all with equanimity.

Looking at my life with fresh eyes, I learned how not to cause myself more pain by diving deeper into the hellhole of San Quentin. I stopped cussing out other prisoners and guards. I discovered that I could save a lot of energy by not becoming angry over small things like the food or the noise. I discovered that it takes a lot more energy to hate than it does to love—and that every bit of love I could conjure up meant that I didn't have to feel hatred.

After a while, I was able to extend some of the love and compassion I was feeling in my predawn hour of practice to others in San Quentin. The practice was to take complete responsibility for my actions. I began to write stories about my life in order to understand it, which has helped me try to use my experience for benefiting others. It feels so much better to use what I've learned to uplift someone else's spirits for even a moment, or to offer an example for others, than to try to hide behind my morning meditation.

CHAPTER 24

Pitbull

Tension in the Yard

IT WAS THE BEGINNING of the day. The morning sun shone through the bars of my cell as I sat calmly on the floor. A guard appeared at my cell door to ask if I was going out or staying in. I sprang up from my cross-legged position, hustling to gather my clothing together. I desperately wanted out—the faster the better. I could almost taste the fresh spring air.

When the back door of the adjustment center finally opened, I saw someone I'd never seen before standing on the yard by the electric entrance gate. *Who's he?* I thought. I'd been hoping to walk quietly around the yard before the fifty-plus other prisoners got outside. As the yard gate locked behind me, I tried to pay the stranger no serious mind. Although his presence made me nervous, I walked past him holding on to my Buddhist vows of nonviolence like an elderly woman clutching her purse.

"Man, where is you from?" he asked in a voice that matched the black cap he had pulled down to his eyelids.

"Huh?" I said, trying to take very deep breaths without detection. "What do you mean, where am I from? Where are *you* from?"

His voice rose. "What set you from, dude? Where you stay at out there?"

I realized he wanted to know what street gang I belonged to. "Hey, shit! I've been in San Quentin for the past seventeen years or so. That's *your* world out there. Mine's in here, you know?"

"Is that right?" he said, his eyes widening. "You been down that long?"

"I been down a long while," I said. "Too damn long."

"Uh-huh," he mumbled. "So what else is out here?" he then asked, wanting to know who and from what towns would be coming out to the yard.

"Hey, man," I said, "just guys who wants to do their own thing, their own time, with anybody who wants to get along with them, you know? Why do you ask?"

" 'Cause, man," he said, with rage in his voice, "I've been gettin' 'em up, stabbin' and fightin' all these punk motherfuckers talkin' that beaucoup-ass shit all up in this here joint, you know? 'Cause I don't get along with none of 'em. It's to the death with them and me—"

"Man," I interrupted, "who you talkin' about?"

"Dudes from all over," he said. "I hate all them punk-ass bitches— from Los Angeles, Bakersfield, Fresno, and the whole damn Bay Area. In every unit I been in, dudes been thinkin' I'm a punk, callin' me a bunch of cowards, and I'm no punk or coward! You hear me, dude? I'm a pit-motherfuckin'-bull! And I don't give a mad fuck either. Them polices knows what time it is, 'cause I be spittin' in their damn faces each 'n' every chance I get!"

"Oh, is that right, is that right?" I kept repeating as this new prisoner went on raging. If only I had stayed locked in my cell, sitting right there on my ass! But no! I just had to come out here to shake hands with a maniac, a real-life maniac! And why? To say: Hello there. My name is Jarvis. I am a Buddhist! No, this can't be real.

"So, hey, dude," said Pitbull, "you feel where I'm comin' from, huh? I'm no punk. I'm no coward. I stay ready. You hear me, dude?"

"Yeah, I hear you, Pitbull," I said. "But, man, slow down. It ain't that kind of party out here. The folks coming out to this yard don't even know you, let alone want problems with you. You can see that I don't want no problems, right?"

"I hear what you're saying," he said. "But I've been tricked before. The police don't like me 'cause I been spittin' in all their faces, and they always tryin' to send other inmates to do their dirty work."

"Well, man," I said, "if that's the case, I advise you to wait until someone moves on you, because out here, if you attack first, the gun towers are goin' to shoot to kill you."

"Yeah, I know," he said. "So I'm just going to stand right here like I am now, and let it be known where I'm comin' from."

"No, not right in front of the yard gate," I said to him. "You want to wait in the back of the yard, with your back against the fence—way over there, where you can see everybody and can't anyone get you from behind, you know?" I pointed.

"You right about that!" he said. "I'm goin' right over there and just wait for someone to run up on me. And boy, when they do, I'ma show them fools a thing or two. Bam! Bam!" He was swinging his fists, shadowboxing his way to the yard's far corner.

Over the years in San Quentin, I had seen a lot of mental cases, but this was the worst I'd ever seen on an exercise yard. The authorities usually place severe mental cases on "walk-alone" yards.

Watching Pitbull fight his own demons, I didn't know what to think. At least he was moving away from the entrance gate, not forcing the others walking out into a physical confrontation. I felt relieved, but also afraid I'd only postponed the inevitable. Would this dude get off the yard alive?

Pacing up and down along the fence, I greeted my friends with a warning look as I saw them observe Pitbull in the corner. Everybody on the yard grouped up in lion packs, some of them circling and positioning to block off escape routes. The strongest—Malcolm, Jambo, and Insane—were poised not more than a few feet from me. Pitbull still stood in the corner, shadowboxing with the devil. This was real prison.

"Say, Jambo." I walked over to where Jambo, Malcolm, and Insane were standing. "Man, what are you guys getting ready to do? I spoke with that dude before everybody was out today, and I think he is more bark than anything else—"

"Check this out, Jarvis," Jambo interrupted. I felt relief because I didn't know what else to say. "This dude cannot stay out here. No way! And, man, you know I love you like a brotha. But all that Buddhist shit you gettin' ready to run on us is not workin' this time, not today."

"He's right, Jarvis," Malcolm joined in. " 'Cause, man, just look at that dude. He's over there fist-fightin' the damn air, man, talkin' to himself like he is killin' somebody."

"And look at us," added Insane. "We're standin' here on this side of the yard while that jack-ass fool is trying to pump fear into us so we don't put a cold piece of penitentiary steel in his ass. We'll just have to see about this, 'cause, man, I'm about ready to bum-rush over there and rip a hole in his guts with this shank and leave it for the pigs to pull out! They had no damn business puttin' him out here with us."

"Hold the fuck on, Insane!" I said in total anger, seeing the blade peeking out of his coat sleeve. "That nut don't need to be killed. He only needs to be let off this yard. If he wasn't on this yard, all this stuff about killing wouldn't even be on our minds. I'd be taking your ass on this basketball court, while Jambo and Malcolm, you guys would be working out over there on the pull-up bars. We'd all just be glad to be out those damn cells."

"But that's not the case," said Jambo.

"Yeah, I know," I said. "But the problem is gettin' that nut off the yard and not standing over here waiting for the perfect time to kill someone. Man, you guys going to have to slow your roll and take three long deep breaths. And this is not my Buddhist shit either! It's called *thinking*. But, man, if none of you guys brought your thinking caps out today," I said, becoming more angry and frustrated, "and if you want to go over there and kill just to kill, go right ahead! 'Cause it's none of my business. I'll let the chips fall, you know? Even so," I was almost talking out loud to myself now, "this guy should not be stabbed."

"Well, I tell you what," said Jambo. "The three of us are going to go over there, but not to just kill that fool. No! We're going over there to ask this dude to leave the yard. And I swear, if he so much as swings at a fly, Jarvis, we're going to break him off another asshole!"

"I hear what you're saying, Jambo," I said. "But still, man, it doesn't sound like you guys are gonna give him a real chance to leave the yard. Hey, let me go over there with—"

"Hell, no!" said Insane. "You just gonna be in the way in case this nut tries somethin'. Seriously, Jarvis, you be talkin' too damn much."

"Okay, okay!" I said. "But you guys have to give this dude—his name is Pitbull—a chance to leave the yard."

"Check this out," Malcolm said angrily. "If we weren't goin' to give this Pitbull a chance . . . shit, man, we'd jus' tell you that, hey, we goin' to blast holes in his ass. It's that simple."

"Okay, I hear what you're sayin,'" I said, empty of words. All my Buddhist convincing had run its course. My friends' minds had been pulled back only a little. Was it enough? I watched them walk straight to Pitbull's corner.

As the yard fell deep into silence watching the lion pack's jaws slowly opening as Jambo, Insane, and Malcolm headed toward the corner of the yard, I glanced up at the gunman standing in the tower shack doorway. He quickly lit a cigarette, took two deep inhales, and flicked it to the ground from the tower. Then he went inside the tower shack and closed the door. That meant, *Do what you want to do. I'm not watching.* There was nothing standing in the way of violence in the yard now.

I thought of Pitbull saying that the guards send inmates to do their dirty work. His paranoia was playing into this whole thing. In seconds, he and my friends were standing face-to-face. He was no longer shadow-boxing. I started mumbling to myself: "Man, you jackass, leave the yard. Come on, man, you can do it, just leave." I felt the pounding of my heart.

Then a miracle happened. I watched Jambo point to the yard gate. Pitbull slowly walked in that direction, raising his hands over his shoulders and shouting loudly, getting the attention of the tower gunman, that he was the "greatest, the champion of the world," and wanted off the yard. I sighed in relief. Through the tower window I could see the gunman phone the adjustment center for someone to come take Pitbull back to the housing unit.

I began to suspect that everything Pitbull had said was true as I watched how the two guards who escorted him away were roughing him up, mocking him, and calling him names under their breath. I didn't know if they wanted to see him simply beaten up or, worse, stabbed and killed. This question still lingers in my mind.

After the tension subsided and everyone went about their business—playing cards, basketball, and handball—I went over to the pull-up bars to thank Jambo for asking this person to leave the yard instead of resorting to violence as the only way. I didn't use this particular language—it felt too flat and awkward for my longtime friend, who had been born into violence, as I had. I just thanked him for using his head instead of the sword. Jambo appreciated this. We spent the rest of our yard time talking about his Vietnam experiences and working out together on the pull-up bars.

Why, Man, Why?

SEVERAL DAYS LATER I again traded in my meditation cushion for the exercise yard. When the adjustment center door opened, I choked at the sight of Pitbull, pacing up and down on the yard, enraged.

Rather than ask the smirking guard escorting me, "What in hell is *he* doing out here again?" I kept walking toward the yard gate. With each step, I took a deep breath, trying to control my steaming anger. I had never hated San Quentin more.

I walked straight up to Pitbull and said, "Why, man, why? Why did you come out here again? Don't you know how lucky you were the last time?"

"Man, dude," he said, shouting in my face, "them police been callin' me a bunch of cowards and shit. They said, 'If you a man you go back out there and prove it!' Man, I'm no motherfuckin' coward. And I'm not scared of any motherfuckin' body out here."

"So you goin' to wait till everybody come back out here to prove to the guards you ain't a coward?" I asked.

"You fuckin' right!" Pitbull answered. "That one guard said, 'A real man with real nuts is goin' to do what he have to do.'"

"Pitbull, damn that!" I said, my adrenaline boiling. "I can't let you stay out here just so you can prove your manhood to everybody."

"Dude! I don't give a husky fuck about what you not goin' to do," he blurted, inching up to my face with rage in his eyes. "Dude, I do what the fuck I wanna do, and, dude, we don't even need *everybody*."

"Hmmm," I mumbled, clenching my fist tightly. "You right! We don't need everybody." *Bam!* My fist landed squarely on his chin. I coldcocked Pitbull flat on the prison asphalt. With my adrenaline still pumping, I could only stare down at him.

The scream of the tower whistle woke me up to what I'd done. I looked up, expecting to see a gun on me. The officer just gave a slight smile and walked into his shack. I had hit someone on the yard—for years something I'd worked hard to convince others not to do. I stared down at Pitbull. *Man, I just punched the lights out of someone. What is Chagdud Rinpoche going to say now? And what about my court appeals?* My mind overflowed with shame at my action, and anger at San Quentin.

Trying to explain all this to myself felt like bending something inside my heart, but on a deeper level something about what I'd just done felt good. I couldn't undo it, nor did I want to. I could have held back, but why? To prove to everyone outside myself that I was a true Buddhist? To strictly keep to my vows of nonviolence, even at the cost of watching this human being get stabbed? *No way,* I resolved. *Not today. Buddhist or not!*

"And I am not returning my vows either." I said the last part aloud when I noticed Pitbull barely lifting himself to a clumsy sitting position on the asphalt. We stared at each other.

"Shit, man!" he mumbled, holding his chin in pain. "What did you hit me with?"

"A straight left, I think."

"So you's a southpaw, huh?" he said, with a broken half-smile. "That's how you got me. But now you see that I am a man, not a coward, don't you? You tell 'em fools that I am a real fuckin' man, will you?"

Pitbull's almost childlike voice awakened my memories of two boys inside the circle at the academy being cheered into violence for our manhood. Seeing him sitting there, asking me to see him as a man, I wondered: Was *I* a man? Was I a Buddhist?

I opened my next meditation session with this contemplation:

Oh, affirmation to life, steady me: keep me balanced and poised. Cushion me. Lessen my load. Seat me upright in lotus posture, seeing only emptiness, not despair, I pray. Teach me your benefits, deep and simple. Benefit this injustice with a change of every heart. Affirm all reasons for being. Let every circumstance, in every depth—pain and joy both—bring to practice you, me, all beings. Let us affirm lifetimes to steady every breath, making peace—and peacemaking—the companion to every heart.

CHAPTER 25

A Mirror into Anger

Little Floyd's Birthday

I HAD JUST COPIED down all the information I needed from the JC Penney catalog when Bork, in a cell down the tier, asked me if he could use the catalog when I was done. "Sure, no problem," I said. I had no reason to keep it any longer. All I had left to do was decide on a toy for my nephew Little Floyd's ninth birthday. Now that I'd written down the possibilities, the faster I could get the catalog out of my cell, the less chance I'd have to revisit it and change my mind.

Later that evening I asked a guard prowling down the tier if she could open my food port and take the catalog to Bork. I thought of striking up a conversation with him, asking him to look at the toys I had in mind and give me his honest opinion: would it be better to get the Pokemon bank or the train that turned into a robot? But it was already late in the evening, and the quietness on the tier changed my mind.

Early the following morning, after my meditation practice, I was surprised to see the JC Penney catalog sitting on my opened food port along with my breakfast. Bork had given it to one of the officers, who gave it back to me. I decided to double-check all the information from the catalog that I'd copied the day before.

When I opened the catalog, I noticed that many of its pages had been torn out from the children's clothing section. I stared down at the ripped paper. It didn't make sense. For all I cared, Bork could have kept the whole thing—it wasn't mine. The prison keeps many catalogs so that inmates can make special purchases through their trust accounts. We can send a gift outside the prison to anyone we choose.

I forgot about the missing catalog pages until one winter day a month later. Standing next to the yard fence, waiting around with other prisoners to be taken back inside when the "yard recall" bell rang, I overheard someone saying to his friend, "Man, that dude Bork is a fuckin' serial child rapist and killer—that's why he's on death row."

Without thinking, I turned to the voice, a big "Huuuuh?" caught in my throat. I lost my breath as if I had just been sucker-punched. My mouth began to twitch as the force of my silent outrage pushed me against the yard fence. I could feel the eyes of my fellow prisoners on me, wondering what had happened. Instead of explaining, I looked up at the sky, gray with moving clouds. *For all this time*, I thought, *this guy Bork has lived only a few cells from me, and never did I know why he was on death row.*

Finally the bell sounded. I moved quickly to be first to leave the yard. I was feeling a strange kind of emptiness, which began to fill with anger when I approached Bork's cell on the way to my own. Seeing him standing there next to the bars, I walked by instead of stopping to say hello as usual. I didn't trust myself to hide my rising anger, much less to say a friendly word.

When the steel cell door slammed shut behind me, the echo told me to lie down for a nap. I pulled my rolled-up mattress and bedding out from under my bunk, where I keep them so that I can use my steel slab bunk as a writing desk. Then I lay staring up at the ceiling.

In front of me floated images of this person down the tier, only a few cells away. Now that I thought about it, everything started to make sense. Bork had always seemed like some kind of mad scientist turned killer. Why was he assigned to an exercise yard by himself? Even then, why did he rarely go outside or even leave his cell?

Bork was afraid of being attacked by prisoners, who hate anyone who hurts children. Living here, I've realized that we despise the child killers among us because most of us were hurt as children. And those prisoners who are fathers can imagine their own children becoming victims while they're in prison.

I lay on my bed, tossed and turned by these thoughts, anger boiling inside me. Now I realized why very few prisoners or guards spoke to Bork, and why he usually slept all day and stayed up all night talking to himself. More sinisterly, I realized why he'd ripped out the pages from the catalog.

Then I heard Bork down the tier, talking and laughing with someone nearby. Sitting up, I listened to every word with cold annoyance. Bork's voice had found my ears and was crawling inside my mind. It stung me with venom, locking my jaws into a tight rage. Later that evening, when the whole tier was eating, I could hear Bork laughing with food in his mouth. My stomach turned at the thought of the kids he had raped and killed. My hatred toward him had turned to poison, and the poison was making me sick.

Contemplation

WHEN NIGHT CAME, I longed for the opportunity to begin my meditation practice. Finally, the tier became quiet enough.

At the back of my cell, I sat on the floor with my folded blanket beneath me. Squeezed between the bunk and the toilet, I faced the wall. This was my one chance to simmer down, to manage this anger that was getting the best of me.

An hour passed. I heard Bork moving around in his cell down the quiet tier. Failing miserably to silence my thoughts, I invoked the compassion of Red Tara, the female Buddha, asking her to enter and bless the tiny sacred space I had made. But all the discomforts, both mental and physical, just squeezed me tighter. The sound of Bork's voice boot-kicked me further out into the dirty sea of my own pain, where I risked drowning in hatred.

Again I invoked Tara. I tried to visualize her navigating me out of this slough of poison and toward the bright images of my nephews and nieces, who suddenly appeared before me like angels. But then I would think of the faces of all the children in that JC Penney catalog and feel my desire to kick Bork's teeth in.

I had come to the very limits of my compassion. At one point I stood up to stretch and rinse my face. As I pushed the cold water button, a haunted thought broke open: the chess games Bork and I played! We each had a chess set, and weekly he and I would pick an early evening and play a game. We numbered each square on our boards and called out the numbers of each of our moves over the tier.

I would always get so close to winning, but then Bork's shrewd calculations would somehow bait and corner me as I struggled desperately to protect my king. *Damn*, I wondered, *was that how Bork lured kids into his web before raping and killing them?* Rinsing my face and hands, I expected to see blood streaming from my eyes, but I saw only my stress and the steam of my anger being cooled.

Once more I squeezed in between the bunk and toilet to work on removing this huge obstacle called Bork that was wreaking havoc in my mind. I bore down hard with my thoughts, as if I lived only a few cells from Satan himself.

For close to two weeks I sat like this each day, struggling against this destroyer of life's innocence, falling deeper and deeper into the place where I could imagine being the parent, uncle, aunt, or sibling of every child raped and killed by the likes of Bork.

Then, thinking of the dharma, I was no longer able to hold on to my indignation. Now I tried to envision myself as Bork's mother or father, sister or brother, and even as Bork as a child. It was scary to be without the ground of a righteous stand, floating in a cesspool of pain and suffering.

Still, for all those days, I continued to sit and invoke my prayers of compassion. Then gradually, for seconds at a time, I was able to feel the sickness so deep and absolute that it could cause a human being like Bork to prey upon children. In the beginning, the sickness I imagined repulsed me. I couldn't take too much. I felt as if I were undergoing spiritual chemotherapy, attached to an intravenous tube that dripped a poisonous substance into my veins.

But as I breathed slowly in and out, absorbed by my anger toward Bork, I saw all the things I didn't want to see. On the screen between my closed eyes, I saw my own anger. I saw the viciousness of my own pain, like those people I sometimes see on TV who have no compassion. I was ugly, shaken, no good to myself. The structure of my face had changed. All the thin frown lines in my face seemed permanent, and the muscles in my jaw were as tight as clenched fists.

To have dedicated my spiritual practice to the end of all beings' suffering and then to see that I still had these very ugly feelings of hatred and the wish to kick someone's teeth in, shamed me to the core. *Damn*, I thought, as one angry feeling was replaced by another, *this isn't good*. It seemed like all my righteous anger hadn't helped Bork, me, or anybody else.

Then a bigger feeling broke through as I plugged into all the human suffering throughout the world. Why hadn't I seen Bork as part of it? Why hadn't I seen myself as part of it, here in this prison? In the whole world? I felt a mental clarity that lifted me above all the clouds of my own making.

When I got a visit from one of my dharma teachers and spent the whole time explaining my Bork ordeal in detail, I experienced another profound awakening.

My teacher said, "Jarvis, that very same anger and rage that you felt in your heart at the beginning, that is what almost everybody out in society is feeling about you—all those people who believe in capital punishment and who are screaming for executions."

I sat there speechless, shocked by it all. But it was true. I live here on death row, alongside Bork. My hatred for Bork now turned its face on me.

CHAPTER 26

Another June

The Garbage Bin

LATE ONE SPRING SEVERAL guards came to my cell with empty boxes and told me that I was to pack up all my belongings. After several years, I was being transferred to another cell in the adjustment center, "as a convenience move," they said. Since other prisoners were also being moved, I didn't take it personally. *Maybe*, I thought, *it's because of the construction work in the unit.* I boxed up all my belongings, and on that same day I was moved into another cell.

When the new cell door clanged shut behind me, I looked around. I could not believe the filth and the stench! I looked under the bunk, the source of the awful odor, and saw at least fifty old trays holding the remains of breakfasts and dinners long gone. They'd been left there like unwashed dishes, stacked on top of each other for months and months.

The rest of the space under the bunk was filled with loads of dirty wet laundry—all state-issued—sheets, towels, underwear, socks, shirts, and jeans—smelling real bad. Rust and mildew had grown like cobwebs on the piles. There were even rolls of wet and dirty toilet paper mixed in with the laundry. Whoever had lived here had used the space under the bed as one big garbage dump. I had to bring my head up quickly before the smell traveled down into my stomach and made me vomit.

On the walls I noticed a paste of dry snot all over, as if whoever had been living here had been in the habit of blowing his nose on the wall. It felt like I was trapped in a hazardous waste container. Throughout my many years in prison, I've moved into some pretty awful cells, but no twenty of those cells combined could ever compare to this one.

I resolved not to sleep before cleaning the place; I was prepared to stay up however long it took. And oddly enough, looking very foreign amid the filth, a surprisingly clean pile of folded towels sat neatly at the foot of the steel bunk, beside two paper bowls filled with detergent and brand-new scrubbing pads. They had all been placed there for *me*.

It dawned on me that I had been put in this garbage dump for the sole purpose of cleaning it up. The unit staff had known perfectly well that this cell was a pig sty and had intentionally chosen me to move into it.

The guards knew I was a Buddhist. They figured I wouldn't spin out and go into a fit of rage, threatening staff, kicking the cell bars, and demanding they move me to another cell, as any of the other inmates would have responded had they been suddenly thrown into a garbage bin like this, and as I myself would have responded many years ago.

Staring down at the clean towels, detergent, and scrub pads, I didn't know what stank the most, the cell or the attitudes of the guards. It burned me up. I felt the impulse to pick these things up and slam them against the wall in disgust. They had trapped me inside a disease chamber! The dry snot and webs of mildew on the walls were like signs flashing DANGER! BEWARE! HAZARDOUS SUBSTANCES! I wanted out of this damn cell!

It was then that I closed my eyes and gave my patience to try to understand. *What kind of human being*, I asked myself, *could have lived for twenty-three hours a day, seven days a week, year after year, in a cell like this?* The anger that had been percolating inside me seemed to dissolve as I wondered who could have slept and eaten here among these fumes of rot.

A New Neighbor

I HEARD MY NEIGHBOR call over to me. "Jarvis! Man, I'm so glad I got you as my new neighbor."

"Who's that?" I asked. I had been staring deep into the gutter of filth, and I hadn't even thought about who was in the next cell.

"Man, this is Norm," the voice called back.

"Oh, Norman!" I said. "That's you over there, huh? How you doing?"

"Man, I'm all right! But how are *you* doing? The guy that was in that cell—did he leave the cell clean or real fucked up? 'Cause, man, he never took showers, not one! Hell, the dude never even put out his trash in the whole year we were neighbors. Plus, man, all he did was beg, beg, beg for cigarettes and coffee. That's it, Jarvis! He begged me to death, you know?"

"Oh, is that right?" I asked. I realized Norman wasn't just talking to me. By the tone in his voice, I could tell he had the ear of the whole tier. They were all listening. He was leading me into an ongoing discussion that he and the whole tier had been having about whoever had lived in that cell. I felt a tinge of insult that Norman would try to use my arrival to ridicule his old neighbor.

Standing in the middle of the cell, looking around, I could feel that something was awfully wrong with whoever lived like this and that somehow it was not entirely his own fault. It seemed sadder by the second. It wasn't something to ridicule.

"Hey, Norman," I shouted out over the tier, knowing others would hear me. "Nah, man, the cell isn't that dirty. It needs a lot of work, but most cells need that spick-and-span touch that only the person moving in can bring to it, you know?"

"So it isn't that funky?" Norm asked me.

"Not really, Norm," I called back. "I mean, you will definitely hear me over here washing down the walls for the next couple of days and getting all my things in order. But I do that in whatever cell I move into, you know? This cell isn't that dirty." And to myself I said, *What a bold-faced lie!* But I didn't want to take part in the tier drama of character assassination.

I could have created a bunch of laughter on the tier if I had told the truth, but to me that would have made the filth all too real. None of it was funny. It would have been like laughing at a person who was mentally ill or physically disabled. The very prints of his sickness were plastered everywhere.

It took me three whole days of cleaning before I could finally rest and find some measure of comfort. And during all the hard scrubbing with deodorant soap and shampoo, washing up and down the walls and floor to rid the place of the filth and odor, I never stopped wondering about the person who had been in this cell, which told a horrific tale of someone's inner life. Who was he? Why was he on death row? What was his story? Day in, day out, scrubbing and cleaning, I wondered: How had this person felt? What was his breathing existence?

Into Another Cell

AFTER A WEEK, I finally felt comfortable enough to put some pictures on the walls, to make this tiny place a bit homier. It was in the morning hour, and I was putting up a picture of Bob Marley, using the gummed paper on the margins of the sheets of stamps, my carefully saved version of scotch tape. At that moment two guards came onto the tier and stepped up to my cell bars. They told me to pack up all my belongings; I would be moving down to the first tier, into another cell.

Countless times, the guards had prowled down the tier and observed me sweating, a towel wrapped around my face to avoid the awful stench. They had seen me climbing up the cell walls, and down on my knees, tirelessly scrubbing. They hadn't been able to hide their shock and distaste as they provided me with more and more clean rags, as well as the bags I needed for all the garbage. I told myself they had to be joking.

But when I looked one of the guards in the eye, he repeated, "Hey! Get all your shit together. Pack up! We're moving you down to the first tier."

In that instant I remembered. It was June! June is the very worst part of the year for me. Ever since June 1985, when the prison guard was killed, San Quentin takes this month to memorialize not only that guard but all guards who have been killed in the line of duty.

The unit staff was going to harass me until they created the reaction they wanted. They needed me to spin out so they could justify their intention to do far worse to me. I saw this desire in their eyes and felt it in the way they stood there smiling in front of my newly cleaned cell, waiting for me to explode into a violent uproar. But I held on to the hope that this was a joke, as if I needed these extra moments to take in what I had just been told.

"What do you mean?" I heard myself ask. "Pack up? Why?"

"Don't know," said one guard flatly.

"You don't know why I'm moving?" I asked again.

"We do not! Are you gonna comply? Yes or no?" the other guard shouted.

It was clear then that I had been moved into this cell as a form of harassment.

The anchor of my spiritual practice dropped. I needed it to steady me, to help me see the nature of things as they really were, in these early days of June.

"What the fuck you mean—yes or no?" yelled Norman suddenly. His voice, like a fist of rage, caused me to jump with surprise. I could tell he was standing at his cell bars, only a few feet away.

"Listen!" said Norman in total fury. "You two punk-bitches don't come up here trying to harass somebody. Who you fools think you are, huh? Yeah, I'm talkin' to you two clowns out on the tier. Now, after he did all your dirty work, scrubbing for days, you two punk-bitches want to move him again! Man, Jarvis," Norm went on, "you tell them bitches to get the fuck away from your cell and leave you the fuck alone!"

"Say, Norm," I interrupted him, surprised by this sudden burst of anger. "Chill out over there, man. Let me handle this. Hey, if they want to move me again, well, hell, man, ain't nothing to it but to do it, you know?"

"Nah, fuck these fools!" hollered Norm. "I'm not going to let these jerks put another nasty motherfucker in that cell again and every night I'm close to throwin' up, smelling all that foul shit! Hell, Jarvis! They got you to clean up all that nasty-ass stuff, and now they wanna move you. That's straight bullshit! I wish like fuck they'd try to put *me* in a cell like that—it'd be the last thing they'd ever do."

"Hey, you two punks out on the tier," Norman went on, now fuming. "You can take that 'comply or not comply' and stick it up your motherfuckin' ass! And if you put another nasty, stinkin', foul-smellin' dude next to me again, I'm goin' to make you move *me*!"

I almost wanted to laugh. It was obvious that Norm had known I was telling a bold-faced lie about the state of the place and now he was afraid that if I left he might get another filthy neighbor. He was only looking out for his own interests.

The guards waited in front of my cell while I packed all my belongings in boxes. An hour later I was on my way to the first tier, the tier I dreaded most. As I was escorted down the clanging stairs, the noise grew louder and louder. I felt like I was descending straight into a riot of inmates cursing each other out, kicking and banging on their cell bars. My new home was in the worst hellhole of San Quentin.

Walking down the tier toward my assigned cell, seeing the twisted faces of inmates as I passed, their hands angrily rattling the bars of their cells, I imagined that I'd mistakenly turned the wrong corner and found myself in the midst of an insane asylum. What saddened me most were the faces I recognized—people I had known in the past who had since gone crazy.

What If Hawk Was Right?

THE FIRST TIER IS where all the inmates are housed who are medicated for psychiatric reasons or who have suicidal tendencies, a high propensity for violence, or serious health issues. If they suffer from seizures, have heart problems that need close observation, or need constant medications, San Quentin keeps them on the first tier in order for staff to be able to respond quickly to medical emergencies. From the first tier an inmate can get to the prison hospital in less time than from the second or third tier. So why was my new home on the first tier?

I fully expected to find my new cell as filthy as the one before, especially when I learned that I would be moving into Hawk's old cell. I've known Hawk longer than almost anyone else on death row, and he's probably the craziest friend I have. He suffers from an extreme case of paranoia.

Hawk believes that the government placed a satellite in his light-bulb, a camera in his television, and listening devices throughout his cell. To top it off, he believes that during a brain operation he had as a teenager they stole his original brain and replaced it with a madman's. Because I've always accepted his truths as his, we've been close. I can talk to Hawk for hours and not have a bored moment.

He's always full of theories about what is *really* going on. But when I was told I'd be moving into Hawk's old cell, I figured it would be several more hell-days of cleaning.

Lo and behold, Hawk's cell was the cleanest place I had ever moved into. I couldn't find a spot on the wall or a crumb of dust on the floor, which looked almost polished. Then I realized that Hawk's cell reflected his paranoia. He feared germs and dirt too. Once the cell bars shut behind me, I smelled disinfectant. Only later did I realize that the guards were using Hawk as a one-man cell-cleaning operation, moving him from dirty cell to dirty cell.

The worst part about being on the first tier was the windows. In my previous cells, I had been able to look far beyond the barbed wire, at the sunset. Closer to hand, in San Quentin's grassy courtyard, I'd seen prisoners being baptized in the baptismal pool and heard the preacher's voice calling out, "This man is giving his heart to Jesus." But here on the first tier the windows were all painted over so you couldn't see outside. That meant I was no longer able to reach beyond this place with my eyes. I didn't know if the skies were blue or cloudy. I had to search for the time of day. These painted windows boarded me up inside.

As I unboxed my belongings and settled in, the noise level continued to climb and I noticed that the cell was a little smaller than what I'd had before. For one thing, the ceiling was lower. Because all the cells are small, a little bit makes a big difference. On the first tier, the "bunk" is a cement block that measures six feet by three, and maybe two feet high. Since the cell is only six feet long, it cuts the cell in half.

On the second and third tiers, the bunks are flat plates of steel bolted to the cell walls. The storage room under the bunk is a valuable feature in a tiny cell. Now I had to stack all my boxes on top of each other, which made my cell even smaller. I felt bunched up; I had no idea where to put anything. With the slab of cement lying lengthwise, there was no room to sort things out. In this first-tier cell, I'd also lost the pleasure of being able to sit on the floor and stretch my legs out under the bunk.

Meanwhile, all the men on the tier were calling out my name. "Hey, Jarvis, do you have any magazines or books?" "Coffee or tobacco?" "Top Ramen soup or crackers?" The voices echoed up and down the tier.

The men thought of me as a kind of goodwill freebie store. Over the years everyone had come to count on me for such things, because I made a practice of collecting magazines and books I thought someone else could use. I would always find ways to get these materials down to the first tier, to people I knew could use them the most.

I had known a lot of these guys before they'd lost their minds. But hearing them calling out my name in joy that I was now among them just didn't sit well with me. It felt like the floor of the stock exchange, with everyone competing for my books and magazines, coffee and cigarettes, each saying he'd known me better and longer, which gave him first option on the bid.

Everyone was benefiting from my agonies. First the guards took advantage of me when they knew I'd clean up that cell, and then they moved me here where everyone was yelling my name, wanting something from me. I needed to take a breath, to go about putting my things in order for a moment, to disappear within myself.

It took me about a week to finally feel settled enough to put Bob Marley back on the wall.

CHAPTER 27

Freedom Ride

Carrot on a Chain

ONE MORNING I'D AWAKENED to another day when a guard called down the tier, "Masters, you have a medical escort. We'll be down in five minutes to pull you out!"

What medical escort? I thought to myself. *Can't be me! I'm not sick!* I couldn't help but feel suspicious. It was June again, always the hardest month.

"Wait! Hold up!" I yelled as the guards opened the front gate of the tier. "I never asked to see a doctor!"

"Are you going or not?" was the cold response. "It's up to you, Masters! Are you refusing?"

A few seconds passed. "Yeah, yeah, I'm going," I answered. "Whenever you guys are ready, I'm ready." And to myself, *Let's just get whatever this might be over with.*

Two guards came onto the tier and ordered me to undress. I pushed my clothes through the slot and turned around, naked, in front of them. After searching through the clothes, they pushed them back in. Then they reached through the slot and placed me in hand restraints. They called out my cell number to another guard off the tier who controlled the switch for the door to come open.

As I was being escorted off the tier, all my senses panned for even the slightest of unusual vibes that would tell me something, anything. But there were no clues. They placed me in a "waiting cell" without saying a single word to me, and I began silently reciting the Buddhist Red Tara mantra, *Om Tare Tam Soha*.

My vajrayana Buddhist teacher Chagdud Tulku Rinpoche had given me many meditation prayers to say in moments just like this. I thought this prayer to Tara, the female Buddha, the embodiment of wisdom, might help the most. *Om Tare Tam Soha*—"Please be aware of me; remove whatever obstacles I'm here to face." As I said it, my eyes welled up as the image of Chagdud came over me.

On death row your closest fear is of your own death. This can be so consuming that it seems as if everyone you love on the outside is guaranteed to outlive you. They seem immortal. But Chagdud Rinpoche had recently died.

I adored him as both my teacher and my father. I felt so blessed that he had walked inside San Quentin to sit with me. In later years, through all his illnesses, Chagdud had rolled his wheelchair into the visiting room. He was the one who gave me my spiritual path. His students and other Buddhist practitioners had become my friends, forming the core of a support group that has worked tirelessly to appeal my death sentence.

A guard I'd never seen before took off my hand restraints and handed me an orange jumpsuit. It looked like a carrot costume. "What the hell is this?" I asked. "Where am I going?"

"Put it on," he commanded.

The words *Om Tare Tam Soha* struggled against *What the fuck is going on?!* The last time I'd worn a jumpsuit was over a decade earlier, during my death penalty trial. So where was I going now? I'd heard rumors that some death row prisoners were transferred to Pelican Bay, another prison many hours' drive north.

I was placed in a waist-chain—a chain fitted around the waist with hand restraints welded to it. It kept my hands close to my sides but allowed more movement than handcuffs.

Hearing Aids

THREE GUARDS ESCORTED ME out the front door of the adjustment center. A small car was waiting for me, its four doors already open. As I sat down in the backseat, a guard reached over me and pulled a strap across my chest. I felt like an astronaut being prepared for liftoff. I'd never worn a seat belt before.

One guard took the driver's seat, one took the passenger seat, and the third got into the backseat with me. The driver spoke into his handheld radio, and off we drove toward the back of the prison. Unfamiliar sights—the general population lower-yard, the prison industry buildings—passed by my window like a movie. I hadn't been in a regular car in over twenty-two years. The ride was so smooth, without the slightest sound—only by looking out my window could I *tell* we were moving. It felt dreamlike.

We drove on a narrow street along the shore of the bay, uphill toward the visitors' entrance. We were going a lot faster than I would have preferred. Being shackled in waist restraints with a weird seat belt across my chest while speeding around narrow lanes made me nervous.

We passed through several security gates—I could see Mount Tamalpais right across San Francisco Bay—to get to the front gate. We passed the prison parking lot, and there was my unit counselor, briefcase in hand, closing the trunk of his car. I made a mental note to tell him later that I'd seen him. I was trying to distract myself from the feeling that I was in a car with three *assassins*—a car that made no sounds and told no tales.

When the east security gate swung open, we proceeded down the street to a stop sign, turned left onto a ramp, and then drove onto the freeway. I vaguely remembered this from when I'd gone to court. *So maybe*, I thought, *I'm going back to court.* But noticing more and more sights I hadn't seen before, I felt a sick sway inside: this was not the direction of the Marin County courthouse.

A sign on the freeway made my heart drop. It read EUREKA. I knew that was next to the Oregon border.

So that's it, I told myself. *I'm being transferred to Pelican Bay, all the way up north, far from my friends in the Bay Area.*

At that moment the guard in the backseat spoke for the first time. "So, Mr. Masters, what's going on with you? What's the problem with your ears?"

Seconds passed. I could hardly piece together the words. "What?" I said. "My ears?"

"Yeah, your ears," he said. "Why are we taking you to see a hearing specialist?"

"Whoa! Wait a minute!" I said. "Is that where I'm going? To see a hearing specialist?"

"Yeah. We have you scheduled to be at Marin General Hospital for a nine-thirty appointment."

"You're shitting me!" I said. I tried to bring my hand up to my head to scratch my brains clean, but the chain from my waist didn't reach half that high.

"Nah! I wouldn't do that," he answered flatly. "You have an outside appointment to be examined by a hearing specialist."

More seconds passed. Then it all came back to me.

Nine months before, I'd gone to see a doctor in order to get authorization to use the visiting phone for people with impaired hearing. I'd been having serious difficulty hearing my visitors in the noncontact visiting booths. The only visiting booth with a telephone was designated for the hearing-impaired. But the doctor said that he couldn't provide me the permission slip I requested; I would need to be examined by a "hearing specialist." It never occurred to me that he'd place me on a list to be seen by one, let alone that I'd be taken out of prison to go to Marin General Hospital.

I felt light as a feather. I wanted to fly, to open my eyes, to look around and remember everything. I couldn't shift gears fast enough! Now I was on an outing, a sightseeing tour of the world that I hadn't seen since I was a teenager. The summer sun reflected off the car window, and as I peered out I wished everything could slow down. My eyes became a camera lens, snapping pictures of cars, trees, and houses. I could breathe the air of freedom—sweeter than anything I could remember.

As I stayed glued to the window, I also began to remember how I'd lost my freedom, and all the pain I'd caused for so many people—those awful times. I felt the violence crushing me. As we passed a supermarket, I remembered how I'd once jumped up on a store counter shooting a gun. The thought froze me. How could I have done something like that? I became scared of myself, scared by those years. How could I have compromised my freedom, my sanity?

My spirit was now struggling to be free—free from the chain tight around my waist, free from the handcuffs, free from the conversations I was having with myself, free from the conversation with the guard about my ears and the hearing specialist.

Minutes passed. We got off the freeway and came into a lot of traffic. People of all ages were walking down the street, riding their bikes, sitting and waiting for the bus.

"So, Masters," said the guard, "do you know how long this examination is going to take?"

My nose was almost pressed against the window as I focused on a shopping center. "Well," I said, "let's hope you guys won't get back in time to be reassigned to more work, and let's hope I won't get back to my cell too soon, you know? Hell, guys," I asked, "isn't there some *long* way we could take?"

Along Sir Francis Drake Boulevard I saw all different types of cars. I once knew the make of every single car I saw, but now I couldn't tell a Chevy from a Toyota. I saw joggers, some wheeling strollers as they jogged, while others ran with their dog on a leash. As we drove through the midst of everything and I looked at all the people, I felt that each one was sharing that day in their life with me. *What if it had been them, these real faces, that I had stolen from? That I had shot at?* I thought to myself. I didn't know how I could have done what I did. I felt so much regret. *How was I not able to feel all this before?* I wondered.

Whenever we came to a red light, I was in a best moment—being there, not going anyplace, just waiting, thinking. Narrowing my focus, I could see small things like the names of businesses on building walls. Widening my lens, I could take in the bus benches and the pair of gray pigeons walking along as if they owned the sidewalk. I saw the beauty of life inside the canvas I wanted so much to be a part of. I wondered: *Would I, could I, ever fit back into society again after so damn long?* I really felt that I could. But would I ever be allowed to?

Every time we drove through a green signal, I felt a bit disappointed. I even wished we'd find ourselves in a traffic jam for hours. I know such waiting usually frustrates people, but it is heavenly compared to San Quentin's death row.

It didn't take as long as I wished to get to Marin General Hospital. The car parked in front of the lobby door, and I got out, looking like an overgrown carrot with legs in my orange jumpsuit. In the hospital lobby sat a large number of people, including children. Walking in wearing that orange jumpsuit, under the escort of three uniformed guards, I felt like a character from *The Silence of the Lambs*. People stared at my waist-chains. I wasn't sure if a smile would make things better or worse.

A man reading the *Marin Independent Journal* slightly lowered the newspaper as I walked by. For an instant we looked at each other. Then he hid behind his sunglasses. Something was wrong, but what? I could swear I'd seen the ghost of my adjustment center counselor; I'd just seen him in the prison parking lot. No way could my counselor be sitting there.

We went down a hallway to the hearing specialist's waiting room, where a middle-aged white woman finally came out and called my name. She explained the tests she would do and asked me if I had any questions. She acted as if she hadn't noticed that I was a prisoner. The guards escorting me stood down from their "this is a hardened criminal" attitude.

The testing area was a space no larger than my prison cell, all decorated like a children's nursery. The specialist put earphones on my head, instructing me to raise my hand whenever I heard a sound. Then she and the guards left the room.

While I was listening for beeps to come into my ears, the word "sunglasses!" inadvertently came out of my mouth. The man reading the newspaper had been wearing sunglasses—that's what was bothering me. Why would somebody wear sunglasses while reading a newspaper inside a hospital lobby?

When my hearing test ended, the specialist said there were still many charts she needed to read, but already she could see I had some deficiencies. She assured me that her final assessment would be forwarded to the prison.

"In a month or so?" I asked her.

"No, not even that long," she replied as I walked out of her office into the hallway.

Speaking so comfortably to the hearing specialist gave me the courage to speak again, despite my carrot jumpsuit. I noticed an elderly lady walking by, completely bent over her cane. She was struggling so painfully with every tiny step, I wanted to reach out. I stopped, caught her eye, and asked, "And how are you today? You look so beautiful this morning, ma'am." And she did look beautiful to me, walking like I could imagine my own grandmother walking.

She beamed up at me. Then, nearly in tears, she responded, "Oh, thank you, young man," in a voice so loud that everyone in the lobby spun around, including the hospital employees behind their desks. Then I noticed her hearing aids; she wasn't aware of how loud her voice carried. Some of the people in the lobby were smiling at our exchange.

I knew I'd been impulsive, but I just had to say something to somebody out there! Outside the prison people didn't seem to talk to each other. Was it the orange jumpsuit, the several pounds of chains around my waist, and the restraints on my hands that were to blame for the hush-hush in the lobby? Everyone in the lobby kept their own space, even when they were seated next to each other. Nobody seemed to acknowledge that someone else was sitting right there—not even the kids! I would have been so hyper at their age, but they weren't saying anything, not even bouncing around in their chairs. They were too well behaved, just frozen stiff.

As I was escorted out, I again noticed the guy with the newspaper held up over his face. I couldn't help but ask, "Dickerson, is that you? Is that you, Dickerson?" He didn't look up at first. I could feel a guard giving my waist-chain a tiny push to say, *Keep moving*, when the newspaper came down. Behind the glasses was my counselor, cracking a smile. He let the glasses slide down his nose so I could see his eyes.

"Man, Dickerson," I said. "I thought that was you! What in the world you doin' here?"

My counselor still didn't say a word, but gestured to the guards that I could stop walking. He looked down, folded the newspaper, then looked up at me again, leaning back into his seat, grinning. His eyes were signaling me to take a look around and see for myself why he was there. In the thin second it took me to scan the lobby, I saw familiar faces here and there—even behind the front desk—of both men and women. They were all prison guards dressed in plain clothes, scattered all over the lobby.

Holy shit! I said to myself. I couldn't believe my eyes. *Where did they all come from?* My counselor got up from his seat. Through subtle hand movements, quietly and effortlessly, he directed all the guards to begin their exits, with some in front of me and others behind. There were more guards stationed outside in the parking lot.

When my escorts put me back in the car, I saw the plainclothesmen searching the bushes around the parking lot. Then state cars pulled up alongside them, picking them up one by one. I turned to the guard beside me. "Man, what is all this secret service stuff? Some sort of presidential escort you guys got goin' on?"

"Well, Mr. Masters," he answered, "you're a very important person to the state of California. We don't want to lose you."

"Aw, come on! Give me a break!"

"No, seriously," the guard responded. "We know your supporters want you out of San Quentin. We just tryin' to make sure it doesn't happen today!"

"You thought my supporters would be here at the hospital waiting to break me out? Is that why you were all hush-hush about where I was going?" I asked.

"All I can tell you," he said, "is that we'd rather be safe than sorry! Whenever we transport a prisoner outside the prison, especially a condemned prisoner, every precaution is taken to ensure that we get you where you're going and return you safely."

As we drove out of the parking lot, I saw a state car in front of us and two others directly behind, all carrying plainclothes guards. "Tell me something," I asked the guard. "Have all these other cars been with us since we left San Quentin? Because I know I saw Dickerson walking out of the prison parking lot, and I've been wondering how he could have been sittin' in the lobby when we arrived."

"You're goin' to have to ask Dickerson that," he answered.

I hoped the ride would be slowed by lots of red lights.

I watched the walkers, joggers, and bicycle riders with such a smile across my face, as if this was my own walk on the boulevard. I also noticed the lack of social interaction among people, which was painful. *Where has all of that gone—turning to talk to each other?* I seriously wondered.

I saw whole groups of people waiting together to cross the street without looking at each other or speaking. People sitting right next to each other on a bench waiting for the bus just looked ahead straight as an arrow, as if nobody spoke the same language. They seemed robotic. It reminded me of a science fiction episode on television, "The Outer Limits."

I watched two sets of parents almost side by side, pushing their babies in strollers. Only the babies tried to communicate, their tiny hands reaching toward each other, gesturing in thin air while the parents ignored each other. Drivers in the cars alongside us wouldn't turn their heads to look at me, though some of them seemed to be talking to themselves. I could relate to that.

"Well, I guess folks would just rather talk to themselves nowadays—they've just become more accustomed to talkin' to themselves!" I mumbled. The guard beside me started laughing. I laughed too. It was sort of crazy, like San Quentin.

"Nah, that's not true," he said.

"Oh, yes, it is!" I insisted.

A minute later a car drove up beside us, as if to prove my point. There it was again—another person talking to herself. I made double-sure she didn't have a cell phone in one hand before I pointed her out to the guard. "So, hey—you tryin' to say she's not, that she's singin' or somethin'?"

The guard started laughing again. "Mr. Masters, how long you been in prison?"

"Doesn't matter," I said. "I know what I see! And she, that woman, is holdin' a serious discussion with herself! Can't you see? She has both hands on the steering wheel. And look, just look, she's in some serious discussion, just a-laughing and giggling to herself."

"Look closely," the guard told me. "Look very closely, Masters. There's a pair of thin headphones on top of her head. You see 'em? And right in front of her mouth, look real closely. You see that little piece of equipment?"

"Yeah, I think I can see something. You're talkin' about that curled piece of wire in front of her mouth, right?"

"Yeah, that's it," said the guard. "That's a telephone. That's an actual cell phone."

"Nah, you kidding me," I said, embarrassed. "You mean to tell me all the people I saw that I thought were talking to themselves had on somethin' like that?"

"Mr. Masters, this is Marin County," explained the guard driving the car. "If it's out there, you'll see it first in this county!"

"Well, I guess you learn somethin' new every day, huh?" I mused, wanting to scratch my head again for some reason. At that moment I realized just how distant San Quentin was from this whole society, like an island unto itself, even though it sat right in the center of the Bay Area. And I'd been confined behind its walls for over two decades. On this day I'd seen a world I hadn't known before.

Over the years I've tried hard to remember things as they were, to hold on to something that I could reach back to and reflect upon, so that I might not feel altogether severed from the world I wished to reenter. Now my memories started to shred. The impermanent nature of everything left me nothing to hold on to. Everything had changed. I asked myself: *Hey! Would you want things to stay the same? Especially if that meant you never grow in any way?* When the castlelike shape of San Quentin suddenly came into view, I had so much to think about, so much to reflect upon.

How fortunate I had been compared to all the other condemned inmates on the dreadful first tier of the adjustment center, perhaps the most crazed in all of San Quentin. I'd actually gone outside the prison, if only for a couple hours—and in order to have my ears tested! My spirit soared, wanting to rejoin life, wanting to redeem myself, wanting to do it a different way, regretting that I had not gotten it right the first time, and that I'd terrorized others in the process.

When the cell door slammed shut behind me, I thought I could hear more clearly the noise of the tier. Then I realized that I was hearing the voice of my own heartbeat telling me that I did not belong here in San Quentin or in any other prison—the voice of my longing to be free.

CHAPTER 28

Wings

T HE SPACIOUS BEAUTY OF Mount Tamalpais on this summer
morning was a glorious sight. To the west of where I stood in the
prison yard, the face of the moon, poised high in the sky, invited me
to race over the mountain's rich green ridges in the distance. In the
early morning quiet I faced the peak, now seeming to stretch like an
awakening soul far above the morning fog.

The sight of the mountain reminded me of the day before, when
I'd been taken out for a hearing examination and was able to see
so much that I hadn't for more than twenty years. Those sights had
kept me awake in the night as I replayed them over and over again
in my mind. I could even smell my deeply real yearning to one day
have my physical freedom again.

Now, like a sigh, a new morning greeting passed between the
mountain and me. We seemed as far apart as two different plan-
ets, and yet we were sheltered by the closeness of this day. *If only,*
I thought, *I had the power to take myself there, to soar above this human
minefield of high-powered fences and gun-tower bricks and find my place up
there.* The obstacles seemed so thin and few that without knowing it
I murmured aloud, "Is that all?"

Someone answered, "What do you mean, 'Is that all?'" I hadn't
noticed Freddie, my closest friend, standing in front of me, putting

on his coat. "Man, here I am sayin' top o' the mornin' to you, and you answer, 'Is that all?'"

"It's nothin', Freddie," I said. "My mind was long gone someplace else. I didn't even see you, let alone hear you."

"Oh, I understand," he said, laughing. "Go ahead and get your rap on. I understand. It's the Buddhist way, 'cause y'all talk to everybody. To the skies, deep breaths like this [Freddie made a funny noise]: *MMMmmm*. To the moon, a short breath like this [Freddie made another funny noise]: *Aahhh*. You guys have the whole get-down cosmos down pat. So I'm up, totally knowing how the Buddhist thing works." He bent over, laughing and laughing.

"Man, it wasn't nothin' like that." I tried to ignore his jokes but laughed in spite of myself. I didn't want to try to explain that I'd just been wishing I could fly.

Hoop, one of the youngest prisoners on death row, just eighteen, came hustling across the yard in our direction, bouncing a basketball.

"Who wants to make a bet?" Hoop asked in his high, speedy voice. "I bet I can kill that damn bird over there with this ball." I looked where he was pointing and saw a seagull about ten feet away, walking carefree on the asphalt of the yard, pecking for something to eat. "You guys wanna bet?" Hoop repeated as he jerked his arm back, aiming the ball right at the bird.

Just as he let it fly, I deflected the ball's arc with my arm. "What in the hell?" I hollered. "Geez! What're you doin'?" Our arms entangled above us as the basketball fell like a dud to the ground. "Dude! What's up with you?" I went on. "Just look at that bird. It ain't done shit to you!"

"Hey, man," Hoop muttered, drawing back and looking at me, almost twenty years older than him. "Ain't nothin' up with me, Jarvis."

I kept hold of his arm and looked straight into his face. "Then why in the hell you come runnin' over here like you the devil's son-in-law in the mornin' tryin' to kill that bird? Are you a crazy zip damn fool or somethin'? Huh? Huh?"

"Man, let go my arm," Hoop said, trying to jerk away from me. Then he shouted, "You best let go my fuckin' arm!"

Freddie stepped quickly in between the two of us like a referee and pried our arms apart. "Hey! Hey! Say, fellas," Freddie said, "come on now, y'all. Trip, that bird gots to be crazier than all of us, 'cause it's still there. It ain't worth all this, anyhow, is it?"

Sure enough, the gull was still walking and pecking, minding its own business, not even knowing it had flown into prison, or that its life was in danger.

Hoop was rubbing his right arm. "Yeah, man, you right," he said to Freddie. "That fuckin' bird ain't worth all this. Why you trippin', Jarvis?"

"Why?" I asked. "Man, you ask me *why*? 'Cause, man," I blurted out, "that bird has *my wings*, that's why!"

Speechless, both of them looked down at the bird, then up into the balls of my eyes, then down again. The three of us gathered like tin-can poker players around a table, looking at one another, then at the feeding seagull, and wondering what the hell that meant. What was it all about? And yet, the crazy thing I'd said had made all the sense in the world to us! We just watched the gull spread out its bunched gray feathers and take off over the razor-wire fence toward the bay.

Afterword

Every Child Matters

IT IS FOR THE young children who traveled with me through childhood that I have pried open my heart and relived memories I had suppressed in my soul's stomach—wishing never to digest them—in order to write this book. I wrote also for the young children who today are traveling a painful, violent life road like the one that brought me to death row. These young people, like myself, may not know how to take advantage of windows of opportunity that appear. They often don't have the skills they need to choose, or to do, differently. Although they may sometimes act out in violent and dangerous ways, underneath they are simply longing to be seen for who they truly are: young children with caring hearts who were never given a chance to shine, a chance to succeed, a chance to love and be loved.

My own truth, and the truth I garnered from every other child I've come across on this journey, is that children want to believe that they matter. They want to believe that their lives make a difference

273

in the world. If this book conveys no other message, may it carry the hidden cry of the young people I grew up with—as well as so many others—who for whatever reason have experienced or will experience as much pain or more than I ever did. Like me, they will end up in foster homes, institutions, or prisons. These are the children whose faces I can vividly see and whose names I still remember— kids on their own at nine, ten, or eleven years old, guided only by their inherent knowledge that in a child's innocence the truth bravely shines. The truth whose hand they hold is that they matter, they can change the world, they can fly, regardless of how many times someone has clipped their wings by moving them from one institution to another.

It is my hope that this book will find its way into the hands of professionals and government officials who will hear this message and take responsibility for nurturing the precious lives of the abandoned, abused, and wounded children who, by no fault of their own, become lost in the system, fill up the juvenile centers, and eventually overflow into the most hardened prisons. These are the people most likely to end up on death row.

That I was wrongfully convicted of murder and sent to death row is disheartening, but it's easier than living with the pain of having taken the life of another human being. It is only out of an innate innocence that, in spite of everything, I have never killed a person, nor have I participated in planning to kill someone. It was my youthful pride, desire to belong, and pure survival instinct that led to the actions that implicated me in the murder of a prison guard, which is why I am now on death row. But no matter how out of control I've been, I have never been the kind of person who could plan and commit such an act of violence. For that I am very grateful. But the subtitle of this book, "The Autobiography of an Innocent Man on Death Row," in no way implies that I have not committed other violent acts. It is painful to look back at all the senseless violence that brought me to these prison gates. I've served my time for the original convictions of armed robberies—some of which I did not commit—and I am deeply regretful for the harm and suffering I have caused to others.

In light of my experiences—from living in an attic to living on death row—I feel blessed that my heart is not permanently damaged. I feel grateful for the people who were with me then, and to those who are with me now. I still have my sanity, my ability to learn, and a willingness to look back into my past and visit memories without holding judgments. In this way I can take what I've gone through and learn how to use it for the benefit of those, on death row and elsewhere, who despair of ever caring enough to love again. It is my profound wish that we will all be able to finally accept our wrongs and losses, move into gratefulness for what we have and have had, and embrace the compassion for others and ourselves that opens us to the freedom of forgiveness.

Acknowledgments

With this book I acknowledge all the kids I've ever known. We taught one another how to smile and cling to friendship when there was nothing else. I also want to acknowledge the many others—the Joshes, Pablos, and Freddies—whose lives were shortened by their own taking or by the system that failed to protect them.

While I changed many names in this book to protect people's identities, their characters are intact and real. By telling their childhood stories, I pray that this book provides others who have suffered with the courage to enter their own life experiences. May they take to heart their own value and allow their voices to be heard.

With deep appreciation I acknowledge Freddie L. Taylor, whose many years of friendship in San Quentin have made him a real brother to me. With Freddie, for many years I have been able to separate myself from a prison culture wrapped in an endless cycle of violence and become the person and the Buddhist I am today.

Writing this book has reopened many memories. In every instance I've tried to speak with a voice that carries my spiritual path forward. I've often had to pause. Many times I wanted to quit, to opt instead for meditating on the more comfortable cold floor, rather than be such an attentive listener to my life's painful events. Although it may be difficult to understand how I'm able to count my blessings for most of my life experiences, I do.

I acknowledge those many dear and important people in my life who have encouraged me to take hold of my thin pen filler and write. Although I still wish you hadn't, I love you still more for having done so and am forever grateful. I can easily recall many visits spent with Sarah Paris at San Quentin; through a small glass window in a visiting booth, she kept at me, sometimes pushing me, sometimes bullying me, in her own caring writer's heart, to "Write! Write it!" after I shared the memories of being in the attic with my sisters. From there, we brought many other painful stories of my childhood to paper. Mark Werlin patiently translated my pages and pages of scribbles into a working manuscript and left me with no excuses, no way to turn back. My heart is filled with appreciation for both of them.

More than anyone else, I thank Susan Moon and Kamala Dietz. Without Susan, it would have been impossible to write anything about my life, let alone a whole book. Her love, support, and editing are a debt I can never repay. Susan, I will always love and appreciate you. My love and gratitude also extends to Kamala, who was always there for me, ready to help no matter what direction my mind took. Her patience and trust allowed me to see my own mistakes; without her, many lesser ideas would have gone unchallenged. Susan and Kamala, in giving their time, patience, and energy, nurtured my best effort in bringing myself and my story to paper.

I have been blessed to have Emily Hilburn Sell as my editor. She has done so much to prepare this book for publication. She has been able to read my thoughts and see into my soul, and as we worked together, though thousands of miles apart, I knew that I could trust her with my life story. For this, I am forever grateful. And Eric Brandt gave me the opportunity to share this story with others, but not without first asking me to do some deeper soul searching. Thank you, Eric, for asking the hard questions. To Julie Burton, my publicist at HarperOne, thank you as well.

I deeply appreciate Sarah Jane Freymann, my agent, for her enduring belief in me. Her determination to have my voice heard through the publication of this book, as well as my first book, *Finding Freedom*, has given me strength and encouragement.

No words can truly express how much I appreciate everyone who has supported me over the years. By continually reminding me of the difference this book will make, they have kept me standing. They have welcomed me into their hearts and families. I've been blessed by their love, support, and tolerance—a gift I could never replace. This family includes my loving sister Carlette, as well as Pamela and Marty Krasney, whose consistent love, support, and presence have been so welcome, and Lee and Mark Lesser, on whom I've been able to lean so many times. I always feel blessed by their love in my life. My wider family circle includes Hank Swan, who was like a big brother to me. Sadly, Hank passed away, leaving many fond memories of the times we spent together. He made his own adventures part of my life, and we shared so much. Hank created beautiful cards that combined his photography with my poetry. He and his beautiful partner, my dear longtime friend, Jan Sells, will always be part of my life. My beloved extended family also includes Savitri Burbank and Michael Kilgroe, who do their best to keep me communicating with the world outside San Quentin, and Alan Senauke, the only Buddhist priest who knows how to challenge me in a way that on most occasions frightens me into looking at myself. I am so grateful for the challenge. My gratitude to Dr. Cheri Forrester for keeping me physically strong the times I couldn't do it alone.

My gratitude extends to Marion Foot, whose love, care, and trust in me are a continual blessing. To have such a treasured and loving friend is a true gift; also to Jane Donaldson and Susan Breiding, who have always been able to share with me the nature in the fields of life; William J. Clark, whose travels over the years have included me; Patrice Wynn, whose love and support will forever meet my gratitude; Betsy Dubovsky, who will always be dear to my life; Kathy Weston, whose friendship always makes a difference; and Loraine Campbell, for sometimes only using the pen filler, as I do, so that our writing comes from the same place. How many years have we encouraged each other?

There are many others over these many years who have shared my life: Will Smoky Godfrey, David Platford, Phil Coffin, Hershey Johnson, Angela Farmer, Victor Van Kooten, Leslie Murphy, Carol Dodson, Kelly Hayden, Michele Modena, Elizabeth Forrest, Ronald Jay Campbell Jr., Maryann Comas, Harvey Taylor, Maia Ramsey, Kathy Rowe, Shirley Mayfield, K. Bandell, and Mary Nordkvelle. Their unwavering friendship, heartfelt care, and constant companionship have held me steadfast in my writing. Thanks also to Ann-Ellice Parker, who knows I am forever grateful for her support, and to Beth Clark for her talent and generous spirit.

This book would not be complete without extending my deepest gratitude to the legal team still working tirelessly to prove my innocence, especially Joe Baxter, Rick Targow, Scott Kaufman, Chris Andrian, Ken Ward, Melody Ermachild, and Rachel Sommerville.

I am particularly indebted to everyone at the Buddhist Peace Fellowship in Berkeley, to Chagdud Gonpa in Junction City, and to Lama Shenpen. These centers have kept me grounded in my meditation practice and helped me keep receiving teachings.

As a Buddhist practitioner, I feel so blessed to have Pema Chödrön in my life. No words can express all you have meant to me, Pema—both in my meditation practice and in my daily existence on death row. To have a precious and dear friend in a dharma teacher who on occasion can also care for me like a mother who knows what I think I can get away with—and refuses to let me—has been the biggest benefit to my practice. I am forever grateful to you, Pema, for all your encouragement to write this book so that it may be of benefit to others.

I am eternally grateful to my mother, Cynthia, whom I will forever love. More than anyone, she gave me reason to never stop believing that there was someone, somewhere, who always loved me, long before I ever learned to doubt the world.

I want to thank my precious wife, Kathrin, who will forever be the love of my life. I can't be more blessed to have you in my life. I am grateful to be able to place into your hands the very heart of all my dreams. I trust that you will always know how, in every way, you are so special to me. I love you and wish to share my life with you, always.